I0161147

She Only Wants a Horse

She Only Wants a Horse

Wisdom, humor, horses, family values, and short stories from the farm

Judith Chase

B
P

BRAMBLEWOOD PRESS, LLC
SANTA BARBARA, CALIFORNIA

All rights reserved. No part of this publication, except for brief excerpts for purpose of review, may be reproduced, stored in a retrieval system, or transmitted in any form or by any means, electronic, mechanical, photocopying, recording, or otherwise without express written consent from the publisher.

Copyright © 2007 Judith Parker Chase

Cover and interior layout by Greg Wadsworth.

ISBN 13: 978-0-9797665-0-3 (Previously published by Elderberry Press, Inc, ISBN 13: 978-1-932762-76-1
ISBN 10: 0-9797665-0-8 (Previously published by Elderberry Press, Inc, ISBN 10: 1-932762-76-0)
ISBN 13: 978-0-9797665-1-0 (e-book)
ISBN 10: 0-9797665-1-6 (e-book)

Library of Congress Control Number: 2007922751

Published by
Bramblewood Press, LLC
729 De La Vina Street
Santa Barbara, CA 93101

Printed in the United States of America.

For Nancy Chase Watts

Chapter One

Won't You Come to Dinner?

I picked my way carefully over rotting stacks of limbs and fallen trees and sat down to wait on a large log near the end of the steep trail. High upon the mountainside, the young man in my life slowly hiked his way down the narrow switchbacks of the long, rocky trail, a pillowcase of dirty laundry slung over his shoulder. As I watched his slow progress down the path, I suddenly felt cold and shivery. Surely it wasn't fear or uncertainty that flooded over me; I'd acted cocky enough the night before while having to defend our plans. There was no lack of love between me and Dan, but could Dan's ailing heart possibly stand the strain of part-time jobs, a full load of college courses, a new wife, and starvation? It was hard to ignore these things when thinking of the future.

Certainly pessimism brings nothing good! At least we were taking action, in spite of total ignorance of what lies ahead...but was the timing right? In exactly two weeks I was scheduled to marry this hiker, and everything that came with him.

"After the wedding," I thought to myself, "I'll get employed as his sidekick and join him as he mans the Forestry Service lookout on this mountaintop. We'll save up all our money this summer, and in August we'll leave these familiar mountains where we've lived all our lives and make our way by bus to the unknown hills of Arizona."

Even as I reassured myself, new doubts crept in. How many obstacles could the two of us survive? In addition to Dan's heart problems, we would arrive in Tucson with little money, no car, no place to stay, no jobs, and no local friends. It was also unsettling that Dan kept trying to join some branch of the military to do his part in World War II. No one in Ojai was encouraging us to get married, for in addition to the war, the Great Depression lingered on into the early forties, with jobs hard to find and pay often low.

I remember thinking, "Maybe I don't really want to know what lies ahead. After going steady for five years, we can hardly be accused of spur-of-the-moment foolishness, but what if we can be accused of perpetual foolishness? Surely all actions have consequences of some sort…but, what the heck, I'll keep my cool to get set, get ready, and go!"

Dan was living in a one-room glass house perched on a tall metal derrick high atop a windswept mountain that overlooked a stretch of the Pacific coastline known as the Rincon. An expansive range of coastal mountains surrounded three sides of the building. This lookout job for the Department of Forestry was one Dan had taken in the hopes that he might earn a salary while giving his health a chance to improve. His doctor had ordered complete rest; luckily, this job came close to that. The two men living there took one-man shifts around the clock, reporting any forest fires, airplanes, submarines, ships, or anything else that might spell trouble in the early days of the war.

Some months earlier I had made the pilgrimage up this same tortuous trail to the lookout from the nearby Casitas Pass Road on the inland side of the mountain. I was bringing Dan some laundry and a few packages his mother had given me. Unbeknownst to me, one little box, packaged inside a larger one, held an engagement ring. On a sunny day, with blue sky above and deep blue ocean far below, Dan presented the ring to me on bended knee as I sat on a large rock near the lookout.

"Dear Judy, will you marry me? Even with a damaged heart, I love you so much."

Looking over his shoulder and facing me were several white-faced Hereford cows, coming near to see if he had any carrot tops or apple cores for them. Despite the seriousness of the moment I had to laugh—how many girls get engaged while the eyes of three large brown and white cows join those of the boyfriend in scrutinizing the fiancée-to-be?

With my future bridegroom on the mountaintop, it became my job to orchestrate all plans for the formal church wedding. I had left my dorm at UCLA and hitched a ride home with a dentist who drove back and forth from LA to the nearby Ojai Valley each weekend. On the backseat of his car sat my small travel bag and two large boxes: one containing a white wedding gown, and the other holding my headdress and long train. I would stay with Dan's mom and dad until the wedding.

I was eager to see Dan that day, for a friend of my father's, Mr. Brown, had called and invited me to dinner the night before. With only my school wardrobe to wear—scuffed and dirty saddle shoes, less-than-white bobby sox, a plaid skirt, and a blouse that I covered with a stretched-out sweater—I set out for a dinner I would remember for the rest of my life.

Mr. Brown didn't try to smile when he came to the door to pick me up. With a stern look and pursed lips he delivered me to his home overlooking the valley. "What's wrong?" I thought to myself. "Could he have bad news to tell me? " I started to wonder why my father, after selling our furnishings and moving to Michigan, had chosen this man to handle my school funds and send me small monthly checks for college. Dad, with all his many jokes and funny stories, had played golf with this solemn fellow for many years.

I had never been to the house before. The whole family was there to greet me. All were dressed in their Sunday best. I caught a glimpse of a formal dining room table, set with a white tablecloth, candles, and flowers. Surely, I thought, there must be other guests coming. Mrs. Brown wouldn't set a table like this every night, and certainly not for me. I waited. No other guests came.

I accepted a small glass of apple cider and soon after was led to my seat at the table. The conversation centered around my school schedule, what I would be taking the following year, and in particular, my upcoming wedding. I explained that I was getting married in less than two weeks. I told them how Dan and I would be hired to stay in the U.S. Forestry's lookout tower for the balance of the summer and then leave for the University of Arizona in the fall. Some of this they may have known from the engagement article which had appeared in the local paper several months earlier, but I thought I needed to say it anyway. Besides, I liked talking about our plans.

As soon as Mrs. Brown removed the salad plates and served the main course, the family suddenly shifted gears, and I realized this was to be no happy celebration of my wedding...this dinner was staged as though it were my last meal before a total catastrophe. As if reading lines from a script, each family member took turns voicing their dire predictions.

The older married daughter was first to comment. "Ah, I hope you know how expensive married life is. For instance, you have no idea how expensive dental work can be. I've come back home for several dental appointments this week, and it will break our bank account for months. I've learned the hard way that two can't live as cheaply as one."

Under the table, I turned my engagement ring so that the small diamond would be seen and sparkle, and then I put my hand lightly on the edge of the table. I could only wonder what in the world my teeth had to do with Dan and me becoming a couple. I'll have the same teeth and the same dental bills whether I'm married or single, and so will Dan!

Mrs. Brown began to speak her lines. "It's terrible what groceries cost now, and you'll be paying rent and all the utilities. Even new clothes are such a headache."

Nothing but discouraging remarks. I felt like asking both Mrs. Brown and her daughter, "Then why in the world did you bother getting married?" Surely, our obstacles would be many and difficult, but nothing was haphazard, nothing had been decided at the last moment.

Mr. Brown kept up the heavy and solemn formality and words. Folding his arms across his chest and tipping back his chair slightly, he added "I'll turn the remaining funds in your account over to you now that you're twenty-one." He spoke as though I would never finish school, and warned of the dangers of "blindly falling in love."

Of course he knew how much remained in my college account as he asked, "How're you going to swing it without a car? And how will you rent a place to stay if you're both in school and paying out-of-state tuition? It'll cost you an arm and a leg! There's no such thing as a free lunch. How're you going to eat three meals a day? It'll be a lot different than it's been for you, having a monthly check and just sharing a dorm room at the university."

Even the younger daughter seemed to have been coached. "Judy," she asked me, "where's your horse now?"

"I've finally fallen in love with someone even more special than my horse. But, you know, Ponge was being boarded and died last year while giving birth to a foal." There was no longer a horse to entice me to stay in California. Had they thought it might? I planned on having a horse again, perhaps several, as soon as Dan and I could get the land. That dream, however, was a long way off. Sharing life with animals would have to wait.

"No, there's no way any of you can talk me out of marriage and leaving the Valley. We're soaring in love, not falling, and none of our plans have been made blindly or willy-nilly. Back in tenth grade we became best friends and soon knew that one day we'd get married. We've dated for five years, for heaven's sake—surely that's not like going off half-cocked! In fact, we sat for hundreds of hours down on Creek Road in Dan's car, working out quite detailed plans for the years ahead. We're doing it voluntarily, just step by step. I guess if we starve we can do it together just as easily in Arizona as in California. Actually, with some part-time jobs, we can probably finance degrees eventually. Education is seldom bad or boring, and we have a commitment to work hard and eventually have a farm or ranch."

I put on my sweater to leave. "Thank you so much for the delicious meal and your concern, for sending the monthly checks, and keeping the black steamer trunks full of Mom's books and other things. If I may leave the trunks with you until we take off at the end of the summer it would be very helpful. I promise to pick them up at the end of August."

Maybe this family knew more than they let on, for I was marrying under more than one cloud. Obviously, there was the frightening lack of money, but perhaps they had also heard about the serious heart problems that had kept Dan out of school for a year. We'd told no one about the final remarks of a heart specialist who had warned Dan, "I suspect your life expectancy will be about forty-three years." Maybe the doctor felt that this remark would keep Dan from marrying me and leaving behind a young widow, but, regardless, it was a cruel statement. The Brown family probably didn't know that absence had made my heart grow stronger, and that I'd transferred from Berkeley to UCLA the past year just to be closer to Dan while he struggled to get well. In any case, the whole event was behind me now, and there was much to look forward to.

I smiled about the dinner, but still, the family's onslaught had ruffled my feathers a bit. After all the planning and wishing Dan and I had done, would the getting be as fine?

As soon as my weary hiker flopped down on the log beside me, he asked, "What's the matter? You seem subdued."

Immediately, I blurted out the tale of the Browns' dinner party. "Nothing's wrong…except that dinner last night with the Browns. They seemed so darn rehearsed in their talk against our future and marriage, and all I could do was hold my ground to suggest that we can't plan too far ahead, but surely, school has to be first on the list, and it's no starry-eyed, reckless dream. I didn't have any easy answers, probably because there are none. Even without their scorn and advice it's spooky to be leaving with so little money. The whole family stayed skeptical and didn't appear to believe we're really going off to the U of A. But they must realize that we had to send transcripts and get accepted months ago. What's so hard to believe about that?"

Dan shrugged and replied, "That's a bunch of baloney. Maybe they thought your mind wasn't made up and they were simply playing devil's advocate. After all, it's only the second week of May and they know school doesn't start until fall. But we're not preordained to stay in California. That's crazy! We believe in ourselves; let others doubt all they want! You and I will make the moves and paddle our own canoe. Don't let other people's values or ideas tear you apart!"

"Thanks for the positive thoughts, my soon-to-be-husband. But with their dire predictions about dental bills, we'd better brush our teeth mighty clean twice a day."

"Come on, gal, we're not saying goodbye right now. I think we need to splurge on a gallon of gas and get some pistachio ice-cream cones.

Without even an ice cube up on that mountain, I've been dreaming about that cold, green stuff. Allen can man the lookout for another hour or two."

On the way to the ice-cream parlor, Dan laughed and said, "I can't believe you mentioned Creek Road! Was it for shock effect?" Creek Road was a popular local destination for lovers to be alone.

I grinned. "Well, maybe it was a sudden impulse to startle them. They upset me. I didn't mention campfires, marshmallows, and that your sister or friends usually went with us. I also forgot to tell them that you do own this car.

"We have to do what's best, and that's staying in school...but I have no clear idea of what 'do' means after that. You really think we can go from nothing to owning a farm?" I lacked confidence and high self-esteem, but Dan seemed to be full of both—at least on the surface. I'd try to catch his constant optimism.

"Absolutely, gal. It's like the song, 'All or Nothing at All.' We'll make it work. You and I have dreamt and planned this for years. Keep the belief!"

We'd chosen the University of Arizona because agricultural colleges in California did not admit women in 1942, and Arizona's warm weather was appealing. Out-of-state tuition would wipe out most of our combined savings, but we might have enough for one year if we found part-time jobs. With the new school having somewhat different course requirements, both of us changing majors, and no funds coming from our parents, it would likely take us two or more years to get those sheepskins.

Still licking my green ice cream, I continued to fuss. "Well, we'd flunk a test for aptitude and resources. Ranches or farms take sacks of money, and your teacher was right when he told your class that almost all successful farmers and ranchers either inherit the land they farm or first make a large amount of money in some other occupation. Also, most farm people have parents who taught them the business of farming from the time they were born and have many relatives to give them advice and support. They grow up in the country and learn how to raise crops or animals and how to repair the machinery and countless other things. I'm sure farm wives learn how to cook, plant gardens, and raise chickens and children. Your bride has a high risk for failure. Most farmers also have good health and muscles for dawn-to-dusk hard labor. We score zeroes on all the above—no funds, no muscles, and not a soul in the whole state of Arizona who might give us a few ideas or support our plans."

The two weeks sped by and the day of our wedding arrived. Scared, young, and ignorant of the likely wild and twisting trail ahead, I tried to keep my shoulders back, my head up, and step with confidence as I walked alone down the aisle of the church, while Dan, just as nervous, waited for me at the altar with his best man, my bridesmaids, and the matron of honor. "Well Mrs. C," he quipped, as we left the church, "Now we've done it!"

A honeymoon bus trip to Yosemite at super low war-time rates for a week included a couple of hard and long trail rides on horseback—a first for Dan, poor man. So sore and stiff he could barely stand up or walk at the end of the second ride, Dan practically fell off the horse while hanging on to the saddle horn. He just stood there, holding on to the saddle with both hands, until his wobbly legs would move enough that he could hobble over to a bench. Riding a horse involves using a lot of muscles in ways that they would not ordinarily be used. Furthering this abuse, a novice's behind tends to bounce up and down rather violently with the horse's every step. Dan probably hurt even more than most beginning riders because I had tried to coach him to keep his heels down and his toes pointing straight ahead, plus a stupid string of other hints to help him look like an experienced rider.

"What has my horse-crazy bride done to me?" he moaned over and over. After the horse trips, we stuck to rental bicycles or sat on the porch of the cabin where we watched and fed a friendly semitame chipmunk.

We returned to the Ojai Valley after our honeymoon, and the Forestry Service staff formally hired us for the two-person lookout job. Neither of us mentioned to the ranger who interviewed us that we would be making tracks to school in September. High on the mountain, at the top of a metal tower, we lived in the stark room with floor-to-ceiling glass walls on all sides. It became a time to talk, gain better health, eat apples and heat lots of canned and dried foods that a local ranger drove up to us once a month.

Since the job demanded that one or the other of us be awake at all hours of the day and night, we split the shifts, with Dan giving me the easier ones—one in the afternoon and early evening, and the other one beginning at 5AM. As already mentioned, our job included more than simply searching for wildfires—we also had to watch for all signs of airplanes and ships. After the attack of Pearl Harbor, many people thought the whole West coast was vulnerable to attack, especially after Japanese forces shelled nearby Ellwood in February, 1942. We plotted our sightings on a large topographical map which covered a table in the middle of the room and then phoned the information in to the Forestry Service. The people on the other end of the line then decided if the planes and ships were friend or foe.

Both days and nights were long and boring. The only visitors were the occasional deer, Hereford cattle, goats, horses, and other wild animals who came to sit in a small patch of shade beside the lookout or to rub their bodies against its steel frame. One morning we did get a short visit from a new critter—while we ate cold cereal and changed shifts, I spotted a gopher perched on his mound of dirt far down the hill. "Dan, let me try shooting this big game with your twenty-two. How about showing me how to shoot a gun?" We both went out on the catwalk. I steadied myself against the railing and looked down the sight of the gun.

Never dreaming I could hit anything so far away, I casually pulled the trigger and in a violent flash the gopher was dead. I, who as a little girl had cried when flies were swatted, had killed the poor little guy deader than a doornail. What had he done? Just up from his bed, he was enjoying the beautiful early dawn at his front door; he never had a chance. That was the first and the last time I ever shot a gun.

In the days that followed the shooting incident, I occasionally wondered how I would manage the role of a farmer's wife and help raise animals that had to be killed for food. It would be a time of truth and consequences in the real world, beyond our textbooks. But before long, I put such thoughts out of mind—those days were far, far in the future. And maybe we'd only grow oranges or alfalfa.

Soon it was time to leave behind the village of Ojai where I had lived my entire life before leaving for college. I was parting with my whole childhood and it was an unsettling feeling. Going away to school had been easier, since I could always come back during holidays and stay with friends.

The name "Ojai" comes from a Chumash word meaning "nest." For me, the small town had been like a cozy nest, isolated by its surrounding mountains—by car about thirty miles distant from Santa Barbara and eighty-five from Los Angeles and UCLA. One of the mountains to the northeast of town was six thousand feet high. Called Topa Topa, it was part of the Los Padres National Forest. I had grown up seeing that special mountain each day from the window beside my bed. Its wonderful, rocky, almost sheer face often reflected the rose colors of the sun setting on the opposite side of the valley and I'd often wondered if all the people in Ojai felt the happy contentment that I did when seeing the peak at sundown. It was sort of like watching the colors of dying embers in a fireplace. Topa Topa had been part of my daily life.

Orchards blanketed much of the valley floor, with crops of Valencia oranges ripening in the summer and Navel oranges in the wintertime. Along the main street, the town was unique and lovely, with a park full of oak trees just across from the covered arcade of stores. In residential areas the roads were even occasionally detoured around some of the huge trees.

The sheltering and tranquil village had changed little over the years. Ojai wasn't right beside a highway or at a crossroads. It escaped the constant streams of cars and trucks zooming off in different directions to faraway places. I'd belonged there and had been a nomad in other states and lands only by reading countless books.

Suddenly I didn't belong in the nest, and like a bird learning to fly, I sensed it would be a big step to get up and put our show on the road. Migrating to a new state and life would have to be done by Greyhound Bus. Dan's Model B coupe guzzled cases of oil and tanks of gasoline, and it needed constant small repairs; thus it stayed behind as a second car for his family.

And so, with not much more than dreams and each other, we packed, bought one-way Greyhound tickets to Tucson, and climbed into the bus.

Chapter 2

The Barn before the House

Off and rolling! With wartime speed limits of just thirty-five miles per hour, the hot and stuffy Greyhound bus plodded southeast, bound toward increasing waves of heat from a blinding August sun. We were finally leaving California to finish college at the University of Arizona, in Tucson, only sixty miles north of the Mexican border.

With all the bus seats full, it seemed strangely quiet except for two toddlers in front of us who cried often and frequently turned around to observe us, their wet eyes round and dark, their noses in need of a handkerchief, and their mother spitting out streams of admonitions to them in Spanish. Most of the travelers boarded the bus in Los Angeles and were young men in uniform or families with packages and bags on their laps. Many would probably end their journey at Yuma or Tucson, with a few going on to towns farther east or changing buses to go down to Mexico.

Hopefully the five steamer trunks and my crated cedar chest would be waiting for us at General Delivery, since we hadn't been able to give a street address. There was trust in those trunks—trust that we'd not starve and that I would someday have a bookcase for all Mom's books, plus a closet and drawers for the rest of our scanty belongings.

I found myself wishing I'd been told my family history and when and where my ancestors had traveled with such large trunks. Had they been brought across the Atlantic on a ship? What had they held long before I told my dad that I wanted to keep them to hold these books and other items from my childhood? He had dutifully read my list and filled the trunks and strapped them tightly closed for me before we parted—he to live in Lansing, Michigan and I to attend school in Berkeley, California.

For several hours, Dan and I stared silently through the dirty windows at the small towns the bus passed on the main road to San Diego. Even trying to think or talk took too much energy, but finally, I repeated to Dan, and then over and over again to myself, the words "Thinking will make it so." Back in Ojai it had been easy to dream and plan these first steps, but now we had a lot of hard schooling ahead and had to find part-time jobs without delay.

Dazed, exhausted, and feeling vulnerable, I was hit by a big wave of homesickness, even though I had left home and been away at school for most of the previous three years. Though deeply in love, at that moment I needed reassurance. Right on cue, Dan whispered in my ear, "This is a fine decision; just you wait and see—get a bit more education and the rest will follow."

I nodded and replied, "At least we're off and doing what we want to be doing!" In the past it had been fun to talk about "controlling our own destiny," but then we were still school kids, with no idea of what the future might really bring.

"Quit worrying! No one knows the future," Dan continued. "This is a fine decision. We're not gamblers, but there must be some kinds of probabilities that we won't starve." In fact, I've heard you saying, 'Think big to be big.'"

"I know, Dan. Still, it's these big things that bother me, the hurdles of having daily food and shelter over our heads, plus all the out-of-state tuition."

He shrugged his shoulders, and I suddenly realized he was just as tired as I was. Pulling from a paper bag a bottle of water, two cheese sandwiches, and two apples for our dinner, he suggested, "It's just a matter of mind-set. Sit here and create a picture in your mind of us finishing school, and then create another picture of our first real jobs after we leave the U of A. You gotta see beyond the here-and-now."

In Tucson, we disembarked into a hot, late August evening, with a temperature of at least ninety-five degrees, and waited while the driver pulled out a motley pile of sacks, suitcases, and boxes from the underbelly of the bus. The lighting around the parking area was harsh yet dim, perhaps to avoid attracting more of the large moths that fluttered around and banged into the lights. The other travelers, now dark and shadowy figures, quickly gathered their belongings and quietly disappeared.

It was hard to believe there were no hotels in sight, but one taxi waited at the curb and our bus driver said we'd better take it. We would have to spend precious money just to find lodging for the night.

As we piled our two large suitcases and a bag and our bone-tired selves into the taxi, we must have looked pretty desperate and pitiful: to help us, the taxi driver got out and dashed up to the registration desks of several hotels before finally finding a place for us to stay that was not far from the U of A campus. He said almost all the hotels in town were full and that we were very lucky to get a room. Maybe we got the last room, or the driver had said the right things, for the sign on the registration counter read, NO VACANCY. I bought the local paper and a city map at the hotel desk and marked a couple of ads for housing, but it seemed strange to see so few places listed. It was a good thing I didn't know what the next day would bring.

At daybreak, I broke our last shredded-wheat biscuits into pieces, put them into drinking glasses, added water, and peeled two oranges. The desk clerk agreed to hold our bags for us behind the counter. Dressed to make a good impression on potential landlords, in clothes that were far too dark, too warm, and too dressy for Arizona streets, we began to walk just as the sun came up. We had no way of knowing that we would cover twenty miles or more under a relentless sun with the heat smoldering at one hundred and ten degrees in the shade…and there was almost no shade.

Our first discovery was that the apartments or rooms advertised in the paper were nowhere near campus. As there were no FOR RENT signs on any of the houses we passed by, our only option was to knock at the front door of houses that looked large enough to possibly have a rental room available. Walking in ever-widening circles around the periphery of the campus, we were constantly told, "All rentals—of any size—have been taken." It was wartime, and the growing Davis-Monthan Air Base was just outside Tucson. No one had encouraging words. With the crush of students coming in for the fall term, people living near the big military base, and the workers needed in the growing war industries, there seemed to be not even one room available anywhere. We stopped for Cokes and water several times and trudged on farther and farther from campus; just one long bus ride from California, and already we were down and out, hungry, and without shelter.

We trudged on throughout the day, though our prospects continued to look grimmer and grimmer. Several home owners mentioned "There's a war on, you know. Good luck even finding a room." Complete desperation is a great incentive. We kept putting one blistered foot in front of the other throughout the afternoon. In fact, through most of our lives, we have always answered with the words "desperation" and "perseverance" to explain to friends why we did what we did. There never seemed to be much choice—it was just constant desperation. As the temperature rose even higher in the late afternoon, I grew dizzy and very close to fainting, while our faces, arms, and hands were sunburned to a deep pink. I remarked to Dan, "This next house will have to be my last. It must be eight o'clock."

Dan looked at the watch I'd given him as his engagement present and nodded, "Actually, it's later than that in more ways than one—what can our next step be?" He held my arm and rang the bell.

A kind-faced, middle-aged man opened the door and invited us in to sit down. He brought us large glasses of water and listened to our story.

"Well, yes," he said, "I do have a small furnished rental across the street from campus if you don't mind living in a barn. It's a two-room place with a kitchen and a bath. It's built in one end of a barn. It's good-sized, and there aren't any animals in it. Would you like me to drive you over to see it?" Those words shine like jewels in our memories to this day.

We both answered as one, "Oh, please. If you would!"

He continued to explain the location—"There's a retired teacher, Mrs. Marshall, living in a large house in front next to the street. She doesn't want to ever be disturbed. You would be going through her side gate if you lived there. I'm Mr. Peters, her business manager, and I take care of a number of her rentals and businesses."

"And the rent?" Dan asked.

"What? Oh yes, the rent is twenty-five dollars a month, but that does include your utilities. And I should warn you, there's no air conditioner or heater." We rented it immediately.

No one but the homeless and destitute, and I guess that's what we were, could have been more thrilled with that tiny brick-walled shelter. We were on cloud nine!

The barn appeared to be two stories high and had a pair of large, barn-sized doors in addition to the small door which opened into the apartment. Mr. Peters unlocked the door and ushered us inside. I could tell the structure was single-walled, because three of the inside walls were the same red bricks that were on the outside. The ceiling was the floor of the second story of the barn, and the apartment was partitioned off from the rest of the barn by a wooden wall and a small closet. The room at the back held an iron-framed double bed, a sink with no counter space, a two-burner stove with a small oven, an old refrigerator, and a small round table with two chairs. Beside the stove was a second door that opened to the outside and would let in some fresh air.

The other room—the front room—was smaller. It contained a couch, a wooden chair, one small dresser, and, behind a door, a bathroom the size of a coat closet. The whole apartment was painted an ugly "minesweeper" gray, but I never asked Mr. Peters why, for fear he'd think I was criticizing, which I wasn't. The two rooms, tiny and oven-hot, seemed like heaven to us.

Dan said it all after Mr. Peters took us to retrieve our suitcases and returned us to the apartment. "Mrs. C, we're together in our own home! All the rest will be duck soup. Can you believe it? With the campus across the street we don't even need a car! Let's go outside—I'm going to carry my bride through the doorway. The next thing both of us had better do is say a great big prayer of thanks."

It was a strange day, as if a dress rehearsal and the main performance were opening at the same time. We were students preparing for life, yet we were married and had to face the real world of work and to find paying jobs immediately. It would be mixing dreams with a lot of doing and a lot of crossing of fingers...and I was so bone-tired.

Mr. Peters came by the next day, telling us he had a friend who would pick up our five black trunks and the crated cedar chest. After he showed us where they could be stored in the other part of the barn, I asked whether I could borrow the pick, shovel, and mattock I had seen in there, as I wanted to plant a little flower and vegetable garden around the foundation of the apartment. Maybe I'd prepare the bed now and wait until cooler days to do the actual planting. I was determined to make something out of nothing—even out of this barren, rocklike, big yard without even the fertility to host a single weed. There was one oak tree hanging over part of a tin wash-shed nearby, but its shade would never reach the barn.

My groundbreaking had a hard beginning in the cement-like earth. The shovel was worthless except to remove what the pick and mattock gradually broke up. Every evening I poured water from the dishpan into the slowly deepening ditch, helping to soften the hard-packed earth. Eventually I had a trench, maybe four feet wide, dug out along the wall on both sides of the front door and down the side adjoining the apartment. I then put every bit of kitchen leftovers—potato peelings, carrot and celery tops, cantaloupe rinds—into the trench to help create soil. I then found some thoroughly rusted metal posts at the back of the lot, and I ordered from Sears Roebuck a section of chicken wire that was high and long enough to make a sweet pea trellis. Cutting across a vacant field on the way to the grocery store about two blocks away, we found two empty coffee cans in the weeds. From then on, each trip to the store we used those cans to scoop up the better soil from the field and carry the tiny bit of real dirt back to dump in the garden trench.

After the summer heat lessened a bit, I bought brightly colored seed packets of the flowers, beets, carrots, onions, and squash that I would plant in two crowded rows in front of my future bed of sweet peas. With the help of the dishpans of water I emptied there several times a day, the seeds sprouted and actually grew under that blazing sun. I carefully planted the remaining seeds as soon as we began eating our first servings of garden-fresh vegetables.

Miracle of Miracles! Soon, sweet peas were climbing the chicken wire and blooming along both the front and side of this first home-in-a-barn. Fragrant flowers, in various colors of white, red, pink, purple, and lavender, made our two rooms smell like beauty and love, and softened homecomings after school and work.

"Dan, now I know I can make things grow and become a farmer. There's such magic in seeds! How in the world can a tiny, dry seed hold something alive, something that with just some dirt, water, and sun becomes a beautiful flower or a big red beet? I can hardly wait to have a farm and watch little seeds turn into watermelons, pumpkins, and corn—big stuff. It will be a never-ending miracle!" These plants and flowers were fuel for dreams: a ranch, perhaps on a hill, with gardens, trees, children, and all kinds of animals—especially horses—running in green fields.

There was no way I could have foretold that this first small garden, with its fence placed against the red brick barn, its mass of colorful sweet peas, and its little rows of vegetables, would in just a couple of years become a miracle to us in another way.

Chapter 3

The Power of Sweet Peas

We soon signed up for fall classes and searched the bulletin boards all over campus for part-time jobs. One thumb-tacked sheet advertised for someone to take the official weather reports twice a day. The open shed that housed all the instruments dealing with weather was at the far end of the campus, but we took the job. We were as close to the campus as anyone could get, but when we walked across it twice daily in the searing summer heat it seemed to cover thousands of acres.

Another job listed was for a Soils Chemistry Technician: No Experience Needed. "No experience needed?" I repeated those words several times. "That's for me!" Now I'd really be busy. I'd knitted a lot while in school in California, but clearly, my knitting days were over. "Take good care of these sweaters, Dan—they may be the last you'll ever get that are homemade," I cautioned.

At home other jobs were being learned in the kitchen. "Honey, I can't believe I burned the limas again. I'm so sorry! And you were right—I finally read the directions on the bag: they should have been soaked overnight, and then I should have added fresh water." Our first bridges were burned behind us, but I was still burning beans. I had never cooked before, except for our time in the U.S. Forestry lookout when I had helped Dan heat canned food and had managed to burn some string beans while sitting only a few feet from the stove in the glass-walled room.

I had one big pot, one medium-sized pot, and a frying pan that had come from home in one of the trunks. I cooked enough for three or four suppers at a time in the big pot. Talk about frugality! Our extravagant menu involved preparing and boiling about four choices—dried lima beans, brown-colored beans, stew, or soup. I called it "soup" when there weren't enough vegetables, meat, or rice to put in the water to make stew. Our "stews" contained free soup bones from the butcher in the nearby grocery store, carrots, potatoes, maybe an onion, and a few stalks of celery. I bought milk, but no coffee, tea, or desserts. The budget ruled with an iron fist—every purchase had to stave off hunger with maximum nutrition, and minimum cost and time. My philosophy about small amounts of money never allowed me to think, "It's just chicken feed," or, "It's just nickel-and-dime stuff." Every penny was real money to be saved or spent carefully, then and forevermore. Breakfast was boiled rolled oats, canned grapefruit juice or prunes, and once in a while an egg. Lunch was in a brown bag to take to school and was usually a peanut butter sandwich and a spotty apple. Sometimes there were almost giveaway specials at the store—produce that needed to be sold immediately. In fact, we found that some of the best deals on food at the grocery store were free—the store tossed out boxes of bruised, damaged, wilted, or slightly stale produce—beets and lettuce with limp leaves, soft tomatoes, dark brown soft bananas, spotted peaches, and other surprises. In this manner, I got a few treats.

Popular success stories of the time told of some of the country's early immigrants starting at the bottom and making it to the top. Why couldn't we at least achieve lesser goals, like having enough money for food? Instead, part-time jobs, heavy school loads, and barely enough to eat were immediate problems. A few weeks before Christmas, I had a miscarriage at two months—maybe from skimpy meals and weariness. Increasingly, degrees and a farm seemed a long way off.

Christmas that first year in Tucson also became a time for some un-expected nostalgia for home and Christmases past—memories of my childhood with lots of special holiday meals, carols, whispering and se-crets. "What can I get Daddy?" or, "Can't you just give me a little hint?" I remembered the years of leaving a big stocking for Santa to fill, know-ing that up in a closet was a box with a few wrapped gifts that would appear beside the tree by morning.

Now all we had to celebrate with was a crooked, two-foot-high tree that we pulled out of the trash bin behind the grocery store and carried home. We set it in a glass jar on the dresser in the front room, and I dec-orated it with a short string of popcorn and several tattered ornaments saved from my childhood that were in one of the trunks. Dan's family sent us a Christmas package, but we bought nothing for each other.

For our Christmas dinner I splurged on a small roasting hen on sale and some wilted salad makings. On the table, two half-burned red candles, still in glass candleholders from home, flickered down to nub-bins during my special meal for two.

At this holiday time I worried a bit about Mrs. Marshall, the wom-an who owned the property and lived in the big house in front of our barn. Not once had we seen her, and no cars were ever parked in the yard, though once or twice we'd seen a nurse, or perhaps a cleaning lady, near her back door.

Sears Roebuck hired Dan to help with the extra rush of buyers for the holiday season. He spent much of his paycheck on a heavy wool blanket. Nights in Tucson during winter months can be cold, with the temperature often dipping below freezing, and we had decided that it was dangerous to run the old gas oven for heat while we slept.

Dan couldn't help but ask, "Would you do this over again if you were back in California? I suspect you're stranger than you know, or you'd not be here and married to me. Whatever did you see in me to chance saying, 'I do'?"

"Come on, Dan! I made no mistake, and this is where we belong. I could get down and kiss this floor daily after that first day in town! It's not what we see here, but what can be. Of course, it's quite a challenge to take the part-time jobs for food and rent when I'm so tired. But I'm not the only one who's tired—you look weary and thin, too. New batteries and a few pounds don't seem to come with the work, do they? The solution has simply got to be staying on track and getting those sheep-skins that can turn into jobs and money.

"You know," I continued, "This is a very special Christmas tree—it's a scraggly little thing, but it seems to make the statement that we've made a small step forward this fall. These are the best of times because we're together here and now."

He still wondered. "Sure you don't wish you'd married for money?" Of course, the answer was no.

I asked him the same questions, got the same answers, and we gave tired grins at each other. Dan knew that after my mom died and my dad had planned to leave California when I left for college, I'd turned down one couple's offer to adopt me and another couple's offer to cover my costs at Pomona College. I'd simply felt the need to be in control of my fate. They were nice offers, but I didn't want to let others be in a position to program my life. Moreover, I didn't want to become subject to the whims of benefactors who might mutate into matchmakers—I'd already made my match.

By late spring, the money we'd scraped together or earned during the year was getting low. "Dan, I think we're both happier when there's enough food on the table. Let's try the job our friend Chuck has offered you back in Saticoy. It can be a detour, not a retreat. Since he's promised us a free, furnished house, perhaps we can save enough to come back to school next year." Chuck hadn't described the work, but he owned a feed-lot for cattle and had suggested that a chance for Dan to stay in agricul-ture and save some money at the same time might look good to us. Chuck could use the help. We accepted the offer and quickly found a college student happy to sub-lease our little apartment for the time we'd be away.

With the final dollars I had saved by hoarding some of my monthly checks from jobs, we bought a well-used secondhand baby blue Ford coupe and headed back to California. With a sigh, I asked, "Dreams and finding the right plan to reach them are surely two different things, aren't they?"

Dan agreed, yet he fretted. "It doesn't seem right to quit and leave. I just hope we can save enough money to make this move back to Cali-fornia worthwhile."

In Saticoy, Dan lasted one day on the feedlot job. He was no weight-lifter, and right away the work required him to tote and toss big and heavy bales of hay onto a high truck bed.

He came home to say, "One more day on the job and I'll need a truss plus a new spinal column. I'm sorry to say I have to quit." We offered profuse apologies to Chuck, packed up again, and moved to a small apartment in nearby Ventura.

There were jobs of all kinds available during the war. I read the Help Wanted ads in the paper and soon suggested, "How about both of us working at the U.S. Naval Base in Port Hueneme?" At the beginning of the war, the Navy had taken over Hueneme's deep-water port and the surrounding land to service the Pacific Fleet. This was headquarters for the Navy Construction Battalion, usually called the SEABEES. At the base we found suitable work with no heavy lifting. Both of us worked in the same division, and our days were spent together installing identification numbers and letter tags on trucks, trailers, typewriters, and all sorts of other industrial, office, and war equipment before it was shipped overseas.

I became pregnant for the second time and was so afraid I might again lose a baby that we decided I should quit working and stay in bed until a few disturbing symptoms went away.

Our next-door neighbor passed on to me her copies of the Ventura News Press, and one day I found a want ad for a ranch foreman. Voilà! That experience might look good on Dan's ag teacher résumé, housing would be free, and there would be no driving to work. Dan quit his job at the base, and we moved to a foothill ranch where the owner raised cattle and grew lemons and oranges. The house we moved into was small but new, and I soon felt well enough to shovel over the soil on one side of the house and plant a small green lawn and several bright orange, yellow, and cream calendulas beside the door.

The stern lady who owned the ranch had recently lost both her husband and her brother-in-law, and running the ranch was a new role for her. She may have been imitating the heavy-handed way the men had managed the workers, or perhaps she was just desperate to get things done; she was loud, gruff, and demanding as she tried to oversee the work every minute she was home. She insisted Dan work seven days a week, and only when she left for a few hours could he even dash to town for a haircut. She spoke rudely about the other hired help in front of them, and they, too, were ordered to work ten- to twelve-hour days, seven days a week.

If Dan failed in an attempt to fix a piece of equipment, her perennial comment was, "Well, when we had Joe, he was always able to fix anything with just a piece of baling wire and a hammer."

That comment became a family saying. Can't fix something? All you need is Joe with baling wire and a hammer. One January night, during a hard electrical storm, one of the big steers electrocuted himself on some loose, exposed wiring. "Well," we said to ourselves, "it looks like Joe didn't use the baling wire and hammer quite right on the corral and barn."

On the first day of spring, our daughter Nancy was born. This baby did things her own way, even before she was born—she went four weeks beyond the expected delivery date, at which point my doctor put me in the hospital and prescribed medicine to jump-start the baby's arrival. Nancy arrived looking like she'd made good use of the extra time: lots of thick hair, a strong and healthy body, large round brown eyes that seemed to see the world with happy surprise, and a smile that seemed to signify the words, "Fooled you, didn't I?"

Nothing had equipped me for motherhood. I'd never held a real baby and had seldom even seen one. Immediately overwhelmed and wrought with the fear of not keeping my baby alive and healthy, I hired a neighbor named Gwen to come during my first week at home to help with the housework and show me basic things, like how to hold a baby, bathe her in the kitchen sink, dress and change her on the kitchen counter, and burp her.

After Gwen left, my constant Bible became the Better Homes and Gardens Baby Book. Its brief advice remained my only resource. Years later I read about the author, Dr. Spock, and his advice that parents should trust their own instincts over books. I never trusted myself, but I guessed, fretted perpetually, and learned by doing, which really meant learning from one mistake after another.

When the baby cried, I held her and sang the only songs I seemed to remember—ones I'd learned at Huntington Lake Camp for Girls during my two summers there when growing up. I also told her she'd get a horse, maybe next week, if she'd only start staying dry for at least ten minutes and not demand liquid food every fifteen.

I panicked at the very thought of germs and sterilized almost everything that would fit in a pot of boiling water. Without a screen door, flies got into the house daily, and I considered every one of them an invading enemy loaded with lethal germs. I could regularly be found dashing around the house brandishing a rolled-up newspaper as a flyswatter. I weighed Nancy daily, and felt like a complete failure if she hadn't gained an ounce. Even between feedings at night I got up to see if she was still breathing or if she had kicked the covers off; I was certain that our baby demanded round-the-clock care.

Then, rather unexpectedly, we became a family of four—a small, shaggy, black-and-white dog strayed to our door early one morning. She had no collar, and no ad appeared in the paper for her. I tacked a FOUND DOG notice on a telephone pole up by the road, but no owner came, and the pooch expressed no desire to leave.

Convinced that the baby, who couldn't even sit up yet, needed a pet, and knowing that the dog had to have a home, I started feeding the dog and she immediately became part of the family. We called her Cindy. Her ancestry seemed to be mostly cocker spaniel with a bit of poodle thrown in. She had a tangled mass of curly black hair, long floppy ears, and a bib-like splash of white fur on her chest. Cindy followed Dan around the ranch every day and slept in the kitchen at night. Dan and the workers fed her slices of orange, and she soon grew to love citrus.

The dog seldom barked and seemed to withhold approval of us. I wished I knew what her first home had been like, because she remained a dog who rejected cuddling or even petting, by remaining consistently grouchy. When I was a child we had had a Scottish terrier with the same neurotic temperament, not even giving love to any of her eight beautiful pups.

Meanwhile, the never-ending ranch job was teaching us a valuable lesson. Dan observed, "Guess we were both wrong in thinking a ranch foreman's job might be an alternative if there are no teaching jobs after

I graduate. Other foreman jobs might be better, but here we're living on crumbs with a seven-day work week and dawn-to-dark hours. The owner watches me like a hawk and tries to make every decision, yet knows almost nothing about a citrus or cattle operation! I don't know everything either, but I'm not given time to check with a county farm agent, some of my college ag teachers in Ventura, or even another cattle grower!"

I nodded. "Worst of all, there're no future advancements or career moves that I can see for you. It's no way to graduate to a good job or acquire funds for our own farm or ranch. Of course, I can't think of ever knowing a wealthy teacher, unless it's Mrs. Marshall back in Tucson, but I can't say we know her since we've never even met her. Still, she can be a role model, and teaching may lead to other jobs. At least as a teacher you won't have to be a slave every day of the year."

Dan then voiced the final decision—"Those are my thoughts, too. Let's go back and do our starving and struggling in Tucson. Classes are the only ticket to a better life. It's hard to believe we've only saved three hundred dollars. The living won't be easy, but both of us can work more and take longer to finish. The main thing is to not give up and to stay happy."

Mrs. Marshall sent us word through her manager that little Cindy couldn't live with us. She already had a wire-haired terrier in the jointly shared backyard, and she didn't think it would work out to have two dogs there. What she did do, however, was offer to loan us eighty dollars a month for our senior year. That would pay the rent of twenty-five dollars, food costs, and, hopefully, a bit more.

When her business manager phoned us with the news, he mentioned how much she had admired my persistence in making the "beautiful flower garden." He related, "I rather think that it was actually the memory of that garden of yours that prompted her wish to help you with your senior year." The show-and-tell of my chicken-wire trellis of colorful sweet peas against the barn walls had spoken to the feelings of the never-seen landlady and would make it at least possible for us to finish school the following spring.

I wrote to the student who was subletting our apartment and told her we would be coming back and that she would have to move. Again, in the fiery heat of late August, with both car windows wide open, we chugged back to college at thirty-five miles-per-hour.

Wearing just a diaper, Nancy lay in a cardboard box on the seat beside me, while Cindy panted and drooled on the narrow ledge behind our heads. One-tenth of the money loaned us by Mrs. Marshall would be used to board Cindy with two gray-haired ladies who had small dogs of their own and lived east of the campus. Mrs. Marshall was never told that we brought our Cindy back to Tucson or that part of her loan money was going toward boarding our dog.

The two rooms were still painted their battleship gray—a reminder that World War II continued to rage. In the fall, once more I shoveled over the same garden areas around the front and side of the barn and planted lots of sweet peas and two rows of beets, carrots, chard, onions, and squash. I had no idea that this garden would be like gold to us one more time in our future.

We both took heavy class loads, and the metal gate beside Mrs. Marshall's house clanged open and shut all day as Dan and I rushed back and forth to take turns caring for Nancy between classes and jobs. Occasionally we had to find a student to babysit for us. With a baby in the house and graduation on the horizon, school seemed ever more meaningful to Dan. Trying hard became his lodestar, and he began to get very high grades. Both of us found part-time jobs on campus, and Nancy's indulgent dad worked another Christmas vacation at Sears. One purchase was an early birthday present for Nancy—a small rocking horse, which Dan found on sale for one dollar.

"Now I have two girls dreaming of a horse. It's a long road, but we're getting closer," Dan reassured me. There were no vacation weekends, no radio, no movies, and seldom a magazine or a newspaper. Our only windows to the goings-on in the town and world came when we brought home newspapers or magazines that had been left behind in the university's classrooms we attended. The only glitter and bright lights to our life were the daily shining sun, two bare lightbulbs hanging from the two ceilings, plus one light on the wall in the bathroom...but best of all, we had the vision of gold seals on parchment paper at graduation time in June.

Few friends visited us during the years of gas rationing and the war. There were no neighbors to talk to, and no time to make school friends.

Survival mattered more: something to eat, part-time jobs in school offices or labs, and getting through midterms, finals, and term papers.

Sometimes, I rolled the word "housewife" around in my mind, trying it out for size and meaning. It remained in small print and not too relevant. I liked the "wife" part, but I didn't want to be married to a house. I had a broom and a mop for the wooden floors but used them only when my bare feet became blacker than they would have become in the yard or when friends were coming. Nothing got dusted. I wiped the table off with a washcloth that we renamed "The Dishrag." The tumbleweeds of my dreams were just dust balls under Nancy's crib. I didn't disturb the dust balls, and they multiplied.

Finally, during this last winter, friends came to visit from California. In their car we were finally able to travel beyond the outskirts of Tucson. My favorite class that fall had included the history of the southwestern United States, and I would have been thrilled to travel around in all the adjoining states as well as in Arizona. Fortunately, when Ray and Emily came to see us, they quickly invited us to go with them to see the giant saguaro cacti south of town and the San Xavier Mission. In those early years near Tucson, saguaro cacti formed almost a forest, with long spiny arms branching out from thirty-foot-tall trunks. They were worth seeing, as were many of the other wonderful cacti. I remember yuccas, with their sharp leaves and tall stems of creamy white flowers, and ocotillos with their beautiful red blossoms growing on some mountainsides.

Our second day trip was with my dear friend Babe, who came with her husband, Walt, and their first child. They drove us up the nearby Sabino Canyon where we picnicked beside a small, clear creek that ran among rocks, sycamores, and willow trees. The children sat and splashed in the shallow creek, while a couple of hawks circled lazily overhead, and we reminisced for the afternoon about all our long years together as children and at college.

During the spring semester I had to walk several miles each way to do my practice teaching in a Tucson high school U.S. history class, while Dan was doing his in the high school vo-ag department in the nearby town of Coolidge. He had heard that the year before, students in another Arizona town had hung an ag teacher by his heels outside a second-story window. We wondered and worried how his student-teaching would go. Could this school be subject to a copycat crime? As it turned out, things went smoothly, and Dan did a very good job of teaching. He started each week armed with a stack of detailed lesson plans, all scrutinized and slightly revised by Dr. Cline, Dan's demanding department head. Our excitement was building even as our supply of energy and funds ebbed.

I reveled in the vision of June. "What a delicious thought to have no more tests, midterms, finals, or reports! You'll bring home real checks, while I'll work hundred-hour weeks on some tiny farm, and it will still be better than any more college for me!" How little I knew!

Arriving home from practice teaching one weekend, Dan grinned and asked, "Well, Mrs. C, where in Arizona would you like to move this summer?" While at Coolidge, he had heard about three job openings in the state for the next school year. "Do you fancy Tolleson, Yuma, or Snowflake?"

I replied, "Well, what do you think? Yuma doesn't seem like a good place for us. When we drove through there, that gas station man and the waitress in the little cafe both told us the place gets only three inches of rain each year, and they seemed to almost be bragging when they assured us it gets even hotter there than in Tucson. I guess there's irrigation water from the Colorado River, but the town looked so dry."

I continued in the same critical vein: "Snowflake sounds as if it would snow and be rather isolated. Both you and I would rather be warm than freezing." (Many years later I learned that the town of Snowflake was named after two founders, Erastus Snow and William J. Flake—and not for winter snowstorms.) "Where's Tolleson?"

"Tolleson is a small town just a few miles west of Phoenix in part of the wonderfully rich agricultural area—the Salt River Valley. But I've heard there's another teacher who may apply for that job, and he has a couple of years of teaching experience. Maybe I shouldn't try there."

The next weekend, when Dan came home from his student-teaching, he seemed encouraged and said that a friend, who was a state official in agriculture, had told him to quit hanging back. He then repeated the man's words. "Uh-uh, you listen to me. That job at Tolleson is an extrafine one. You get up there right away and give it a good try. Take my word for it—you'd do well there and like it. That West Side area's got lots of farming and ranching, yet it's nice and close to Phoenix. In fact, the whole Maricopa County is a great area to live in. A lot going on these years. My philosophy is to never wait for the light to turn from green to yellow—get goin'!"

Someone in Coolidge, unfortunately, convinced Dan that there was a train that would stop in Tolleson and that that would be the easiest way to go. Dan took the train, dressed up in his only good suit, an overly starched white shirt, a tie, and wingtip shoes to make himself look older. Finally, the train stopped out in a countryside of fields of grain with not a town in sight. The porter told him this was the stop for Tolleson. "The town's up this road a spell. You can walk to it—others do."

It was a dusty, hot hike on a day that was over a hundred degrees in the shade. Clothes crumpled, perspiring, and a bit dizzy from the heat, Dan walked into the first store he came to and asked for directions to the high school. The man pointed, explained it was just down the street a short distance, and then asked why he was going there. Dan explained, "I've come up to apply for the ag teacher job. That's not much of a train station down the road."

The man laughed and held out his hand. "Sorry about that. I'm on the school board and heard you were coming up." Dan washed up the best he could in the store's bathroom, gulped a Coke, and trudged on through the little town to the high school.

Mr. Wade, the principal of the school, immediately told him, "This vo-ag program has exactly one year to shape up and become one the school can be proud of, or there will be no agriculture program at all, and you'll be out. Think you can do the job?" Dan told him he could.

The principal smiled and nodded. "I'll talk to the Board and get their official OK, but you go ahead and make plans to come. You're hired. Let me show you the shop and ag classrooms, if you have time. There're no classes at this hour."

Back at home, I had done little but fret all day. I knew the approximate time Dan would make it back from the train trip and then home by car from Coolidge. Finally, the door flew open, and my man rushed in, looking both happy and frazzled.

"Have I ever got news! I'd have phoned you if we had a phone, but maybe this is the best way to tell you anyway. Here, let me hug you!" We both stood up, and, though he seemed a bit light-headed, he threw his arms around me.

"I got the job! You're now married to a teacher who won't have to lift and toss bales of hay for a living! Even the salary's way up for a first-year teacher!" Dan still seemed completely flabbergasted that things were finally working out.

Joy of joys! Without waking Nancy, we quietly danced around the apartment and softly sang snatches of "Don't Fence Me In," "Oh Give Me a Home Where the Buffalo Roam," and "Blue Skies." Our new life would finally begin after graduation, which was only a few weeks away.

Without any funds to pay for the caps and gowns for graduation ceremonies, we skipped the rituals and slid straight into summer. While we kept our part-time jobs on campus for the summer months, Dr. Cline insisted that Dan keep on writing lesson plans for all and submit them for his approval and corrections. Dr. Cline's university work seemed to be his whole life, every month of the year. Meanwhile, I would have another baby in late September or October.

Outside our little world, other big things were happening. It was 1945, and the war was ending. Roosevelt, Hitler, and Mussolini had all died in April of that year, and the United Nations officially came into being as its charter took effect. Elizabeth Taylor, in the movie National Velvet, captured the essence of the female passion for horses. The country's people were restless, tired, and ready to get back to normal, war-free civilian life. Many returning vets and other folks swarmed into rural areas seeking a country or suburban life with a job, car, house, and kids. With its mild, dry climate exempt from snow and freezing weather, Arizona's Valley of the Sun became one of the fastest growing areas in the country.

Women were encouraged to leave work and become housewives again, since there was no more need for Rosie-the-Riveter defense factory work. Some vets went to college, but many had a nostalgic vision of just having a good civilian life again free of war. It was a heady and exciting year, full of enormous change for a great many in America.

Meanwhile, Dan and I had to move from Tucson to some kind of a rental house near Tolleson. In Goodyear, just west of Tolleson, we found a duplex surrounded by other duplexes and expansive Bermuda grass lawns. Late that summer we bought an old two-wheeled luggage trailer to move our few belongings, picked up little Cindy from her sitters, and transported our belongings in three round-trips.

Even though I was expecting a baby and Dan wanted to work on reorganizing the ag building rooms at the high school, Dr. Cline insisted that Dan take a trip with him to Cedar Break, Utah, the day after we moved in. Dan couldn't refuse his department head, but it continued to be "blue sky" time—he got home in ample time for Baby Danny's arrival. In fact, this baby, like Nancy, decided to arrive almost a month late. Early habits must be hard to break—to this day Danny often catches planes just before they taxi down runways.

Dan and I had become ever so tired of waiting for the baby's late arrival. However, it had seemed to startle our new neighbors when they saw me pushing a borrowed lawnmower through the thick Bermuda grass that covered our large lot—I was only trying to create labor pains for a baby reluctant to enter the world; they only knew that in my bulging smock and pants, I looked very "with child," or "with several children." Finally, when the delivery time arrived, the doctor was out on a distant fairway playing golf. Regardless of the unusual circumstances preceding and during labor, the baby came into the world in fine shape. Once again, I got up multiple times every night and stole down the hall in the dark to check Baby Danny's breathing and to carefully reposition the sheet or blanket over this miraculous new child.

Dan, meanwhile, only had several days left before classes to begin an overhaul of his classroom and the ag shop. Completely exhausted, he began life as a teacher, and I as a mother of two babies and one not-so-affectionate dog.

Cindy was now part of the family, even though she seemed to thoroughly dislike little Nancy, by growling through bared teeth in a low, long, singsong voice whenever Nancy approached. With no friends yet, except for a young dentist next door (who put in four crowns on Dan's front teeth as one of his first operations), I had time to talk to the pooch, but attempted interactions with the dog were rather frustrating. When I asked "Want to play ball?" she only turned her head and looked the other way, as though to reply, "Naw. Feed me and leave me alone." If I threw a ball or a stick for her to fetch, I was the one who ended up fetching. If I asked, "Cindy, how about a hug?" she pulled away from me in bold defiance. Eventually Cindy became hospitable enough to wag her tail a bit and greet us with a few signs of friendship, if not enthusiasm…but then again, she was probably only thinking about dinner.

We kept Cindy since she never chewed a hunk out of anyone. "Well," we'd say, "kindness surely begins in the home. We'll still keep the dog." While Baby Danny would have no animal preferences for a long time, Nancy already preferred horse stories, horse pictures, and horse rides at the park. I had a growing premonition that if (and when) the time finally arrived for us to have a horse, I might not be the only starry-eyed girl holding the reins.

Chapter 4

Oh Blessed Land

I was still learning unavoidable lessons in what I could do without, although living in a duplex was heaven after the red barn apartment in Tucson. The duplex was quite new and had two bedrooms plus a large living room and dining area. Dan built a sandbox on the back lawn for Nancy, and then made her a small swing. After a neighbor discovered I was still washing all the diapers and the family wash in the bathtub every day, she put me toward the top of the list for a washing machine at her husband's local appliance store. Things like washing machines, refrigerators, tires, and cars were in short supply right after the war, and there were waiting lists for people who wanted to purchase them.

While I plodded along with Nancy, new Baby Danny, and grouchy Cindy, Dan began teaching not only days but evening classes to returning veterans in his high school vo-ag room. It was a subject matter some of these returning farmers knew far better than he—they'd grown up with parents who had raised dairy cows and grown crops like alfalfa, cotton, melons, and sorghum. Some veterans were returning to farms they'd already owned when they went to war. Others abandoned the rural areas for jobs in cities or became employed in ag-related fields, such as farm advisors, insurance agents for farming people, bankers for ag loans, and sales agents for seed or fertilizer companies.

Trying to look a bit older and more knowledgeable than his nighttime students, Dan took to wearing his glasses, and bought a suit to wear with his wing-tip shoes. He also frantically wrote and studied lesson plans to stay one class ahead of these students and brought in a number of more experienced guest teachers who knew a lot about farm machinery, farm credit, and certain crops, to help make the classes more interesting and informative. Lo and behold, the young returning farmers liked him and kept coming. We became friends with some of these vets and their families, and Dan quit tossing and turning in his sleep.

With his daytime vo-ag students, Dan had started out the year with a rousing pep talk. "Gang, much is expected of you and me this year. There will be no more agriculture classes at all at this school next year unless you and I really make things sizzle—Mr. Wade warned me, and I believe him. You're going to change, perform, and succeed, and, what's more, it's going to be fun. Every one of you, whether a freshman, sophomore, junior, or senior, is going to be part of the team and get involved. Not just with farm projects, but with stuff like parliamentary and public speaking teams. You name it, we'll do it. Your blue and yellow Future Farmers of America jackets, which I will make sure each of you own, will be as impressive as any football jacket, and we're beginning right now, this morning."

As leader of his pack of students, Dan continued to spruce up his ag rooms. The school janitor was already overwhelmed with too much work, so Dan made him a loyal fan by telling him he'd sweep and scrub the floors, wash the windows, and paint the blackboards in the shop and ag room. Purina Feed stores handed out small signs with upbeat inspirational sayings, and Dan put them on a corner section of the blackboard each week, along with a schedule of the class lessons and projects. A few of the most popular sayings from the company, now called Purina Mills, were:

WINNERS NEVER QUIT...QUITTERS NEVER WIN!

ASPIRE NOBLY, ADVENTURE DARINGLY, SERVE HUMBLY.

THERE IS NEARLY NOTHING SO CLEVER AS HONESTY AND SINCERITY.

GOOD HABITS ARE LIKE MUSCLES—THE MORE YOU USE THEM, THE STRONGER THEY GROW.

IF AT FIRST YOU DO SUCCEED, TRY SOMETHING HARDER.

A TURTLE GETS NOWHERE UNTIL IT STICKS OUT ITS NECK.

HE WHO ASKS A QUESTION IS A FOOL FOR FIVE MINUTES...HE WHO DOES NOT REMAINS A FOOL FOREVER.

NO ONE OF US IS AS SMART AS ALL OF US!

DON'T BE A CARBON COPY OF SOMEONE ELSE...MAKE YOUR OWN IMPRESSIONS.

With the help of a student who had the tools, Dan built a magazine rack for the classroom. He stocked it with our Time magazines, some agricultural ones, and others that he begged from the staff and students. Next, he and the students created some shelves for agriculture books. He also revived the students' farm machinery co-op, and soon students could rent out an International Harvester Farmall tractor, a plow, a disk, a harrow, and a large pressure sprayer.

At home, who could possibly ask for anything more? Why worry or think about the past or future with the present so full? In just a few fall months we had been granted a second, dearly loved child, enough food to eat, a washing machine, and a two-bedroom home to live in. But we still had dreams for the present.

Our inner clocks were the problem: they ticked loudly, and unseen schedules ordered us: "Go full speed and make more plans and decisions without delay—time involves both living and money, and he who hesitates is lost." Even a few months of rent paid to others seemed to be money wasted. The alarm clocks demanded, "Don't procrastinate; solve any problems later." Every night that Dan wasn't out teaching night classes or going to a Farm Bureau or Lions Club meeting, we plotted various schemes for the next day, for the next month, and for years into the future.

By Christmas we were clear about what we wanted, but less clear about how to achieve it. The washing machine, bought on credit, would soon be paid for, and by almost constant starvation we would have Mrs. Marshall's loans paid off by spring. We had no savings at all; nevertheless, I was to start looking for land and a small house. Oh blessed land!

"It's a matter of priorities, of figuring out what's most important and not putting it off. We've simply got to make a small beginning and not continue paying rent. Wasting time is not the way to go," Dan admonished. Having caught my obsession for land, he had begun to embrace it even more desperately than I.

Beginning a short subscription to the Phoenix paper, I read the listings of farms for sale, but no newspaper would be likely to carry an ad for the kind of place we could afford. Most mornings, the kids and I crowded into the Ford coupe to take Dan to the high school. Then, with sack lunches, jars of juice and water, baby bottles of milk, diapers, and a few toys or picture books, the kids and I roamed the countryside hunting for signs. Baby Danny lay in a cardboard box on the seat, while Nancy crowded in beside him or crawled up on the ledge behind the seat.

Several months passed, and still I couldn't find a tiny plot of land with a house on it for sale. Still, I wasn't allowed to slow up the search no matter how discouraging it became. "Don't worry, honey, the trail is still on the low lands and…"

"You can say that again!"

"Let me finish," Dan quickly insisted. "Don't worry about this flat land and a first place: our trail is just beginning, and the next stop may be in the foothills. But at this juncture we have to continue to be fixated on the here and now. Please, please, hon, keep looking!"

This beautiful Salt River Valley where I searched for our first farm had been inhabited centuries ago by native farmers. On these desert lands, the Hohokam had made their canals and cities with just rock axes and hand-powered tools…yet their ingenuity and knowledge of the land allowed them to successfully grow crops like beans, maize, squash, and cotton.

After the Mexican War of 1848 the Salt River Valley became part of the United States, and some twenty years later, following the U.S. Civil War, veterans and others began to come to the valley. They discovered hay growing wild, and water available for crops. The name Phoenix came from the idea that a new large city could rise on the site of the ancient

Hohokam city, like the mythological bird that rose from its ashes. In 1912, Arizona became a state and was admitted to the Union, the last of the contiguous forty-eight states.

This was still an incredibly young and developing area, although farms, ranches, and towns abounded in the region when we arrived. Phoenix was the capital of the state, as well as the county seat of Maricopa County. Although it was a small city, it was quite cosmopolitan and beautiful, while still retaining a strong agricultural feel—there were farm equipment and feed stores, the county fairgrounds, and a hotel called the Westward Ho.

While agriculture was the city's main reason for being, there were also mining, tourism, and manufacturing. After the Roosevelt Dam was built to hold back the Salt River to the east, water from the Salt and Verde Rivers made the valley green, and a great network of irrigation canals brought water to both city and farm lands. In the wonderful mild climate, crops could grow twelve months a year. There was even the Southern Pacific railway to ship some of the produce out, and Phoenix was the hub of many roads coming in from neighboring towns and the rest of the state. However, many of the areas I searched contained discouragingly large farms of cattle, or row and field crops.

In the town of Tempe, on the east side of Phoenix, was Arizona State College (now Arizona State University), surrounded by farmland. Scottsdale was still a tiny place, notable mainly for its popular Pink Pony Saloon. Other towns nearby, like Glendale, Mesa, and Tolleson, were small western towns surrounded by farms, ranches, or desert. People attended and participated in rodeos, and staged lots of backyard barbeques. Plows and fences had come to much of this land, yet this was a recent enough development that lizards, roadrunners, and cottonwood trees still abounded. The setting seemed perfect, but I just could not find a farm of the type we needed.

I didn't want to get too close to Phoenix, as we knew about cities that gulped up the nearby countryside with industry, tracts of houses, and golf courses. The west side of Phoenix was already developing some industrial sites and urban sprawl, and neither of us wanted a long commute for Dan in our aged Bluebird car.

Finally, I turned down a narrow dirt lane labeled Fowler Lane in a sparsely settled area west of Phoenix. There I finally discovered a recent homemade FOR SALE sign nailed to a fence post. TWO ACRES AND HOUSE, it read, and displayed a phone number. The sign couldn't have touted much more. We'd need no guided tour of either the house or the land to get a good feel for what we were getting ourselves into. The place possessed none of the appealing features cited in newspaper real estate ads: no fireplace, office, garage, balcony, mountain view or charming garden, or any of the other catch-words so dear to the area's Realtors.

The only structure on the property was a tiny, sad house, stark and square, its walls made of unpainted cement blocks, and its roof composed of ugly, roll-on sheets of green asphalt. From the road, I surmised that the only door was at the back far corner of the house where I could see steps leading to a porch. Masses of weeds covered the lot and grew right up to the cement foundation of the house, rustling low and lonely in a slight breeze. The whole landscape was flat and without a single tree.

The house appeared to be unoccupied, but topping the scene were chickens, ducks, and a couple of turkeys and a goose wandering loose on the porch, in the yard, and along the aptly named Fowler Lane. A rather small wooden shed or chicken coop had fallen mostly onto its side in the backyard. While their owners had built the house very close to the dirt lane, I thought that few cars would come that way, as there were only a couple of other houses before the road ended at some kind of a packing shed. Two wires strung to the building indicated the presence of electricity and a phone line.

The place held me like a magnet: would this have to be First Farm? I had a terrible feeling of inevitability as I looked at this wasted land and the dilapidated house, about the size of a double garage. How could I describe it? It wasn't the somewhere of my dreams, with rolling green hills, mature trees, and majestic mountains in the distance. It wasn't a friendly house with verandas and lots of windows. It couldn't be considered quaint, interesting, historical, or unique, unless perhaps in the category of "the ugliest" or "the smallest." Could it have been considered rustic? No, "rustic" sounds a little like fun. What was it? The place couldn't be called a thatched cottage, a log cabin, an adobe hacienda, a

villa, or a Victorian. Was it a homestead? Well it wouldn't have been acquired through the Homestead Act as it certainly didn't have 160 acres,
and I suppose it wasn't as primitive as many homesteaded houses. Another word came to me—the land and shack most appropriately fit the
title "Challenge." Dang it, I'd take it in stride, and there'd be no holding back in the way I'd tackle it!

But how could it lead anywhere? "Maybe," I thought, "this can be
like a campsite on our trail." The whole place was so terrible, it suddenly became funny. Nancy asked why I was laughing. "Well, hon," I
answered, "opportunity doesn't always knock twice, and, to put it simply, this seems to be the only little farm for sale in the whole Salt River
Valley. I think you'll be living here in this bare-bones abode. I'm not
sure I even want to see what's inside. But remember, good things don't
always come in fancy wrappings."

"Can we buy it? Will the chickens and ducks be my ducks? Can I
have those horses in that field? Please?" She had immediately fallen deeply in love with the horses in a neighboring field, and the large number
of chickens, ducks, and a turkey running loose.

Stories my mom had told about walking through snow to school
didn't seem so bad at that moment. Those snow-walkers had often begun their walks from large two-story farm homes, with porches, fire-
places, and nearby barns filled with cows, horses, and hay. Those farms
usually had shade trees, and sometimes a pond for swimming in the
summertime and ice-skating in the winter. Right then, I would have
preferred the farm and home my mom once had, no matter how much
snow came with the property.

I rushed back and reported to Dan, "Bingo! Honey, I've found the
most wonderful farm—a rural hideaway! And you know what? It's in
a prime location because it's close to your job. It's on a little dirt road
you've never even noticed when driving by to Phoenix. A turn to the
right, and a surprise lurks in wait for us on Fowler Lane!"

I continued my enthusiastic presentation: "There are two whole acres,
all strongly fenced, probably by the neighboring ranchers. Nancy went
wild over seeing horses in the field on the north side. I think the house
has at least two rooms. And a bath! At any rate, there was no outhouse.

It looks like some family started there and then ran out of money." ("Or just ran away," I thought to myself.) "Maybe they'd sell with nothing down and just monthly payments."

We all went back to see it. Dan was appalled, even before getting out of the car. When we peered through one of the windows of the house, we could see there was a tiny kitchen, plus one other room and a bathroom. The inside walls were just the other side of the gray cinder block outside. I pointed out brightly that termites would never eat the house down, with those cement floors and cement-block walls. The poultry raced around hither and thither, frightened by us but still looking for some last seeds or bugs to eat before settling down for the night.

Dan blurted out, "Honey, four of us can't live in a two-room shanty! It's all so, so, well…scroungy! This isn't even close to the image of what I've thought of getting. You're crazy!"

"Will it be an embarrassment to you? Believe me, Dan, it'll be a changing scene; I'll make it a different picture. Haven't you heard? Just as great paintings can't be explained, neither can the potential of this place be described."

As we hurried home to eat before the kids started crying and before Dan had to leave to teach a veterans' class, I continued to praise the farm. "Listen, Dan. Sure, it's a grim place now, but it's absolutely delectable because it's doable and maybe a bargain. I'm positive it's the only two acres on this side of the Valley that we stand even a slight chance of buying. Cement blocks are better than sod for walls. What were you expecting? Parquet and marble floors, vaulted ceilings, and spacious rooms? Instead, there'll be spacious skies, green lawns, and gardens. You've got to feel the promises that land makes.

"Please, Dan, we've got to do it. It's got a couple of redeeming features: it's probably supercheap with a chance we can buy it, and it's the only wee farm for sale in this whole area anywhere near Tolleson. I see what you see, but it can be first-class just having our own roof over our heads, beds to sleep in, and good homegrown food. The car still runs. There'll be sunshine, love, and laughter." Beneath this façade I felt frightened and not nearly as certain as I portrayed myself to be.

Dan began mumbling and repeating something about, "Well, I never said I could promise you a rose garden—only love."

Which made me question, "Well, will you still make that promise when we're living in such an unromantic setting, and when I'll never be cutting a very glamorous figure in work garb? I have a horrible vision of the kids and me soon looking like we belong here—that land's not for sissies, and it'll be a hard life."

It only took two votes, mine and Nancy's, to decide to buy the place. (Nancy had seen those horses across the fence.) No time was spent poring over maps, meeting or talking to the neighbors about the area and the water supply, or checking with county offices for any easements or road rights-of-way. I simply phoned the owners immediately.

They insisted they had to have all cash, and that they needed it soon. They were leaving the state, and wanted the flock of chickens, ducks, turkeys, and the goose to stay with the property. The price was low, it seemed to me, but what could we do to get the property? We hadn't a penny of savings in the bank.

We put the kids to bed, and later, when Dan's evening class was over, we lay awake for hours thinking. With a weary sigh, I mused, "When there's opportunity, we've got to see it and run with it. I'll never find anything any better for a first toehold. The price is right, and we can add rooms onto the house. While you're off earning, I can almost feed us there with animals and a garden. It can be made attractive with green lawns, the house painted white, a pink and white oleander hedge along the road, and new sheds for hay and the chickens. The only problem is, where do we get the money?"

Dan shook his head and wondered, "Would a bank give a beginning teacher with a wife and two kids the entire sale price? No way! They'd demand a good-sized down-payment from us; there's no need to even ask. It beats me where we can get the money."

Suddenly I had an idea. "Hey, let's phone Mr. Peters and see if Mrs. Marshall would loan us the money. I've paid off extra on the school loan each month, thank goodness. She knows we can be trusted, and she just might like to help us get a first house. Since her money's in real estate, she might be sympathetic to the idea." Holding that slim possibility in mind, we got several hours of sleep.

With a bit of bravado, I called as soon as I hoped her business manager had eaten his breakfast with a cup of coffee. "Yes, Mr. Peters, I've been looking for months, and it's the least expensive place I could find. Yes, it's well fenced. The house has an almost-new roof and concrete brick walls. It certainly doesn't have a shaky foundation; it's solid concrete… no, the sellers say the water supply is from a neighbor not too far away who has a small dairy farm and a good well. He has an agreement to furnish water to this house and the other two neighbors down the lane. Since there's that much water nearby, I'm sure that if we had to, we could drill a well and find water in the future…Yes, we could pay it off in five years. No problem. It's just that Dan is in his first year of teaching, and we've had to buy appliances and furniture, and we may have to replace our car before long. Beyond that, we have a second child now. But Dan is earning extra by teaching nights as well as days, and we have several other extra jobs in mind…Yes, the teaching is going very well."

Mr. Peters said he would ask Mrs. Marshall. He phoned back and said she would give us the loan. "Oh wonderful, wonderful! Thank you so much, and please thank her!" We discussed the financial arrangements.

Two hours later, Mr. Peters called me back, rather upset and apologetic, to say Mrs. Marshall had changed her mind, and wasn't sure about another loan.

I could only say to him. "Please tell her I understand. Thank her for even considering it. Be sure you give her our thanks again for helping us with our senior-year costs, and tell her not to worry. I don't want her to be upset because she's changed her mind. Don't forget what I've said. And don't you worry, either."

In midafternoon, I got another call. It was from Mr. Peters again. "Judy, I told her what you said, and she's had more time to think it over. She'd like to give you the loan as long as you can pay everything back to her within five years. She still remembers your colorful flower beds, and the present renters in the apartment haven't planted a thing."

For the second time, my old-fashioned sweet peas, other flowers, and vegetables were magically coming to the rescue. Mrs. Marshall became the sponsor of our first farm, giving us a big and heavy cloud of debt with a silver lining.

Dan walked in from school that day to ask, "Well, did you tell Mr. Peters you want a loan to buy a shack the size of a chicken coop?"

"Quit chewing on it like a bone. Celebrate! I got the loan. Our former landlady has become a mortgagor. She's going to help us get our first farm!" Laughing with relief, I wondered aloud whether I'd soon be crying if we couldn't make the high mortgage payments.

"Come on," Dan urged me, "you're the one who's always telling me how good challenges are, and here's the opportunity to take on a whole raft of problems. Though come to think of it, maybe there's not too much to lose when it's good land."

Thank heavens the lender never saw the property, especially at the time she gave us the loan. The kindnesses of Mr. Peters and Mrs. Marshall remain vivid and warm to us to this day; yet we probably saw Mr. Peters in person only half a dozen times, and we never once saw Mrs. Marshall in person in spite of having lived in her backyard barn all the time we were in Tucson. If she ever came to Phoenix and someone drove her by our farm on Fowler Lane, she never stopped to check on us.

This was an early era when people often saved and saved until they had the full price of a house before buying. Any kind of credit, mortgage, or loan seemed risky for both lenders and buyers after the heavy losses during the long years of the Great Depression. Most of us knew there were no free tickets to where we wanted to go or live—it was up to each of us to make things happen. "First Farm" on Fowler Lane became ours, and so did the big, going-out-on-a-limb mortgage.

Still perhaps addled from that day, I had to laugh about the two street signs up at the corner to the lane. One warned, DEAD END STREET, and the other said, FOWLER LANE. My farm would never be a dead end for us, or a "foul" experience, except perhaps for all the chickens. I did, however, jokingly dub the shack our "Road House," because it was built so close to the lane.

There would be scant entertainment for us with the mountain of work ahead. And, in spite of the thrill of owning land, I tried to remember that it would be but a pause, a way station, on our trail to other land, and reminded Dan, "My dear co-owner, we can date future places from the time we got First Farm! It'll be no joke to have so few creature comforts, but it will surely be an affair to remember: two kids, all the animals we can get, and the transformation of land and house into something far more than is there today." All the nervous pressures of my day were blotted out—"Jeepers! We're landowners, that's what we are, and someday far off, it'll be 'the way we were'! My goodness, the finding and purchase of it has all happened so fast—just in the last two days!! Can you see what I see?"

Dan replied, "I'm sure we'll remember it all right; but it's going to be endless hours of work, and with a jam-packed schedule of day and night classes, I'm not going to be able to help you very much. Maybe I'll have some time in the summer, though I might start work on a Master's degree. My school principal just mentioned that my two-week vacation could be three weeks if I go to grad school."

"That's OK, but my cast of characters had better get along well. It'll be awfully up-close, with a good deal of forced intimacy. Four of us, plus Cindy, in this space, won't leave any space for anyone to pout in the wings. Pouters will have to do their pouting outside. I suspect we'll all avoid the tight quarters by trying to keep the two windows and door open and by remaining outside as much as possible."

Fortunately, Nancy had seemed years old the day she was born, and she loved to "mother" her baby brother; they got along well, at that age at least. Cindy's ill temperament would make her rather well suited to the position of being an outside guard dog.

It was reassuring for me to know that I wasn't the first with such dreams. The hope of finding land in the West was what most of the covered wagon treks were all about in the early days of America. Some people went west as trappers, soldiers, or traders. Others searched for gold, or a passage to the Orient. A few were missionaries. But in the end, most were settlers who sought freedom and the chance to create farms, ranches, and a new life.

To go west in those early times had been a hard decision, requiring much daring, spirit, and endurance. A deep urge stirred within those pioneers to find that better land and life. Most of the long migrations were to inhospitable lands, and starvation and death were frequent occurrences, but there were also many winners.

My feelings for the land echoed from those earlier settlers. Why couldn't working hard and long open up opportunities for us, just as it had for those who'd preceded us? Each day can be part of the trail to be traveled and a fine adventure.

Some of my mother's ancestors had come from Europe many generations ago, but the only ancestor I'd ever heard about from those earlier times was John Robinson, who had helped organize the Mayflower's voyage to America, but who himself hadn't made the trip.

At the age of sixteen, my dad had felt the pull to leave England, and without family or friends to accompany him, he had voyaged west to a very young and new world. By the time I was born, my parents had crossed the country to California, making their own "manifest destiny" by settling on the western edge of America beside the Pacific Ocean.

At least for these two acres we hadn't had to clear and level the land, fend off hostile Indians, drill for water, or even build fences. No need to sleep on a straw bed or gather buffalo dung and sagebrush to make a fire to cook by and to keep us warm. Civilization had come to much of the Salt River Valley by the time we bought this little block house. It's true that an Indian Reservation was only a short distance away, and this house was not far removed from being a sod hut, but on our parcel, there were water and electricity to turn on, and a tank of Bu-Gas we could use to heat shower water and to cook with.

Yet, in this different time and way, we too were on a trail that would have to stretch out far beyond the next hill. It was hard to curb my excitement and obsession about how to make First Farm a home for us and lots of critters. Maybe it was a bit like getting religion, having this land and house that called to me; I suddenly felt somehow related to those pioneers, finding communion through a sympathetic spirit.

"Come on, Dan! Let's go see the place again. You've got to be my cohort in this; it's all a matter of trying and doing it our way. It has the bare essentials—bright lights that go on in both rooms, a toilet that flushes, hot and cold water that comes out of the faucets, and a roof that will keep us dry—at least I assume it doesn't leak since it appears to be rather new. This doesn't say 'poverty' to me, it suggests all sorts of wealth, including two whole acres—we're land rich, even if we make headway slowly!"

Chapter 5

A Rooster and His Harem

Taking the homemade trailer we had bought when we moved from Tucson, we arrived at Fowler Lane with our first load, which included a box of Fels Naptha soap, a mop, and a broom. It was an exciting time—my possessions were arriving in my own empire, even though it was happening on borrowed funds.

"Fancy this, guys! We now have our first farm lane, our first rural mailbox, and there's a phone line to the house, so we can get our first phone number in Arizona!"

In sight was even more poultry than we remembered—chickens and ducks, a big goose, a rooster, and two tom turkeys—all wandering around the yard, poking in the weeds or loitering on the porch and steps. I noted, "Maybe they all come home from their daily excursions and roost near the shed for the night. Nancy, look at the sorority of Rhode Island Reds and white Leghorn hens that seem to stay together as a group!"

I continued to watch the poultry from the car while worrying, "Well, I already have my first farm animals, but they can't just run free and live off the land much longer—these birds are probably making it very unsanitary for Nancy to play in the yard. Dan, the sellers have been here today and filled those old washbasins by the shed overflowing with water. We'd better buy chicken feed, and we'll need some wire to patch the pen. The shed must be rebuilt right away. I need those hens to lay their eggs where I can find them. At this point, they're probably laying them indiscriminately down the lane and all over in the fields."

Nancy quickly got out and raced toward the chickens, calling, "Chick, chick, chick. My chick!" In seconds, the big flamboyant rooster, with long flowing feathers, opened his wings to half fly and half run toward Nancy. With long claws extended and vicious spurs exposed on the backs of his legs, he shot airborne and slashed Nancy's face just under her eyes. There were two long, deep gashes, and the poor child fell and screamed in pain and fear as blood streamed down her face and onto her coveralls.

We rushed her to the local Tolleson doctor, who, although it was late in the day, was fortunately still in his office. He took a number of stitches under her eye while we tried to explain to Nancy what had happened. She needed to be told many times for any of it to sink in. I tried to explain, "Honey, that rooster feels he owns those chickens. He had never even seen a little girl before, and he decided that you might hurt his family— he thinks that it's his job to protect and take care of his flock of hens."

"He didn't have to hurt me," she cried, through continuing tears. "I wouldn't hurt the chickens. Why'd he do that? He's bad!"

"Look, Daddy and I will get rid of that mean rooster, and he won't hurt you again." Silently, Dan and I were both deciding that maybe the goose had better go too. Like the rooster, the goose was almost as big as Nancy and might well attack her. We resolved that making pens for the poultry would have to be the first big job on the land.

As the sun went down, we finally unloaded the trailer. My optimism broke for a moment, and I murmured to Dan, "If this is a long-running serial, I hope this isn't an omen of what lies ahead." Bare lightbulbs hung from the ceiling, casting a brittle, unsatisfying light on the cardboard boxes and mounds of clothes in the two rooms. Both Baby Danny and Nancy were whimpering and sorely in need of hugs, food, and sleep.

Immediately, Dan changed from criticizing the property to optimistically defending it. As we headed back to spend our last night or two in the Goodyear duplex, Dan smiled and proclaimed, "Only challenges, as you've mentioned to me. Look at that beautiful pink sky. That's a good sign. Nancy, the chickens have gone to bed, and we're taking you back for din-din and sleep. We won't try another load today. Tomorrow you'll feel better, and we'll get rid of that bad rooster as soon as we can."

Later, as we transported the rest of the loads, I could only feel anger toward that proud, strutting, crowing bird. I kept close tabs on poor Nancy who stayed in the car, or insisted on being carried into the house. Meanwhile, Baby Danny spent most of his day lying in his playpen, set up on the shady side of the house.

Out in the field, the ruler of the barnyard actually looked magnificent as he strutted around, like a big, puffed-up turkey. Adorning his head were his comb and wattles, all a deep red, while his body and tail gleamed in patterns of green, red, orange, and black.

I assumed the rooster would not attack adults, but I wasn't about to test him. Like a well-trained sheep dog on duty, he constantly followed or led the chickens and would surely have gone to battle again to protect his harem. If Dan could take on the challenge the next evening, there would be a rooster to cook in a day or two.

"Come on out and help me," Dan called through the screen door. "We might as well proceed in ignorance and try to use whatever's out there around the shed to fence in the rooster. Anything that will cage him until I get back home tomorrow night. Thank heavens for the hammer. We can use it to take out the old nails in the boards and then we can use them again."

Monday morning, when the rooster had barely had time to crow in the first glimmer of dawn, we managed to corral and fence the cocky bird into our crudely made pen. As for the perky hens, the young fryers, the ducks and the turkeys, for a while, they could continue to roam free during the day, arguing about bits of grain, and at night they could roost in their old nests, made from packing boxes nailed to the back wall of the shed. We would get pens made as soon as possible.

As a child, Dan had helped his father and grandfather butcher poultry, and he had liked no part of it. However, with a big soft spot in his heart for his little daughter, who almost lost an eye to this rooster, he had a good subject on which to relearn the unpleasant chore of butchering poultry. The rooster would crow no more after that evening.

Life is no dress rehearsal, and life on this desolate land would be very much a live show. The first scene had been a disaster, but the sky was blue, and I vowed again that First Farm would become a world of my making. President Herbert Hoover had once promised the nation there would be "a chicken in every pot." There would be lots of chickens in my pot, even if little else at first. I'd already decided where my vegetable garden would be planted and where a cow would have a stack of hay—a piece of cake.

Chapter 6

The Pick-and-Shovel Gal

Plump Rhode Island Red and white Leghorn hens rhythmically bobbed their heads and wandered around the yard, scratching and searching for wild grain or insects. Since all the land, including the area around the house, had been left fallow for a long time, it probably harbored lots of seeds and countless tiny living creatures. And indeed, birds of a feather did seem to flock together: most rushed to see the spot where one hen foraged extra hard in the high weeds, as if she'd discovered an extrafine meal, and only a few took off into the pasture or along the lane.

"I wonder if they'll enjoy having 'hen parties' now, or do you suppose they'll act 'chicken' with no arrogant rooster following them about and trying to keep them herded and safe? Dan, you're not even listening to my lame jokes!"

Already, he was mentally laying the groundwork for chores to be done this first week. "If you take me to school, Mrs. C., you could go into town tomorrow and get this list of chicken wire, nails, staples, and fifteen rough two-by-fours about eight feet long. We can use part of the old lumber that's out there on the ground to fix the corners and most of the roof, but we have to have new posts to shore it up and more posts for the new chicken wire. I'll kill the rooster tonight, and we'll get the rest of the poultry fenced in within a week or two."

The two turkeys and the ducks didn't seem dangerous. They just followed the chickens wherever they roamed and roosted near them at night. They appeared as dumb as I'd read they were, but I'd also read that in earlier times they had been more intelligent—back before they'd been subjected to so much breeding aimed at producing heavier and heavier birds. I'd try to keep the turkeys until Thanksgiving and Christmas. The next afternoon, the big goose went to live with a student's family that kept a flock of them.

To celebrate the closing of escrow on those two gray rooms, a field, and a dream, we'd bought a hammer, hoe, mattock, rake, saw, and shovel. Not knowing how much money we would need for escrow, we had borrowed a few extra dollars. With some of those funds, Nancy and Baby Dan and I rushed to the lumberyard, bought the building materials on Dan's list, and had them loaded in the trailer and car.

As I drove home, I realized I'd be doing much of my talking to the children and animals. It would do them good, and it would help organize my thinking. "Where there's a will, there's a way, you guys. What shall we do after lunch and a nap? We need to make our farm pretty and nice."

Danny didn't talk in sentences yet, but Nancy had lots of thoughts and talked to the point, in short declarative or questioning sentences: "Can the rooster get out? I want sand in the sandbox. I'm awful thirsty. Can we stop for ice-cream cones? We need more horse books from the library. Can I pet the brown horse? I want to feed the horses."

The two mares in the adjacent field would delight Nancy every day, and it was hard to hang on to carrots for dinner after I showed her how to feed them without getting her fingers between their rows of teeth. She was already receiving a motley herd of little toy horses from family and friends, and each day she reminded me often, "I want my horse."

Again and again I had to repeat, "Not yet. You're still only two years old until March. You have to be a lot bigger to get a horse. We will get a cow, and maybe you can ride on the cow's back while I lead her around the field. How about that?" She knew that was a bunch of hocus-pocus.

"No, I want a horse." Nancy was actually a lot like me. Neither she nor I had ever been around live horses when we began to beg for one. Without actually knowing any horses, why did each of us have such a strong craving for them? And, in the same vein, nothing I'd experienced or studied at UC Berkeley, UCLA or the U of A had been about owning land or being a farmer's wife. Yet, for me, this had obviously been a deep yearning.

I didn't roll up my sleeves—rather, I cut them off at the shoulder seams that first afternoon. The vegetable garden would have to be planted and the vegetables growing before I indulged in the luxury of making a lawn. Already, an increasingly warm sun was crossing a brilliant blue sky each day, and before long it would be too late to plant a spring garden.

During that first week, I also helped Dan each evening as he made the chicken pens and coop, built rabbit hutches, and found a cow to buy in several weeks. By the time we started building the chicken and duck pens and shed, I had discovered that ducks and chickens need to be segregated. The ducks made the chickens' drinking pan a muddy mess by walking around in it and dipping their beaks full of mash and grain into the water.

Chickens are territorial animals, as well as social animals; toward evening, they often made their way home as a group, coming home to roost. During the day, the hens continued to sit on and walk over the porch and the steps to the house, with the white Leghorns being somewhat more flighty and nervous, and the Rhode Island Reds more docile and friendly. Some adventurous chickens of both breeds liked to roam in the field, both on our land and on that of our neighbors. In short order, the chickens decided I was the delivery maid of food and not a foe, even when I used a broom to shoo them away from the porch. I continued to have a difficult daily Easter-Egg hunt to find their eggs in the tall grass on the property and down the lane.

When I gave them grain and vegetable peelings they all quarreled, squawking and pecking each other, and it soon became obvious how the term "pecking order" had come about. One extrastrong hen was the number one, dominant hen—just as in a dog or a wolf pack there is one pack leader, or top dog. There appeared to be a complete pecking order from top to bottom, with each hen pecking and fighting those less strong or aggressive in order to get more of the grain. That was hard on the lighter weight or younger chickens, given that food availability was directly proportional to strength and feistiness.

I decided we should build one pen for the hens so they could hen-peck just one another. We'd make another pen for the fryers and the younger birds, and a small pen for the ducks. Around the corner of the shed on the south side, there could be a fourth pen for the turkeys. We were in a hurry and had minimal construction abilities, so the pens were crudely made and somewhat inefficient. Still, they worked, and I turned my attention to the problems of watering and feeding the various groups. I bought a second garden hose to reach the makeshift watering system that consisted of some old kitchen washbasins that I had bought at a farm sale.

The ducks, like the chickens, seemed to have their own language—they quacked and groused each day about the shortcomings of life, probably because they couldn't find a lake to swim in, or any extra food to eat. They bullied each other over any bug or kernel of grain and trailed along behind me single file on their webbed feet whenever and wherever I walked around the yard. I suspected they kept me company not out of friendship, but in hopes that I could magically produce dinner.

The best place for the garden was along the far side of the driveway near the dirt road. I set the sprinkler on the sun-baked land to soften the soil and then hoed out the tall weeds and brush and then shoveled the area.

There were times when I questioned my routine. There were only two acres, but it wasn't part-time farming with so few tools. "Where's all this work going to get me? Where does luck fit in? Am I lucky, or stupid?" Then I scolded myself, "Naw, they say you make your own luck. Maybe future baskets of vegetables, jars of milk, and plenty of meat will be enough payback for my daily fatigue. At least there'll be no bulges around my middle." With that settled, I went out to rake up the chicken manure and set it in a pile next to the garden site to spread or turn under.

Action always seemed better than investigation, study, or procrastination. Why, having gotten through years of classes, did I now refuse to study or research anything or ask for advice? Next week, after another payday, I would buy brightly colored packets of seeds and tomato plants. Planting Victory Gardens had been promoted by the government during the earlier years of the war, but as we didn't take any newspapers or magazines, or even own a working radio at first, I was still in a wilderness of my own making as I planned and planted a rather extensive vegetable garden that could keep a family of four from starving. Dan's books and bulletins seemed too much bother to find and read, so the advice at the feed store and the directions on the back of the seed packets would be my only instructions. It was pretty sketchy—a school of hard knocks, a learn-by-doing life. But what happened would not be judged by others, and buying a few extra seeds to replant or having to nurse a sick calf, wouldn't be a catastrophe. I would invent if I had to, but I would go full steam ahead without delay.

The shack itself was an immediate challenge, with a million things to do all at once. It was too bad I couldn't take quick courses in Basic Homemaking and Farming.

Unfortunately, I had never liked playing house, much less doing housework. I had set up Danny's crib in the kitchen the first day, but it had to be shoved against the kitchen counter every time I opened the refrigerator door. Since the crib had to be rolled aside a thousand times a day, I had to gamble that there would be no scorpions, since the best way to prevent scorpions from making their way into a crib was by placing the crib legs in little jars of water. This was impossible when the crib had to be moved so often.

The dining area, also in the kitchen, was a card table which had to be placed very close to the only door to the outside. We'd acquired four brown folding chairs from a faculty member, but I stored one on the porch until Danny would no longer be confined to a high chair. The secondhand playpen stayed permanently outside on the shady side of the house, where Danny could sleep and play part of each day.

In the other room, Nancy's crib was assembled and placed just beyond the door to the kitchen. Next to it we placed the couch against the north wall, and our bed against the east wall, which had the two windows in the room. The dresser, a cedar chest, and a door to the bathroom were along the south wall.

Part of the tiny bathroom was the clothes closet, with more concrete blocks serving as walls. Since the closet had no door, there was a constant view of the mess of clothes, shoes, and boxes crammed inside. The shower was adjacent to the closet and was also made with unpainted block walls and a cement floor. With such limited space, I couldn't possibly have "a place for everything, and everything in its place," even if I had been so inclined.

"I'm afraid it's all a bit grim," I complained to Dan as he returned one evening from teaching his night class.

He looked around the two rooms and immediately suggested. "I guess the worse things are, the louder we'd better laugh."

I could only agree. "Laughter is better than tears or aspirin. I confess this shack is not exactly a romantic setting and this will be a dismally realistic show, but at least my cast of characters will never show up late. In these few square feet of space we'll all be on stage with the curtains up twenty-four hours a day—a scene of dirty dishes on the counter and stove, all of us dressing and undressing as the days begin and end, and Nancy's toys all over the floor. We are all within eavesdropping distance of every sound and unable to escape the smell of food being prepared, from greasy fried chicken to burned and smoking toast. All I can say is there'd better be no bad behavior!" Up to a point I thought that might become true—with no room and no audience for tantrums, the children might learn there was no reward for putting on crying acts or storming out the door.

I'd only met Dan's fellow teachers and some of the wives for a few minutes when dropping Dan off or picking him up from school.

Nevertheless, one wife by the name of Faye did stop by during our first week on Fowler Lane. She wanted to say hello and bring a mixed bouquet from her garden "for the new house." Oh my!

Escorting her into the kitchen, I laughingly told her, "I haven't had time to redecorate yet." I put the flowers in a Mason jar on the counter and seated her at the kitchen card table. Fortunately, I could offer her a few oatmeal cookies and some coffee, still in the pot—luxuries we never indulged upon in Mrs. Marshall's barn. She tried to say some nice things about our place, but words more or less failed her. I began thinking of the polite words she had probably come with, words such as "Oh how charming! It's lovely! How gorgeous! What a beautiful view! What a priceless dining room set!"

Watching her search for something to admire in my hovel, I tried to think of words to put her at ease. "Certainly," I said, "there are no Screen Actors Guild wages for all my work here, and our dream farm isn't just around the corner, but this is a start, even if it can't be described as lovely, casual, or country-style living. I'm gung-ho over its possibilities; we'll just have to do it on our own, one step at a time."

The poor lady somehow made a quick recovery and managed to say, "Yes, we all have to start somewhere: what fun to have all this land and have your own place so soon! And I believe you're starting a vegetable garden already? It's so nice and quiet here...but will you be lonely?"

"No, I'll be too busy to be lonely. I like the challenge and the quest, if we don't starve." I liked Faye. She had come wearing old jeans, a blue shirt, and brown leather flats, and she was friendly and quick to chuckle. Nancy soon wandered in to demand one of the cookies, and with her came a couple of flies that buzzed around the table in the hot crowded kitchen. I couldn't seem to kill either of them with a folded-up newspaper, and the visit quickly became too much like the story of the city mouse who came out to see how the country mouse lived.

Faye didn't stay long, and she must have told some of the other staff members about our primitive shanty on the West Side's ugliest, smallest farm. Few people would understand our present shortcomings and future plans. Fortunately, no one else from Tolleson came to visit that spring. My education in country living would mostly include just myself and

Dan. Of course, those first years after the war were lean and busy ones for most young people as they tried to get through school, start families, find jobs, and buy homes.

Later that day I began to think again of Faye's visit, and I told myself, "Actually, everyone is alone in various ways…but, no, I'm not lonely and there's no prison of silence. This place is better than a house crowded between others, with barking dogs, door-to-door salesmen, and cars and delivery trucks rumbling down a busy street. Flies must get into expensive houses almost as often as here. Even without a radio, there's a cacophony of different voices: the chickens like to keep busy by cackling and clucking, the ducks love to quack, Cindy barks, Nancy and I talk, Baby Danny cries, and soon there will be a nice cow and a calf or two crooning to us with delicate moos. A few lovely wild birds have started to arrive, including dove and quail. Really, the only awful sound to be heard is my singing—will I ruin the kids' future ear for pitch by always singing off-key?"

I was learning that animals, as well as kids, improvise amazingly well with what they have on hand for entertainment. Even the neighbor's horses whinnied and raced around their big field, chasing each other, tossing their heads, and kicking up their heels just for the heck of it.

Without manufactured toys and games, Nancy quickly became a budding scientist, spending a lot of research time in the classroom that lay just outside the back door. "Mom, if you won't get me a horse, will you buy me the butterfly and grasshopper net daddy said I needed?"

She had the right idea to make the most of the current natural life, and many mornings she became engrossed in finding a number of insects to study in the tangled mass of weeds and brush out back. With a never-ending interest, she squatted on her heels, jar and lid in hand, to watch a caterpillar humping his way along the ground, a black shiny beetle of some kind, or a fickle and fleeting grasshopper. She giggled as she followed several ants struggling through the weeds with their tremendous loads, trekking away on some dim trail to get their find of melon seeds or a dead bug back to the anthill.

I bought my budding entomologist a butterfly net and a small magnifying glass that continually got lost in the yard. Fearing the hot sun on the glass could start a fire in the weeds, I tied a long red ribbon around the handle in order to be able to find it when Nancy finished her daily research. Soon, some of Nancy's ants, bees, beetles, butterflies, moths, and spiders were lined up in jars along the back side of the kitchen counter, on the windowsill, and on the dresser. I named Nancy's morning research a "field trip" when she ventured out into the back pasture.

Nancy also searched the yard and field for botanical wonders and brought me bouquets of many spring weeds. I acted thrilled to get lots of thistle, mustard flowers, and wild radish. Additional jars soon contained wilted and drying blooms. She created fun out of almost anything. Sometimes the offerings came with roots and mud still attached—trophies from areas I had watered in order to shovel and hoe.

Nancy tried to give Cindy flowers by pushing some in the dog's face and up her nose. "Smell, Cindy, smell them!" she demanded. In her tenderness toward all animals she was trying to share something precious with unfriendly Cindy, but the dog jumped up growling. Fun could be created out of almost anything, but not with Cindy.

Nancy must have inherited the bouquet-giving gene from her dad. Except for my sweet pea ventures, I'd shown a very limited appreciation for flowers and had made a tremendous blunder when Nancy was born. Dan brought me a big beautiful bouquet to the hospital at a time when we barely had enough to eat and my worn-out tennis shoes had cardboard stuffed inside for soles. I looked at the expensive bouquet and could only think how much I had dreamt of new, snowy white tennis shoes nestling in a box. I must have said so, for it was pretty much the last bouquet Dan ever gave me.

Clothes were a challenge, especially when company was coming. It seemed a waste of scarce money to buy whole new outfits when the kids were outgrowing their clothes almost daily. Hopefully, Dan would stay the same size. In those days, teachers wore suits or jackets, with slacks, long-sleeved shirts, and ties, while I planned to wear my high school and college clothes for many years. I did a lot of washing and ironing. For the rest of us, I devised several clothing strategies. First, I would buy clothes two sizes too large for the kids. Second, the clothes I did buy would be mostly unisex. Nancy's shirts, corduroy coveralls, socks, shoes, and pajamas would be passed down to Danny. In my mind's eye, I decided that on this bleached, dun-colored plot of land, the kids should have bright, primary-colored clothes whenever possible. I bought red and blue coveralls, bright plaid shirts, and summer shorts in greens, blues, reds, or yellows. They would each have just one dress-up outfit—a dress for Nancy and slacks and a dress shirt for Danny. Sometimes they had better shoes, sometimes only farm shoes. Third, I accepted with great appreciation every hand-me-down mailed to the kids by long-time friends. Somehow, my sincere and gushing thank-yous kept the donations coming in.

I became the primary farmer because I was the only adult on the premises during long days and many evenings. Dan was in his classroom by 7:45AM and often visited his students' FFA projects after the school doors closed in the afternoons. He became president of the local Lions Club and of the Arizona Vocational Education Association. Just to be able to spend some time with him, the kids and I tagged along to Farm Bureau potlucks.

Often he came home to ask, "How's my pick-and-shovel gal? Tired? Maybe this is too much of a good thing!"

The answer was in front of him, with me slumped over, elbows on the table and red eyes drooping half-shut—the result of working in the blazing sun without a hat or sunglasses…I owned neither.

All creatures, human and animal, like to be appreciated, and his concerns came at a good time of the day. "No, I'm just chugging along. I suspect I'm never going to be a fancy lady of the house for you, but I can play the part of the farmer, gardener, plant manager, personnel arbitrator, scheduler, and so on. I can't say 'I've had it!' and quit, but I can't be fired either. Well, I suppose you could fire me since there's no union for people like me." I managed a grin.

Dan nodded. "OK, hang in there. Right now I can't do much more on the home front."

I'd always loved recess periods at school—they were a chance to run outside for games. Now I had recess most days, and I was content, even if the time was spent wielding a pick-and-shovel. I had caught some kind of work ethic bug, and, crazy as it seemed, I liked the work and had few qualms. At least I wasn't knocking my brains out memorizing all the battles of the Civil War or the date of every happening in the history of the world for some class exam.

There was a lot leaning on my shovel. First Farm had to be the headwaters of our plan, a large and unpredictable first step. I constantly felt the need to rush because I was haunted by the many, many miles that lay ahead. To produce food it was critical to quickly get the garden plot cleared of weeds and the soil shoveled over and mixed with the chicken fertilizer. Soon the vegetable seeds and tomato plants were growing in small, straight rows.

The tall weeds that grew right up to the foundation of the house were also of concern, and I became increasingly worried about scorpions, snakes, and other creatures that might inhabit the yard. I started wetting the ground with a sprinkler and picking and hoeing out all the weeds.

Practicality was my motto and was foremost in my mind: "Dan, let's not try for a tender, fine grass lawn. I'm going to buy Bermuda grass; it's tough enough for the rough life here and won't need much water. Since they say this area hardly ever freezes, the lawn may stay green much of the year, rather like it did in Goodyear."

Soon, another project loomed. In order to have good grazing land for a future cow and calves and to save on the cost of baled hay, our land needed to receive its share of water from the West Side area's irrigation district. Flooding the field would grow some pastureland.

Starting at the driveway and going north beside the road next to the barbed wire boundary, I dug and dug. I wet the ground as far as the hoses would reach, but, after that point, it took the pick and mattock to make progress. I had to dig the ditch all the way to the back of the property and then along the back fence line. The sun became hot, days melted one into the other, and weeks passed. Often I didn't even know what day it was.

At some point I discovered the phenomenon of a "second wind." Many days, I started out with little energy, but the harder and longer the workday, the better I began to feel, and my strength grew, even though I saw no bulging muscles. The secret to a second wind is to just automatically get up and go, and go, and go.

There wasn't even a swamp cooler for the house that first year, and by early summer both rooms felt like ovens set to cook a roast. Options were few: shut the windows at about 6:30 AM to keep the cool night air in, cover the windows with aluminum foil to keep the sun out and be in perpetual darkness, or keep the windows and door open and hope for some breezes to blow through the house. None of these possibilities worked well, and we pretty much stayed outside on the shady side of the house most of the day.

As I dug the irrigation ditch (which we renamed the "Panama Canal") there was a lot of time to think. Every time Nancy wandered out she asked the exact same question, "Whatcha doing?" She never seemed to have any other random thoughts or inquiries; maybe she hoped to catch me with a different answer sometime. Yet it was a good question, and I had to laugh. Why was this constant plowing ahead with what is usually a man's job giving me such pleasure and contentment? It was simple and straightforward labor—digging back and across a seemingly infinite, rock-hard wilderness. It was hardly glamorous or heroic! I envisioned countless easier and more fun ways to build strong muscles—things like playing tennis, or swimming in a cool, cool lake. Then reality took over as I realized I was the only laborer available.

"Honey," I would reply, "I'm making hay while the sun shines! Do you see the hay? I don't either, but I'm thinking about it. A man called a zanjero will open the canal gate to let the water flow into this ditch. Water will come pouring down this ditch and cover all this pasture and soak into the soil. Hay seeds will drink the water, and that will make the seeds grow into green grass for the cow and a couple of little calves to eat. We'll buy the cow and a calf or two before long. I'm leaning on the post to rest my shovel. Is your red wagon tired?"

"No."

"Well, let's go in and fix lunch. I'll read you and Danny a story before naps." After eating, I would prop Danny up and held him against my chest, while Nancy and I sat against pillows on the bed, and I read aloud, over and over again, an endless number of books for preschoolers at nap and bedtime. Danny couldn't understand the stories, but Nancy made sure he looked at all the pictures until both of them became sleepy.

In our straitened circumstances, it helped some that I held the belief that "Only people who don't read books are truly poor." I discovered that idea wasn't exactly true when I really thought about how difficult it was to pay for even such a meager shelter, and when food was so hard to come by.

"Dan, I've a fleeting thought. You don't think we were dumb to push so hard for this place? We both seem to be forging ahead with such rigid goals, and only the kids will have a filling supper tonight."

"Naw, this way's fun. Taking chances may bring a lot more surprises. Even next month may be somewhat better, though you're the one keeping the books."

I gave a feeble laugh.

In the heat of summer we took our suppers later and sometimes alfresco as the sky darkened. Nights remained somewhat cool on this bit of desert, and the clear Arizona sky was spectacular, with a sky full of billions of stars shining and often a big moon throwing a soft glow over our very own property. Our world would have been pitch-black when the moon was absent, if not for the faint glow of the city in the distance. The occasional falling star became a big event for Nancy. Everything was completely still except for Nancy's chatter before bedtime and the faraway hum of a few cars on Van Buren Avenue.

I sometimes questioned, "Would there be such a wonderful feeling of resting and giving in to this time of day if I had done nothing but sit around all day?"

Dan grinned. "You'll never know."

Chapter 7

A Rabbit Triplex with Basements

There would be no more searching for eggs in the yard, the pasture, and the sides of the lane. All the chickens, ducks, and turkeys were in their pens. Like our house, the poultry shed was no fancy home, but I could soon find the eggs just by checking the apple boxes I had filled with hay and nailed to the back wall of the new three-sided shed. Besides, the yard where Nancy played would also be clean and safe before long.

Still, the farmwork had really just begun, and already this establishment seemed seriously understaffed and filled with endlessly hard workdays. The kids and I desperately needed a diversion, a change—some kind of outing—and it couldn't be deferred another day.

"Nancy and Danny, let's go find a bunny. Won't that be fun?"

No rabbit hutches had been built, but what the heck, I'd just forge ahead. With no knowledge about rabbits and no one handy to ask, it was really a silly impulse. But still, the idea of having rabbits had come to me years before we ever found First Farm. Somewhere, deep within the five big steamer trunks, there was probably information on rabbits in one of Dan's agriculture books…but the trunks were too heavy to unstack and search without help. More to the point, ready or not, I suddenly and impulsively felt I had to get rabbits right away that day.

As I explained to Dan, "We can't live just on chicken, eggs, and beans. A bunch of bunnies would be fun for the children. I'll drive you to school today and then go out and find a pregnant rabbit." No time to fret about the butchering process; later on that would be Dan's department.

There was a rabbit breeder listed in the Yellow Pages, and I told him my kids and I wanted a bred, white, momma rabbit with pink eyes. "No, I just want to buy one rabbit—the minimum. Are the white ones a sturdy and easily raised breed?" As usual, I got an "A" for action and work, but not even a passing grade for preparation and knowledge. I shuddered at my language—the language of a two-year-old—as I ordered "a white, pink-eyed bunny" later that day.

This large, white, velvety soft mother-to-be left all her friends and a large, completely air-conditioned building for the rather inhospitable land of First Farm. The seller gave me no tips on keeping rabbits, although there were lots of things he could have mentioned. For example, the need for an air-conditioning system in the fast-approaching summer heat would have been a nice warning.

Bunny came home in a cardboard box, with Nancy holding the precious heavy cargo on her little lap. I did stop at the feed store to buy two crocks to hold the doe's food and water, a bag of rabbit food pellets, and one bale of extrafine alfalfa hay. I only bought one bale of hay because I figured that by the end of the week we would surely have found a cow and would have to buy many bales of hay.

What a lovely creature this snow-white rabbit was! She would be easy to love, and I knew her babies would delight Nancy and Danny. Nancy, who had eaten her first marshmallows at a friend's home a few nights earlier, quickly came up with Marshmallow as a suitable name. This was a happy improvement over all the chicken names like Browny, Whitey, and Henny. The doe had a funny short nose, long soft ears, bright pink eyes, and, except for being heavy and pregnant, she seemed perfectly designed for hugging.

As I sat her down on the kitchen floor, instead of racing off to hide, she groomed herself a bit by licking her paws and rubbing her face and body. As she hopped about after her wash, she didn't seem at all dumb, but rather determined and inquisitive. She watched us carefully, wiggled her nose to test all the new odors around her, and seemed to listen acutely for any signs of danger. Finally, she explored the whole house.

At this point, there was just no place for Mother Rabbit to live except inside the house. Nancy was thrilled. Marshmallow had the run of both rooms and the bathroom. Nancy and I put newspapers all around on the floor for her use, while I crossed my fingers. As the rabbit explored, she didn't seem to mind that Nancy spent the rest of the evening on her hands and knees following along behind her on the floor, trying to imitate her hip-hopping leg action. Bunny eventually nibbled the alfalfa-scented pellet food I'd bought and ate a small piece of carrot.

"Don't you even try to pick up this rabbit, Nancy. She's way too heavy for you to carry, and don't forget, she's soon going to have a bunch of baby bunnies."

"OK. Can she talk?"

"I don't believe so. At least not often." I was guessing—what kind of voice does a rabbit have?

With the joyful nonsense of a live rabbit having free rein of the house, Dan suddenly found time that evening to dig out of a trunk a USDA bulletin on rabbits, and he started making a list of supplies he would need for her cage: lumber, woven wire, nails, some sheets of roofing tin, and latches. Then he read about the need to keep rabbits in a comfortable temperature range, and I remembered the air-conditioner on the roof of the barn where I had bought her.

Dan suggested, "We'd better find out more. There's no air-conditioning here yet, even for us. We'd better not get the wood and wire for hutches until someone can tell us where and how to keep this rabbit—and her soon-to-be-babies—cool."

It was easier to wait for that bit of information because rabbits are instinctively potty-trained and try to make just one place their bathroom. This doe used only one newspaper in the far corner of the bathroom and never went anywhere else. This was indeed a most happy discovery.

I splurged on another short subscription to the Arizona Republic, not so much to read, but to have paper to use for daily cleaning of the doe's bathroom. Thanks to the rabbit's need for newspaper, I began to scan the front page to read a bit about world affairs, as well as some state and local happenings.

It was a happy household until the next morning when I discovered Marshmallow had chewed up a significant portion of my Joy of Cooking and Fanny Farmer cookbooks. On top of that, she had attacked the electric light cord (lucky for us—and her—it hadn't killed her). She had also gnawed maliciously on a leg of the bed. Help! Marshmallow would have to stay in the bathroom unless she was being watched. Otherwise, the legs of the bed would grow smaller and smaller in diameter, and before long we'd be sleeping on the floor. At that point I remembered that rabbits are nocturnal animals; while we slept, Marshmallow's sharp teeth had been extremely busy.

Dan asked his students if any of them knew anyone who raised rabbits. They didn't, but the father of one of the students put us in touch with a man whose children raised rabbits for their 4-H project.

Before we discussed the chilling of rabbits during sizzling Arizona summers, I tried asking this rabbit owner, Mr. Blake, why our bunny often stamped her foot. He only seemed to guess as he answered, "My kids might know. Maybe she feels insecure and a bit threatened being in your nonrabbity environment."

Mr. Blake then gave discouraging news. "For people like you, having rabbits poses difficult problems. Such a small project can't justify a barn with roof sprinklers, air-conditioning, or even fans."

For his kids' rabbitry, he had converted a portion of his large garage from its former use as a woodworking area, and put a swamp cooler through the back wall to cool the room. The only thing he could think of that we could do was to keep wet gunny sacks over and around the cages. I couldn't spend every fiery hot summer day constantly hosing down gunny sacks hung over cages, and there wasn't a shade tree on the farm. What to do? Soon our whole world would become bleached under a relentless sun, and my daily washes would dry on the clotheslines in minutes. A caged rabbit could not survive Arizona's summer heat without a way to stay cool. Furthermore, there was a whole litter of bunnies coming soon, ever so soon.

"Acting first and thinking later has drawbacks, doesn't it?" I noted at breakfast.

"Naw, it's more fun this way, in fact, hilarious. Did you ever think your living quarters might be two rooms shared with a pregnant rabbit and two kids under three?"

With Marshmallow underfoot and about to produce a large litter at any moment, it didn't take long for inspiration to come to me. I worried that the doe might have a very large litter, and I had no idea what date she was due to give birth. Not only that, she constantly entertained herself by chewing everything within reach, and although she had a large, heavy tummy, she could still stand up on her hind legs to reach things. One morning I found she had spent the night chewing on a bath mat and towel. Next, it was another book with half its front cover gone. Arizona had a way of testing one: we needed to live in new ways to deal with the tremendous heat, limited water, and undeveloped land. But it was a darned strange place if I couldn't somehow create a home for a rabbit!

The morning paper carried a news article that day about some troubles occurring in the basement parking area of a large apartment building. A basement! "Hey, Dan, let's build the bunnies some 'apartments' with underground rooms! Heat rises, and if the bunny basements are deep enough so that there can be lots of dirt piled on top, and are built under the shade of the hutches, and if the backs of the hutches are built against the north side of the chicken shed, it might stay cool. Don't ground squirrels, gophers, and other animals survive heat or cold by tunneling beneath the ground? Sure!

"We can build boxed-in ramps, like tunnels, going down beneath the earth from the cages, and nail little cleats made of pieces of wood or metal across the ramps so they won't be on a bunny-slide going down, and the rabbits will be able to climb back up. I can feed and water them upstairs and carpet their basement bedrooms with straw or alfalfa once we get the cow and some hay. If we make the basement ceiling out of sheets of tin roofing, I can put some dirt on top of it and take the roofs off now and then to change the hay. In fact, we can make the basement's bottom and sides, as well as the tops, out of sheets of tin roofing. Or are those sheets made of aluminum?"

Dan gave me an OK. "Sounds possible. I hope you're right."

Any trip away from the homestead, for any reason, continued to be a welcome change for Nancy and me. The kids and I piled into the Bluebird, with the trailer behind, and I bought the lumber, roofing, and other materials for the triplex apartment hutches and three basements. I figured there had to be one pen for Momma Rabbit and her babies, one smaller one for a future Daddy Rabbit, and the largest pen for their growing children.

Still, I had no idea how fast the picture-book-pretty babies could multiply. Eureka! Soon the pens were full of snow-white, fluffy, hopping balls of ever-so-soft fur—all with pink eyes and noses. Very soon after, a Daddy Rabbit came to reside in the adjoining smaller pen to ensure even more babies.

While it wasn't posh, the rabbit triplex, with basements, worked perfectly. The rabbits stayed cool by sleeping in their "burrows." As soon as the afternoon sun lay low on the horizon, the whole rabbit population scrambled upstairs to eat, hop and play, and use one corner of the upstairs hutch area as a restroom. This valuable fertilizer fell through the hutches' wire mesh floors and onto the ground, where I shoveled it into the wheelbarrow to spread around the yard for an extra green lawn and garden.

"Nancy, Momma Bunny needs a nice friend to give her fresh water and pellets. You might dip this can in the sack and pour one can of supper into her dish while I fill her water crock." Nancy was great about wanting to help care for her brother, but I hoped that a bit of responsibility and knowing how to do a few easy chores might seem more like play than work and make her feel important and caring.

One thing always led to other things, and these "other things" usually involved money. Rabbits don't gauge supply and demand very well. Fixated on supply, Momma Rabbit's generations came quickly, one after the other. Before I could save enough money to buy a deep-freeze, there was a rapidly growing surplus of rabbits. Neighbors down the lane bought some fryers, as did several teachers in Tolleson, but I had no adequate distribution network.

Money or not, I was soon forced to find the "best buy" on the biggest deep-freeze possible. A long white Sears freezer was delivered, and the driver and his helper placed it on boards against the shady, north side of the house. For insulation, I covered it with a piece of carpeting and an old spread.

The investments in things like the freezer used up funds we could have used to buy food. I didn't need to look back to see what was catching up with us. I was facing it day by day, and it was hunger. It was time to buy a cow and to order hay, and I knew we'd be even hungrier as a result. It was hard to chew on just hope and real estate, but there remained that overpowering addiction for land and farm. There continued to be no waste. Lean meals not only continued, but became more and more meager, and there were many days when Mom and Dad ate little or consumed a diet that was anything but balanced. We were actually "bankrupt" and the bank balance reached about two dollars before another check arrived each month.

Chapter 8

Too Green for Auctions

Isn't milk an almost complete food? And if we, meaning Dan, milked a cow, wouldn't there be the fringe benefits of lots of cream and butter? Excess milk could be sold to neighbors or fed to a couple of young calves. Chickens and rabbits didn't seem to quite make a farm, because they were often just backyard projects on local town and suburban lots. However, the resident chickens, ducks and turkeys were doing well, and the rabbits now had their bunny hotel with basements. With the coming of a cow, I figured we would have a farm, if not much of a farmer. After another paycheck, a milk cow went to the top of our list of necessities.

Fortunately, we didn't go to an auction for the cow. We would have been babes in the woods. Too often the animals taken to auction have some kind of problem: they're runts, have ailments, are nonbreeders, or are too old. Auctions give out no money-back guarantees.

We couldn't find a small breed of cow, such as a Jersey, but one of Dan's evening students, a fellow we called Farmer Bill, sold us a just-freshened big Holstein cow and helped us find a Hereford-cross bull-calf so we would have at least one animal to share the extra buckets of milk. We named the cow Maude, and within days, she provided us with so much milk that the refrigerator was overflowing. Two neighbors down the lane began buying some, and the red Hereford calf was drinking his fill. Still, finding mostly milk in the fridge, Dan decided, "Let's get another calf to drink Maude's extra milk—this time we can buy it at auction. I can't bring myself to bother Bill again. We won't lose too much on one calf if something's wrong with it. And besides, an auction should be educational and fun!"

We had heard about a couple of auctions in the Valley, and the following Saturday we headed there with the luggage trailer on our bumper hitch.

Most of the auctions we attended in later years sold horses, ponies, sheep, goats, pigs, calves, cows, and steers. But at this auction, other things were also sold—things like farm or ranch equipment—tractors, harvesters, trailers, and combines. Last to be auctioned that day were the contents of a large farm home, including an old hat rack, a rocker, a barbeque setup for feeding large numbers of people, a large wagon, and antique wagon wheels that might be used as decoration in a Western historical setting. There was living room and bedroom furniture, including a long dining room table with fifteen chairs. Finally, there were many boxes of old issues of National Geographic, Western Horseman, and the Saturday Evening Post. The contents of the last box were free: tumbly black puppies about six or seven weeks old.

It was heartbreaking to know that some family's lifetime possessions had to be sold off, especially for so little money that it would scarcely help the sellers. All the equipment, the furniture, and the magazines went quickly. Some of these things might have been passed down for several generations. Now, I guessed, there were no heirs, or no heirs wanting the accumulated possessions...only strangers, wanting bargains.

It would have been easy to be flummoxed and carried away by the hearty and glib chatter of the auctioneer. In his fast and singsong voice, he tempted the crowd constantly with, "Three, who'll give me three?

Four? Four and a half? Five. Who'll give me five? Five? Sold to the lady in the green shirt," as he pointed to me. I'd bought a lovely antique-appearing rocking chair.

We contented ourselves by getting just one lively, and seemingly healthy, white-faced, black calf. After the gavel banged down for the last time, we waited our turn in the loading area out back, standing next to our two-wheeled trailer. It was a sad time—calves were bawling excitedly and desperately for their moms, and their moms were bawling back to them just as heartbreakingly. Frantic horses and colts whinnied shrilly with fright, as they, too, protested the loading process in the increasingly dusty area. Trucks and trailers waited their turns to back up to the loading chutes, while the auctioned-off animals were loaded in with end-of-the-day impatience and force.

We went to a number of auctions after that and I always found this sort of subculture both fun and sad. Some farm people were going home with much-dreamt-of purchases and emptier pocketbooks, while others were selling a horse they loved but could no longer afford, or a bunch of cattle that had to go to market early so the sellers could make mortgage payments, or perhaps buy seed for the next crop. For five dollars I got a fine antique oak rocker that at one time may have held many a fretful baby and his mom, or a wistful grandfather who spent his final years rocking on some ranch-house porch and watched the world go by. Did the family who sold the National Geographic magazines ever travel the world, or did they only dream of it by reading the articles and studying those wonderful pictures?

Back home, the calf, whom we'd named Blackie, didn't seem to grow. I also decided he was much older than we'd thought. He was a hit with Nancy, however, and I let her lead him around in the yard like a dog. She fed and hugged him often...until she developed an eye infection that doctor after doctor seemed unable to cure. Diagnosis and cure finally came after some strong X-ray treatments that were probably risky in that early period. I could think of no way Nancy could have gotten the infection except from the auction-calf, so we took Blackie back to the same auction, told them the problem, and sold him. Experience is a hard teacher at times.

Nancy was so saddened and upset at losing Blackie that when one of the feed store clerks had to part with her purebred collie named Heidi, I was tempted. Our little dog Cindy had been a thorn in my side for a long time: neither child could pet or hug the family dog. Surely having another dog could be classed as a necessity.

On our next visit to the feed store, Heidi was still there, asleep in front of the counter. This collie, only about two years old, was Lassie-beautiful, needed a home, and was the exact image of the wonderful collie I'd had as my first dog.

"Oh, Mom, I wanna take her now!"

"Let's ask Dad tonight, and we'll get her on Friday if he agrees. There are an awful lot of animals for me to take care of. If we get this dog, will you feed her each morning for me?" That would always be one of my more stupid questions, because in spite of promises made by the kids, Mom always ended up feeding the critters.

So we sold a dog-sized calf and acquired a calf-sized dog. I quickly realized that Heidi's beauty was only fur-deep. Pedigrees don't guarantee brains, and it was soon evident that the dog was not only a rather stupid dolt, but also a rather touchy one, though she usually let Nancy pet her. Dan and I agreed that in Heidi's case, there must have been too much in-breeding for looks and not enough breeding for health, intelligence, temperament, performance, or even common sense. Still, Heidi was now part of the family, and, needless to say, we kept her and gave her lots of love.

I often wondered about the process by which these dogs arrive at their hierarchical ranking. Dogs are very civilized, and normally choose one dog as leader of the pack. But here was one dog who was indifferent, grouchy, and little, and another who was ever so large, beautiful, and terribly dumb. Except at mealtime, neither dog seemed to pay much attention to me, so clearly they didn't view me as their leader. Eventually, the two of them seemed to decide that little Cindy would be top dog, and Heidi kept out of her way most of the time.

Chapter 9

His Name Is Sage

Even before I pulled on a pair of jeans, a flannel shirt, and slippers, I knew there was another surprise or crisis outside, and, of course, it couldn't wait until night had given way to morning. Cindy and Heidi were performing a serenade with a duet of low whimpering growls and yips, as though they really didn't want to wake us up, but were too excited to stay silent.

Intent on something at the top of the big steamer trunks stacked on the outside back porch, the dogs showed me their find. On the highest trunk was a huge, agitated, gray cat, staring down at the dogs below with round owl-like eyes that glowed green in the darkness. In time with the dogs' chorus, the cat talked back at them with a deep, rumbling growl and a high wailing cry, followed by an occasional hiss. Puffed up with fear and anger, he was like a Halloween cutout—his hair almost standing on end over his highly arched back, his bushy tail twitching back and forth, emphasizing his statements. "You beasts may have chased me up here, but you'd better think twice about me. I fight like a lion and will make you run for your life if you come any closer."

It seemed like a good idea to ask the dogs to get in the car before I introduced myself to this elegant monster. It would also give me time to think. So many creatures arriving for me to take care of, so much time necessary to feed, clean, and make good homes for all of them, and often food was scant for us humans.

"Well, come on, pussy, will you let me carry you into the house and let the rest of the family meet you? We'll have to wake everyone up, if you haven't already done the job. You don't look a bit like a wild stray, even with your ferocious act. You've had a home."

I'd seen other cats in the area that seemed like wild strays, or maybe belonged to the dairy not far away, but Cindy and Heidi never let any of them feel welcome in the yard. Town people, hoping that every farmhouse could take in more and more cats, just didn't understand the fright, suffering, and sometimes deaths of many of the cats they tossed out along rural or town roads. Equally horrible were the number of dogs also dropped off in the countryside. Unless people possess the capability and willingness to care for and love their pets, they should never acquire them, as animals have just as many feelings and as much capacity to suffer as humans. This puss was lucky to have survived. Most likely he had been a Phoenix city cat and had been taken to the county and left beside the road to find a home, a near impossibility for a cat who had never hunted daily for food, shelter, and water. Traffic on Van Buren Boulevard was often heavy and fast, and the cat must have given up trying to find his way home or he wouldn't have risked coming to our back door as dawn approached.

With the dogs locked in the car, there was a little more meowing while the cat explained that he didn't really want to be here at all, but that he had really had a frightful night, with cars racing by up on the road, dogs barking at every house, and some huge four-legged monsters walking around in several fields.

I assured him that he was quite right, but we could be friends. After I talked to him a few minutes, he came willingly to the edge of the trunk and didn't need to be coerced to let me carry him into the house. This exquisite animal had really been just setting the rules for me to follow, making me know he would be picked up only when he was ready.

Danny and Nancy, still in their pajamas, were at the kitchen door with Dan and were about to come out as I opened the door while holding the huge, still slightly quivering cat. It was only then that I learned that cats were not one of Daddy's favorite animals. In all the years we had dated and been married, how could he and I have not talked about cats? Nancy, however, was wild with excitement. If the cat stayed, we would need a crash course for the kids on how to treat a cat, another course to teach the cat how to treat the children, and a third program to convince Daddy that cats are wonderful creatures and should be part of this growing potpourri of a family.

The cat seemed ever so soft and vulnerable. His paws were cut up and caked with dried mud. He looked sore and had probably walked a lot farther than I thought at first. I held him as he steadily viewed the family with an unwinking, suspicious stare, obviously deciding if this just might make a home. He was luxuriantly dressed in a long, thick coat of gray—fancy bloodlines of some sort. Perhaps a Persian? No, his face wasn't the round Persian shape. I smiled to think that, along with Heidi, our elegant purebred collie, I might acquire another creature with stylish and beautiful clothes to be one of the classy members in the family—totally unlike our ugly home, ancient scratched furniture, and our old and faded clothing. Even star performer Dan had few costumes in his closet. His were of the conservative, dressed-up style of teachers of that era—one tan suit, two sport jackets, and three pairs of slacks. The dressy dark blue suit of our wedding day languished in the cedar chest along with my wedding dress and a white Palm Beach suit that had been Dan's attire when he'd had a dance band during high school and the first year of college.

I figured this cat's coat had been tailored by many matings—matings arranged by humans in order to achieve this long, beautiful, and impractical fur. Both the cat and Heidi had wonderful coats that were very unsuited to the Arizona heat or to walking through the stickers and burrs on this land.

The vote was three to one to keep the elegant cat if the owners couldn't be found, but Dan's non-yes vote wasn't an actual no. He suggested that it could become an outdoor cat, and that we might advertise to try to find the owners. Meanwhile, I would keep Pussy inside to become used to the dogs and to make sure he would stay and know that this was home.

This was the first cat I'd ever owned, but as a child I had read books about cats, and we had friends who had owned them. Even with my skimpy knowledge, I somehow felt that this cat would make quick and sound decisions. I slowly set him down in front of some leftover chicken and a saucer of milk. After one careful appraisal of the kitchen, he daintily ate all the meat and licked up the milk with a little pink tongue. No thought of racing off to hide under a bed or to look for an exit. Cats, I'd read, are complex creatures, and soon he would be teaching me how well he could cope with the dogs, kids, and Dan.

After the cat dined, he licked his chops, paws, and thick coat and then reconnoitered every part of the house, including an inspection of our bed, likely to test its softness and possibilities. As he explored, I apologized, "Dear Puss, don't knock it. The house is small and will always be a mess, but you'll be ever so loved, and you'll never be dropped off again out on some strange and dangerous road."

Thankfully, Dan had left to teach that evening, but I worried— would he ever let a cat sleep on the bed?

"Mom, what can we call him? How about Pussy?" Nancy clamored. A moment later, she changed her mind. "No, I want to call him Pretty. Is he a boy or a girl?"

Suddenly, I decided this guy, or gal, wasn't going to be called something like Pussy. "Aw, come on, Nancy, hold it. This time, Mom gets to choose the name." Actually, I had been mulling over names for him from the moment my eyes met his steady, round-eyed gaze of appraisal out on the porch. He was obviously a deep thinker and a talker who would make his own decisions, but I knew little of his personality. Maybe I should concentrate on his looks; fur doesn't make a cat, but my, he was lovely.

"Aw, come on, what things are gray, you guys? Clouds, doves, rocks, sagebrush…Hey, you've lost your chance. I want this gorgeous cat to be called Sage! Not only is he sage gray in color, but he is obviously a very wise cat. You've learned a new word; now you'll know what sage means because this kitty is smart and wise. Sage is also the color and name of a wonderful mountain shrub where Mom and Dad grew up. And sage has an interesting hissing sound, a sound that the kitty may like, especially if you say 'S-s-sage' with lots of love and kindness."

After the kids were in bed, Sage padded over to me, jumped onto my lap, and happily sank heavy and deep into my pajamas. With his soft purring motor turned on and his eyes closed, his singing was surely of relief and safety. Later, he settled down on the rug and slept with all four paws tucked under him. His body moved slightly, and he twitched his nose and whiskers now and then, as though remembering his recent trek and fright. Again I wondered how long he'd been lost. This was his castle now, but could he already trust us and consider this place home? Somehow he knew to stay off the bed, perhaps because he had never been allowed on one, or because he realized that Dan slept there and was not yet his friend.

Schooling started the next morning. I had to teach Heidi and Cindy that this cat was now family and was not to be chased. Sage needed little help from me: he played his part with great bravado, as though taking on two dogs, two preschoolers, and two adults—including one who disliked him—was all part of an ordinary routine. By an extremely showy repeat performance—hissing, growling, and making his tail stand up in the air—he let it be known that he'd rather fight than run. With all that hair on end he was almost as large as Cindy, and it only took a swat or two of his tiger-sharp claws to persuade the dogs to ignore him. Actually, the dogs were normally amiable animals—laid-back critters who learned earlier that no animals, whether cow, calf, chicken, or duck, were to be chased or hurt in any way.

Maybe times had changed somewhat for cats. I'd read that, while a dog is man's best friend, dogs are cats' worst enemies. However, among the farm families we knew, the cats and dogs got along well together. Sage immediately decided that it was Heidi and Cindy who had to adapt to him, and, even then, he would reserve judgment about them. He had an enormous and effective presence; perhaps he had lived with dogs before.

Cats don't have to save or protect humans to be heroic: just putting up with a house full of children and dogs every day is heroic. However, I'm sure cats appreciate it when adults in the family teach the children how to treat them gently and hold them carefully. Convincing Nancy to be gentle at all times and to not keep trying to pick Sage up by the tummy or neck took days. The children currently insist that all their lives I've said, "Now, cool it!" and I probably started then. "You've got to cool it and just pat and stroke the cat. Will ya please quit trying to pick him up!?" If Sage was on the bed asleep, Nancy pulled him to the floor. If he was on the floor, she tried to lift him to the bed. Since Cindy had never let Nancy hug and hold her, and since Heidi was big and indifferent, the kids were in heaven with an indoor cuddly cat—indoors, at least, while Daddy was at work.

Why is it that many cats know the difference between little children and adults? Nancy's stroking, pulling, lifting, and hugging could be rough and clumsy, but Sage accepted it. He wasn't the only cat that I'd seen dragged all over the place and carried in an uncomfortable manner by kids. The cats stayed limp and put up with it if it was a child doing it.

Lack of kindness always bothered me, so proper-care-of-Sage lessons continued for weeks. Finally I relented a little, and on several occasions I let Nancy dress Sage up in a doll hat and place some of her old baby blankets around him and put him in the baby buggy for several rides around the yard. He submitted with only a few verbal complaints, but for a good spell afterward he washed and rearranged his tousled hair with tongue and paws.

Having known only uncooperative dogs in the past, Nancy wanted to teach Sage to sit up, roll over, and do things that one of her friend's dogs could do. I suggested right away, "Nancy, Sage will never roll over or sit up for you. He would just ask you 'Why?' if he could. The cat doesn't see any reason to do it. Don't you sort of agree with him?"

Sage agreed to accept his name, but all of us would have to shape up and do our best to make this an acceptable home. With an easy confidence, he soon began to choose which foods he would eat, and his bed would have to become our bed, though he wouldn't get nighttimes on our bed until he won over Dan's heart. This canny cat knew what his first job would have to be, and he started on that project just as soon as he was permitted outside.

Perhaps Sage made a carefully reasoned decision, "It's good to be impartial and accommodating to all the family, but my first work here has to be winning over the cat-hater." With fascinating ingenuity and persistence, Sage began courting Dan's love. No matter that I was the one who had gotten him accepted in this nice home and was feeding and talking to him all the time—morning and night, Sage followed Dan as he went out to do the chores. The cat really made a hit when he let Dan try to squirt the cow's milk into his mouth, even when it left his face and chest dripping wet with milk.

Sage's strategy was to persistently show Dan that he favored him above all others, and, after all, this love was special, for obviously Sage was a discriminating cat. He rubbed against Dan's legs after edging into the house alongside Dan and the full milk pail. Then, with loud murmurings of "I think you're special," he gracefully jumped on Dan's lap the moment he sat down and continued to purr the "I think you're wonderful" song while gazing up at him with hope and trust. Talk about a snow job! And what a relief for me—with this going on, there was no way Dan could boot Sage out the door.

It didn't take long at all before Dan and Sage adopted each other and were the best of friends. Actually, this regal cat had performed a miracle that converted Dan for life—in future years, all cats would be welcome in our home. I kept quiet, but continued to feel this might well be a ploy, a part Sage was playing to make life easier for himself with this new family that included a difficult man. Most animals don't fake their feelings, but was this one an exception?

The cat obviously thought well of himself and firmly believed that he was no puppet; no one would pull his strings if he could help it. Thus, it must have been he who had chosen us: he was in control and should make the decisions. With that attitude of power he probably felt he could love us and still be independent. Sage finally began to play, relax, and sleep soundly. Not having lived with a cat before, I was constantly intrigued by this beautiful, graceful, and mysterious creature, and I always looked forward to what he might do next.

Cats are classed as domesticated animals, like dogs, but Sage didn't easily adopt our domestic schedules and habits. He liked to sleep days and go out to prowl our field at night. Inside the house he chose places like the kitchen counter, the dresser, or even Danny's crib for his bed. It was he who went bump in the night as he jumped to the floor to change sleeping arrangements. He liked to eat when we did, as well as about six other times a day, but he didn't clean his plate unless he liked the menu. While Kitty dawdled and ate tiny bites, the dogs, of course, gobbled their meals in seconds.

Sage hated the phone, the car, and definitely detested getting wet (as I learned the first and only time I tried to give him a bath). He seldom came when called, unless chicken was frying in the pan, and by not following any rules, he became a terrible model for the kids. "Get off the counter this minute!" was an order he never learned, though he did learn to jump down when I came into the kitchen. Since I assumed Sage was a rather typical cat I wondered whether indeed he was domesticated. Not very well, it seemed, in this home.

The conniving guy became a finicky eater in stages, and I became a slave to him in roughly the same stages. Those first days, any table scrap was fine, along with some milk. Then, to entice me to share more of our dinner of chicken, rabbit, or beef stew, this cat, who must have been a born actor, started turning and walking away from his dish of food now and then, his tail twitching a "yuck, yuck, bad food" message.

In many ways he seemed like a very well adjusted human. I loved to watch him do his morning or evening stretching exercises and washing-up rituals, and pull out lots of stickers and burrs without my help. When finished with his grooming and breakfast, he usually sat or stretched out on the counter or dresser to meditate or nap. He would have gone higher, but the house provided few places for solitude or safety from Nancy's reach. He'd tried the top of the refrigerator with a jump from the crib, but I had stacked it with boxes and bags of cereal, flour, sugar, and potatoes, since there was only one cupboard in the tiny kitchen.

Even outside, there were few high places to climb for fun or safety. In the early mornings, and in the late afternoons after Dan came home, Sage often sat on the hood or roof of the car. Once in a while he tried the top of the baled hay, but Nancy could usually climb up there. The deep-freeze, covered with a carpet remnant, was on the shady north side of the house and became his usual command post and sleeping area during the heat of the day. Sage probably joined me in dreaming of huge shady trees hanging over and around the house...surely this elegant cat had lived in a more affluent neighborhood, one with trees and gardens that provided cover and shade.

In time, the cat became a sociable fellow and followed me around during the hot, sunny Arizona days, or loitered around the garden as I planted, hoed, or picked vegetables for dinner. Sage was a born naturalist and student of all that was in the garden, yard, and fields; he spent hours carefully smelling the soil, nibbling plant leaves for taste tests, and sniffing flowers. Every insect was of interest, and he would patiently sit and watch one beetle for ages, sometimes touching it lightly with a front paw to see what might happen. Gradually, the neighboring horse field and the dairy fields across the lane became his domain; all had to be explored and thought about—after all, life is an adventure. Sage was never a big hunter, but now and then he brought a few trophies to the back steps. Dan or I always tried to take the bird or mouse away before the children saw it.

Cat companions can cure much loneliness; as I wrote letters, paid bills, typed, and read the daily paper, Sage often came in to ham it up—jumping to the tabletop, knocking off papers, trying to grab my pen as I wrote, or even just watching the pen move across the page with a mesmerized stare. He also liked to stare down at the messes he made on the floor, his eyes bright and intent, and his tail swishing back and forth as though he were considering the additional effect he'd make if he jumped down into the mess. He lived happily in the moment and, as far as I could tell, never fretted about the past or the future.

Dan lamented, "I don't like to nitpick, but is there some good reason I seldom get an entire neat paper to read? The news must turn you violent." I would never tattle on this cat; he'd worked too hard to gain Dan's approval.

Mostly I gave the cat praise; he obviously knew the general tenor of remarks like, "What a good, good kitty!" or, "Aren't you a beautiful cat!" Sage sometimes answered by rubbing against my legs or jumping into my lap to purr—this fellow-being was giving love or approval back.

Sage loved playing with empty grocery bags. I put several on the floor after returning from shopping, and he stalked them, crawled in them, and rattled them all he could. If I laughed and became his audience, he seemed to savor the game even more. Then suddenly he would quit, jump to a chair, and carefully groom his coat and wash his face and ears.

On extracold nights, Sage agreed to stay in, and even with Dan's snoring and my tossing and turning, he remained on the double bed, either stretching out between us in the center or across the bottom part of the bed. Softly purring and kneading the covers with his paws, he nestled deeper and deeper into the bedding, his purring ending with a funny little hiccup just as he fell soundly asleep. Even with only about a fourth of the bed left for me to sleep on, this cat's complete relaxation made him a teacher par excellence for me, and I tossed less while he was there.

Cats really do sleep a lot, or so it seemed, and I never was able to keep Sage from sleeping on the kitchen counter in a splash of sunlight on cool winter days. At least he was a great role model and salesman for the kids, taking long siestas morning, noon, and afternoon. I could point to him and plead with the kids, "Come on, you kids. Lie down and sleep. Sage knows it's time for a catnap."

One morning he explored the kitchen counter—for food, of course—and stopped to smell a bouquet of flowers in the one small vase I'd brought from home. He liked flowers both outside and inside the house, but apparently he did not feel the same way about vases. With a sudden move he knocked over the lovely blue vase, sending water flowing around his feet and over the pieces of broken crockery. This cat was seldom without dignity, but the noise and water clearly made him anxious to go outside and seek more predictable wonders of life. Sage's tail immediately began to jerk back and forth in irritation, and he gave me a look as if to say, "Did you have something to do with a booby-trapped bunch of flowers?"

We changed him a little, perhaps, but this calm and quiet fellow changed all of us more. He reinforced the children's patience and curiosity in watching and catching butterflies and bugs, and taught them to be calm and playful friends. In spite of constantly washing himself to stay fastidiously clean and neat, he wasn't afraid to be a clown and tomboy part of the time as he raced around, tumbled, and leapt high for pieces of hay, twine, or Nancy's rag doll dangling above him. In high spirits, Sage played hide-and-seek with the kids, racing and jumping to the top of the dresser, table, or chair, only to jump down when they found him, after which he would try to hide somewhere else. Often, he just played alone, rolling around on his back with happiness. I had to shout a big "No!" to shoelace entertainment when he tried to separate laces from shoes, or, failing that, chew them to bits.

Sage became a seeker of food, relaxation, fun, and excitement, and he got love from all the family. At bedtimes he always listened to the books I read to the children, and his calm, relaxed, heavy body on the bed made wakeful eyes sleepy and my job easier.

One day I noticed that he had finally begun to catch the grasshoppers that had invaded my vegetable garden like an army; he would crouch for long periods, watching for the right moment to suddenly pounce on and eat one of the destructive insects. I joked, "Humans may have crisp crackers, cheese, or peanuts as a predinner snack, while this lordly fellow likes to crunch and munch the hard shells and bodies of a few grasshoppers for his hors d'oeuvres."

Then one sad morning, when I went out to the yard I found Sage, cold and dead in the garden. I decided his death must have been caused by poisoned grasshoppers. The insects were like a plague upon the land that year, so to save the garden I had put out grasshopper bait under the vegetable plants' leaves. Countless grasshoppers had been eating the bait, but it had never occurred to me that Sage, too, was being poisoned by eating the infected grasshoppers. The guilt that Dan and I bore from this was heavy.

Together, Nancy and I buried Sage near the garden. I wrapped him in an ancient work sweater of Dan's, one that this puss had stubbornly claimed as his own until Dan finally gave up and decided the cat might as well keep it. Nancy was encouraged to pick every flower that she could find out in the field and put a large bouquet on Sage's grave.

We both cried, and, as I dabbed away Nancy's tears, I wondered what life on this farm was doing to a small, sensitive child.

As a child, I'd lost pet dogs and a horse—what in the world had my parents said to me then about what it means to live and die? I couldn't remember, but I tried to tell Nancy my thoughts. "Let's talk about it, hon. All over the country, in towns, cities, farms, and houses, most people own a dog, a cat, or some other animal, and all of those animals live much shorter lives than people. We have to learn to face death as a part of living; it's sort of like a big circle we all make. Life isn't always fair—sometimes sad things just happen. I really loved that cat.

"Sage was very lucky to live with us and to have a good life after being lost and hungry, and we've been richer for having him in our family. The main thing is to be kind to all creatures and try to make them happy as long as they live. It'll be nice if we all remember Sage. Now, let's go see what I can fix for lunch. Tell Daddy about it when he gets home. Tell him Sage has gone to heaven, or greener pastures, and tell him why he died. Daddy will be really sad, too."

Chapter 10

Mom Says It's Six

My biological clock, or circadian rhythms, made me well suited to be a farmer. I was always awake long before daybreak and began every day at a full gallop. Forever, for me, it had been "early to bed and early to rise," but so far the "wealthy and wise" ending to Franklin's verse eluded me.

"Good morning, Dan. Wake up! Whatever success I'll have as the farmer-on-the-site may be due to my choosing a mate whose clock runs more or less on the same schedule as mine and some of the animal kingdom. Don't you agree?"

"Yeah, but did you plan on daily shifts of fifteen to eighteen hours?"

It was 5:30 AM, and Dan quickly shook his head and began dressing in his faded jeans, wrinkled shirt, and sneakers before taking the pail out to milk Maude while I started breakfast. Maybe my philosophizing was all just sales talk, but I'd been lying awake thinking and had to finish.

"You and I and the animals have the sense to go to sleep when it gets dark and to get up when it gets light. To keep these hours, there need to be reasons, and now we've got many reasons seven days a week. Sure, there are nocturnal predatory animals, like owls, foxes, lions, and cats, who hunt in the dim light of the moon or stars, and there are rabbits, guinea pigs, and deer, who like to munch grass after the sun sets or in the predawn hours, but I'm so happy that we keep the early morning routines along with our animals. Early birds get the worms, you know."

Dan replied, "Don't give me too much credit. You'd find me sleeping till noon and letting you milk the cow if I weren't such a nice guy. If early birds get the worms, as you're telling me, maybe late birds get more sleep plus the late-to-rise worms—not that I want any worms."

Friends continued to think it was almost indecent and certainly not normal for us to go to bed at the same time as small children and chickens. Yet even many plants, with their chlorophyll and photosynthesis, have sense enough to close their flowers or do some sleeping at night. What did those night-owl friends of ours think their ancestors did before electricity, oil lanterns or candles?

For some time I had been puzzling over the confusion and stress that cows must experience if they wake up at dawn expecting to be milked and fed and their owners with late-morning clocks force them to wait until nine or ten. Are there farmers like that?

I had always lived in a world dictated by clocks. Noisy Big Ben alarm clocks had clanged most mornings to get me out of bed and to school on time. Bells and buzzers had marked the end and beginning of every class. In college there was sometimes barely time to run from the second floor of one building to the next class on the third floor of a building across campus. It was also a world of deadlines for assignments and final exams. I had actually signed up for those schedules and kept full appointment calendars. When I crowded part-time jobs into my life, they called for even more alarm clocks. Sometimes I set three clocks in different spots in my room to make sure I wouldn't sleepily turn all of them off and go back to sleep.

Now we had reasons to go to sleep early and to wake early—naturally. The nighttime lighting was horrible, consisting of three bare bulbs hanging by electric cords. Plus, I had one table lamp that sat either on an upended apple box or a dresser by the bed, with its cord plugged into the only wall outlet in the room. Besides, we were both bone tired by sundown, and always in need of sleep. Moreover, there could be no lights shining in the house until after the children were asleep. With Danny's crib in the kitchen and Nancy's bed in the other room with us, it just made sense to go to bed at the children's hour and to get up at the first hint of light. It was an excuse to do what our inner clocks wanted anyway. Vestiges of those earlier alarm clocks seemed to have been planted deep within me. If I had started setting an alarm again I surely would have reached out and turned it off shortly before it started clanging. There was no money for me to have a wristwatch, but when I was out in the yard working, again something told me when it was time to come in to fix lunch or dinner.

Maybe it was just easier to feel time when living in the country. Our dogs did—they seemed to know exactly when Dan would arrive home. The whole world has rhythms, seasons, and cycles—rains and snows come in certain seasons, the sun and moon have their phases, and the timing of ocean tides is predictable and inexorable. The rabbits munching their pellets, the chickens scratching for grain, and the cow and calves grazing in the field, all follow inner clocks. Whales go south to calve during certain months and swim north in the spring. Many birds and wild animals migrate on rigid schedules. Even the horses across the fence began growing winter coats before the nights became cold.

Of course, many people can't avoid readjusting their inner clocks to fit work or play schedules. Dan had to milk the cow twice a day, seven days a week, get to work by 7:30 or 8:00 AM, go to nighttime meetings, and teach his evening classes usually at 7:00 PM. Still, the schedules were sometimes flexible—many a night all of us yawned at the same time, and went to sleep at a time most people considered their dinner hour.

Dan observed, "You don't have to stick to any fast schedule, you know. Why not be flexible and do these dishes tomorrow?"

"I guess you know you've just given me a great excuse to turn into a goof-off. Be flexible? Sure, I'll try to think more about the moment, not the future—shift into low gear and hear the birds sing and see the clouds now and then."

"Absolutely. Why don't you try to become less tired? Take a nap."

Naps for me would have felt like failure, like lessening my commitment to make dreams come true, and replacing it with limp creature comforts.

In Tucson I had buried my head in books and almost never gotten away from school buildings to see the sky and countryside. Except for having felt cold or hot, I would hardly have known what the weather was like. Work, study, class schedules, and Baby Nancy dictated the days and nights. Now, I did concede that no matter how much needed to be done, there had to be time to at least look up and revel at the Arizona sky with its constant show. White clouds frequently billowed into all sorts of shapes as they sailed slowly across the sky, and at night the air was so clear that the moon seemed to have grown, and even the stars lit up our farm. Maybe this was what serendipity was all about—about finding these happy and simple moments. Serendipity was a new word to me then, and I began to think about it often.

"Kids, look at that solitary hawk silently circling up over your heads. Perhaps he's wondering about the hens. Look up some of the time. No one should go through life with his head down."

And Dan was right about my schedule: maybe I would enjoy this farm more if I revised my schedule now and then, at least at times when kids and animals wouldn't holler. I could do the supper dishes after breakfast the next morning, wash clothes in the cool of the evening and hang them in the early morning. Tennis shoes needed not go in the wash until they were completely brown. Large-sized safety pins could hold up the kids' red corduroy coveralls for a while longer. I could read and write from 4 AM to 6 AM, and now and then, feel free to eat a piece of fried chicken for breakfast and a bowl of cold cereal at bedtime. With any time saved, I would give the children a surprise party of frozen juice sticks, or let Nancy bring a young bunny into the kitchen to feed it a pie tin of lettuce, carrots, or celery tops.

I was lucky to have a mate who was scornful of domesticity, of too much housework, and who had always favored my spending as little time as possible cooking, sewing, ironing, or cleaning. Fortunately he never changed. We didn't eat out for many, many years, but he always made things easier when he said "Get out in the fresh air: the wash and ironing will be there tomorrow." Fortunately, there were no bosses, no timecards, and no deadlines to create a fear of being late.

Yet, I'm bragging. Too often I forgot these ideas and worked for weeks at a time as if I were on a chain gang. Since we kept adding and adding to the schedules, I couldn't just lock the store door and go home early. It was also hard to take Dan's advice and still be that model farmer, mother, and wife. On the nights Dan taught, as soon as Baby Danny slept I made pies (if I had enough ingredients), ironed shirts and several of the little tablecloths from a wedding shower that covered the card table, and tried to sweep, mop, and dust the house. Most days remained full as I took care of the kids, mowed and watered the new lawn, tended the vegetable garden and the animals, cooked meals, and ran errands. Procrastination and flexibility constantly did battle with duty and obligation.

On the bright side, overcast days in the desert were rare, and, as the sun came up, there were often vast morning displays of color in the sky—blazing shades of yellow, orange, coral, crimson and pink. This was another reason to rise early. At that special hour it seemed as though the entire sky became my personal stage set. In addition to the show of colors across the sky, the birds and animals began to tune up their voices, starting with the clucks, chirps, and cooing of the chickens and wild birds, who were soon joined by the cow and calves with their tentative snorts and gentle calls. Sometimes the neighbors' horses came to the fence to snort and whinny, feeling that they too had rights to a sociable part of our life. When Dan went out and let the back door bang shut he was like a conductor increasing the volume of the music: all the animals became louder as they insisted on being fed immediately. Even blasé Cindy and Heidi gave excited yips. I loved it—breakfast time on a little farm in the country! Over the many years to come, there was an ongoing payback from our having lived on those specks of Arizona land—my memory still holds clear the colors of those wonderful clouds and the sky as the sun rose at dawn or slipped out of sight at the end of the day. Sometimes, I must have looked up.

Chapter 11

Sure You're Not Living Beyond Your Means?

There's a saying, "Less is more," but that became hard to believe. In spite of an improved yard, for months there remained a famine on Fowler Lane—the Great Depression played over again. I'd read a saying once that warned, "One should never eat the seeds for next year's crop." That year, I'd have cooked whole buckets of seeds if I'd had them. There was no adequate diet or bounty in my farm basket, with just eggs, milk, chicken, rabbit, and a meager $4.83 in my purse by the 17th of the month. It became a constant juggling act: "Shall I skip the toilet paper and buy a bag of potatoes? How embarrassing if I can't make the small payment on the cow! Shall I send postcards instead of letters to my dad and to Dan's folks? " I'd already crossed off all long-distance phone calls. I knew, without long columns of figures in any budget book that the First Farm economy was in dire straights.

Some economists say figures don't lie; others say figures can lie. Either way, I discovered that a good teaching salary plus the extra money from the night classes didn't equal a living for four on this heavily mortgaged land. Somehow, I would have to produce more and save more, and Dan would have to bring home more bacon. We needed a lot more bacon. The saying, "If you can't do, teach," was not true. It took a lot of doing to teach, but it wasn't a job that made one wealthy, not even when teaching nights as well as days.

With only two weeks of vacation each summer, or three if he was attending college, Dan couldn't take summer jobs the way the other teachers sometimes did. It would take all his three-week vacations for five years for him to get a Master's degree.

"I'd be stopped in my tracks with despair," I told Dan, "if I ever took time to study all our economic facts. I'm not ever, ever going to write down a budget, when every penny is already so carefully spent!" Dan agreed, but we often talked about food late at night.

Our time was also not squandered: even if it seemed cheap, time was in as short supply as money, unless I was talking about money owed. It would be a waste of time to find totals of assets, disbursements, and debts owed, since the balance would obviously be a negative one. And why spend time and money on a cute little budget book in which to record figures for food, water, mortgage payments, and basic phone service?

I knew the amount of our hefty mortgage payment, and dirt-cheap didn't apply. It was a lousy, huge hunk out of Dan's school checks. The only land that was cheap was actually free—much of the dirt from the unpaved lane and the farm drifted into the house at no charge, covering floors and curtains, and coloring the water in the washing machine a muddy brown—especially in summer when the melon trucks drove by daily, raising thick clouds of dust. Our one small double window facing the lane was always opaque with dirt, and the kids drew pictures on them with their fingers, then wiped their hands off on their pants or a bath towel. Even the inside dirt got recycled.

"Oh brother, what's for supper?" Dan came in to ask as he opened the refrigerator door. It was hard to be masters of our fate when there was not even cereal on hand. The Crisco can on the one high shelf contained chicken feed savings for emergencies between paychecks. "It's just chicken feed" never became my philosophy. It might mean small change to some, but to me, every penny was (and still is) real money. When Dan's school checks arrived, I saw them just long enough to make out a deposit slip before taking them to the bank.

It didn't take a written record to know where the money went, and it was never under a heading called "recreation." Deposit bank slips were record enough of income; but the bank also sent out monthly, bright yellow sheets, all nicely printed with a careful bookkeeping of deposits and checks written—all totaled and giving me the sad news that I had $4.91 remaining in the account. Since I felt an overdrawn notice would be the same as death, I tried hard to not go below the $1 level, since I wondered if the bank even counted sums under one dollar as money.

"Look here, hon," I told Dan, "we've gone for broke on this primitive place, and we're almost there. I don't even dream about frivolous purchases. I dream about potatoes, beans, and soap for the washing machine."

Dan merely sighed, opened the fridge to see again what food was there, and murmured, "So I see. Your low-budget show doesn't even have the props for eating tonight, except for more eggs, milk, and leftover fried chicken."

Shopping in a grocery store was weird. Beans were more filling than oranges. Always there were comparisons to be made and the recurring question: which necessity is the biggest? Or it became a matter of substitutions: "If I don't buy needed socks, maybe I can buy some flour or potatoes." Every two weeks or so, I dashed down the aisles of the grocery store for the basics, with few choices to be made; flour was flour, and sugar was sugar; I bought big bags only if they were necessities. Bananas were purchased only when mostly brown and marked down, or when they were a weekend special. I tried to avoid overly treated or overly wrapped food, on the premise that the less processed and handled the items, the cheaper they would probably be.

Other customers usually ambled up and down the aisles and left with full baskets, but I was out of the store in minutes and always took the same route. I knew if I slowed down I might be hypnotized by a thousand items. I also tried to shop early in the day to avoid queuing in long checkout lines. Standing there waiting, I'd be tempted to fill another basket with impulse items that the store stacked seductively at eyeball level near the cash register.

Meanwhile, back at the farm there was finally an element of timing that could help or hurt the bank balance. I suggested, "Chickens don't need a new roof this time of year, but we'd better buy that old bathtub for a watering trough for the cow. The permanent roofing for the shed can go on in the fall." This turned out to be a poor conclusion reached in ignorance, and we had a close call with one of the few rains of the season.

This was not a home with wall-to-wall carpeting tacked to the floors. My one threadbare nine-by-twelve rug was all I had over the concrete. The rug was a tweed of reds and tans. It had absorbed its share of dirt, and not much more could be swept under it or ground into it from above. The rug's condition finally got to me, so I rolled it up and dragged it outside. By setting one end of the rolled-up rug against the clothesline, I got it draped over the first two lines, hoping that the 4" x 4" posts, the cross-pieces at each end, and the lines would hold. I had heard you could beat rugs, so the dust began to fly as I whipped this one with the broom. Even so, it still showed spots and looked dirty—a year of constant use by toddlers, assorted animals, and two farmers had created a need for special treatment.

Thus, after brushing pails of soapy water over the rug and scrubbing the worst spots with a bar of soap, I turned the hose on it full-force to rinse away the suds. Immediately, the added water weighed the rug down, and the two end posts of the clothesline fell inward, even though they had been set deep in cement. The whole mess of posts, wire clotheslines, and rug suddenly lay on the lawn.

I simply could not have Dan come home and see how stupid I'd been. "Dash it, Nancy, I've got to tough this out before Daddy arrives, and you've got to help me." Just re-setting the posts would be hard enough for Dan to figure out, since the balls of cement were still tightly around the two posts. Tears would only add water, I thought, and that made me laugh a bit hysterically. Even Nancy was in awe of my mess, and recognized my predicament.

Working quickly, I cut off the wires fastened to the posts. Then, my two-and-a-half-year-old helper and I rolled the posts off the rug, left the wire with the posts, and rolled up the rug. We dragged and rolled the rug over to the gravel driveway, spread it out, hosed it off again, turned it over, and hosed the other side, then left it there to dry.

Dan stopped just short of driving over the rug when he got home. He came into the house saying, "I know I'm a nice guy, but you've got to stop giving me this red-carpet treatment."

Fortunately, there wasn't much that could break down besides those clothesline posts. Our toaster was simply a little tin box with slitted sides—it sat over a stove burner and burned four slices of bread at a time. We were both full-fledged klutzes about anything mechanical. I might break down, but we didn't own a lot of machines that could. The only batteries we had were in the flashlight and the car. As far as mechanical equipment, there was the washing machine, the car, the refrigerator, the freezer, and the muscle-powered lawnmower that I'd used at Goodyear Park.

There was a funny thing about having so little: there was also very little garbage. The current fervor to recycle, reduce, and reuse didn't exist then. Both farm people and town people, just as a matter of course, reused what they could. On Fowler Lane, even what garbage there was had a way of looking good, so I'd mutter, "Let's see, would the cow eat carrot tops and these dried pieces of bread?" or, "No, Nancy, I'll save your old clothes—your brother can wear them before long since they're made for either girls or boys."

We burned papers in a rusted metal barrel and buried a few cans and old tennis shoes in a small dip in the land out in the field. Not even Cindy or Heidi would have wanted to chew on our old shoes; they would have taken them out and buried them.

Rubber bands collected in a kitchen drawer until they melted together, pens stayed in that same drawer long after they quit writing, and paper clips collected until they were black and rusty. Slivers of soap pressed together made a bar that came apart when used, and the soapy sliver had a tendency to fall on the shower floor, get stuck in the drain, and back the water up.

Too often I could be heard uttering "Oops" as I tried to fix something. "Oops" became one of Danny's first words. Feeling guilty, I bought new handles for broken shovels, hoes, and rakes after giving up trying to fix the old ones, and even then I struggled to keep the wooden handles attached to the metal parts. Today, without a backward glance, people throw away just about everything, from slightly used cars to long-term spouses.

I continued to worry about finances, and I observed to Dan, "Selling milk to neighbors and growing vegetables just isn't doing the job. You and I have got to make something new happen, because at this point we don't even have pennies to pinch!"

Long into the hot summer nights, our talks evolved into Econ 1-A sessions. I ventured to say, "As you and I both know, it's about supply and demand: we must supply more money and demand even less than we are doing now. The problem is, I've no area of excess spending; many times, even now I can't spend on anything but the necessities. But boy, do we have demands! The car's going to give out soon, we've got to pay off Mrs. Marshall as soon as possible, and then we've got to enlarge the house. You're planning on starting a Master's program this summer, and that will require tuition—and that's just for starters! There's simply got to be another game in town!"

With a tired sigh, Dan responded, "Well, when we're on the bottom, there's only one way to go, and that's up. I've got to earn more. The veteran classes have been a good idea. What else can we do?"

It seemed strange how one thing always led to another. I'd subscribed to the newspaper because we needed paper for the rabbit's potty in the bathroom, and that was good because she used it as intended. Receiving the paper had prompted me to scan it when I had time. Now I had an idea, based on what the paper didn't have. "Dan, in reading the Sunday copies of the Arizona Republic, I've noticed there isn't much written on agriculture. It's your field and we both would really like to read about what's going on across this 'fruited plain.' Wouldn't everyone in agriculture feel the same way? And wouldn't it also be interesting to non-ag people in small towns, and even Phoenix? It's your field—maybe you could do a weekly column or something. We'd both learn a lot if you interviewed farmers. Think of the incredible number of things grown in this valley plus all the ag businesses you could write about in a column. I'd help with your rough drafts and type the finished ones to hand in."

He was quiet for a moment, then pushed his chair back from the table to grin and say, "I like the idea. Sure, we can sell words, and the main cost will just be gas to get the articles. However, I'm not sure the newspaper pays much."

"I agree about the low pay," I continued, "but you could tell upbeat success stories that would not only inform but would give ideas and hope to others. Make it more readable with personalities—write about the most successful growers, dairymen, horse breeders, cattlemen, and even the man who sold me the rabbit. We would learn so much and meet such interesting people. We could get the articles and write the stuff on weekends!"

Dan agreed and added, "Maybe I could take pictures, too; the paper would pay extra for that...except that we have no decent camera. Well, I'll talk to them."

The editor of the paper thought the idea of an agricultural section featuring articles and pictures was a good idea for the Sunday paper. Dan talked him into financing a good camera, saying his better one had been lost. The kids toyed around with our old, box-shaped Kodak camera while Dan and I learned to use a fine new one.

At the same time, Dan told a company that sold tanks of propane and helium gas that it needed a bit of advertising and that, for very little cost, we could produce a one-page flyer with a photograph and blurb for them. I hung up a white sheet on the porch of the house for a plain background and tied brightly colored balloons with a bow of ribbon to float above the tank of helium the company lent us. Dan bought several rolls of the suggested film from the camera shop and practiced with the lens and several extra ones he'd bought, plus the range finder, the viewfinder, and the synchronized flash attachment at different times of day and at varying distances. The propane company liked the advertising, and their small check paid us for the rolls of film and flashbulbs. Not much training, but Dan decided he knew enough to start phoning farmers and ranchers for articles. Weekends became even more busy than weekdays.

At that point, I realized both of us had either inherited a strong work ethic or had caught the work bug early on. I shuddered with guilt to think how skillfully I'd evaded home chores while growing up. I was an only child, yet had never been made to wash or dry dishes or even to fold a load of laundry. Mom had been busy teaching long hours, and my more elderly dad had become the cook, housekeeper, and taxi driver.

"Dan, we don't know how to slow down. You've already got a full day of teaching plus night classes and meetings, and you help out on the home front every moment you can. Now we're going to get up at 5 AM on Saturdays to rush off on these weekend journeys!"

He tipped back in the folding chair and replied, "I thought this was all your idea."

"No," I continued, "hunger is a problem, but everyone must have some kind of problem. We've always just called problems 'challenges.' I close my eyes or read to the kids when I don't know what to do about something.

"The trouble with becoming slaves is that the work is endless. If we're not careful, it'll become an end in itself. I already feel like a draft horse with fields all the way to the horizon to plow each day. I bet you do, too."

Friends in town enjoyed relaxing on Saturdays and Sundays, getting up late, reading the paper, going to church, going to ball games, visiting friends, making special meals, or fishing. On our Saturdays, we fed the animals, milked the cow, ate breakfast, made sack lunches, cleaned the kitchen, and then the kids and I got dressed in our only decent, clean clothes, in order not to embarrass Dan when meeting the people he would be interviewing. Then all four of us squeezed into the Bluebird coupe and tackled the long day.

As Dan narrowed his eyes and peered at the notepad on his lap, his answer was a vague, "Maybe. Where's the darn map? I don't know this Mesa area very well."

Dan took along the name and directions for some successful farming or ranching operation or ag-related business, and toted a camera and notepad in a professional-looking new camera bag, which he stored under his seat. At first, both kids curled up with their knees under their chins on the Bluebird's shelf behind the front seat, but eventually, one of them sat on my lap or squeezed in between us. A slave or not, I began to relish Saturdays. "Dan, having nothing to do must eventually be the worst thing there is."

He agreed, "Yeah, all this action is kinda fun, isn't it?"

Much of the time it was broiling hot. I often felt half-baked even before the breakfast dishes were washed and put away. Each year the Phoenix area has nintey-one days of hundred-degree temperatures or higher, and sometimes the thermometer goes up to one hundred and fifteen degrees. I always insisted, when talking to friends from cooler areas, that "The heat's not so bad because it's a dry heat," but we seldom arrived at our destinations feeling very dry. We unfolded our cramped bodies and tumbled out of the coupe with damp and wrinkled clothing, flushed red faces, and wind-tousled hair. Without going near a seashore or a lake, we all kept permanently weathered and the color of burned toast.

"Sure you're not living beyond your means?" One jolly farmer, who knew Dan slightly, scratched his head and popped that ironic question as we all spilled out of the car to meet him. He probably spoke without a clue as to how terribly right he was.

Dan and I laughed politely, while the farmer gave a good belly laugh at his own joke. This man had no way of knowing that our house on Fowler Lane wasn't much roomier than the car and had an equal lack of elegance.

"We're going to get a bigger car."

The farmer punched Dan's arm and replied, "That's what I figured."

Dan interviewed outstanding farmers of many breeds of sheep, dairy cows, beef cattle, horses, rabbits, chickens, goats, and sheep. We went to ranchers who raised alfalfa, cantaloupes, cotton, dates, and seed grains. We stopped at cooperatives, at a broom-making plant, and at packing plants. Come hell or high water, we ferreted out something different every week for every Sunday edition for five years of feature writing and photography—without ever missing even a single week of submitting photos and text for the column. All of our columns and pictures were used.

Zooming back to Phoenix we dropped the film off to be developed, picked up animal feed, groceries, and any other necessities for the week, and rushed home. In the late afternoon or evening it was important for Dan to sit down and try to come up with a title, some good lead sentences, and an ending. That way, the easier writing, with a pencil and eraser, could be done on Sunday. The interviews were mostly to gather interesting and factual information, quotes, and pictures, but Dan often reorganized the material to be more like a story and sometimes included some of his own comments and research on the topic.

On Mondays I pounded out the final version of the column on my old portable typewriter, and that evening we all drove in to pick up the photo prints, select the best ones, and turn in the photographs, the negatives, and the article to the offices of the Arizona Republic on East Van Buren Street.

Combining work with pleasure, Dan then slowly drove the main street so we could all see the city lights and lick ice-cream cones. It was our celebration of making it through another weekly deadline. Ice-cream cones were progress in our Spartan life, and for them we broke my rule that no food was to be eaten in the car. The combination of ice-cream cones and small children in a tiny two-seater car was not a good one: the cones mixed, melted, stuck, stained, spread, flowed, dripped, trickled, and ran together all over the children and the car. However, Monday nights only came once a week, and a family needs to celebrate, a trade-off of mess for fun. I vowed to myself to always bite my lip and keep still over little stuff.

The interviews and photos appeared in the paper the following Sunday. The newspaper checks paid for the treats, if not for the extra cleaning I had to do inside the car.

Dr. Cline, Dan's department head at the university down in Tucson, drove up soon after the first articles appeared. He was completely discombobulated by Dan's feature writing. "You'd better not do any more articles! It's impossible to write correctly about agriculture after talking to just one farmer and not doing extensive research; it's bound to jeopardize your teaching position." He was a man oriented to much research and study.

For the first time, Dan didn't take Dr. Cline's advice, much as he liked the man. Neither of us thought it would harm his teaching job, nor did we believe Dan would fail as a farm writer and photographer, although an English teacher we knew suggested Dan might fail for lack of writing skills, because what does an ag teacher know about writing? Despite these doomsayers, becoming a part-time journalist worked out just fine. During those five years of weekly articles, only once was there even a smidgen of a complaint, and that was over a couple of very minor points. Dr. Cline continued to grumble. Nevertheless, he also continued to assign student teachers to do their practice teaching under Dan's supervision.

Our long relationship with the Ford coupe finally ended due to its old age, compounded by the weekly struggle of getting the photos and articles delivered, and the packed-together-like-sardines nights at the drive-in movies. We swapped Bluebird for a two-door, green Chevy sedan. Absolute luxury! Each of us could have our own seat and window, and, like the coupe, the Chevy became a trusty and faithful vehicle. I often told the children, "It's Saturday and time to go a-roving." Perhaps that's why the car was soon named Rover, though the name may have come from a book featuring a wandering dog named Rover.

For years getting interviews continued to be our only escape to a bigger world, mainly that of the Salt River Valley. From an agricultural perspective, we came to know Maricopa County very well, but there was never money or time to travel throughout the wonderful Apache State. Not until years later did we visit the great Colorado River, the Grand Canyon, the Petrified Forest, the Painted Desert, and other scenic areas. We didn't even take the time to visit an Indian reservation just a dozen miles away.

Chapter 12

Friendly Fertilizer

From day one on our little farm I had my own brand of free fertilizer, and I continued to shovel up a growing pile of this wonderful stuff for the growing garden, the new lawn area, and a hedge. "This land is my land," I would think, "and it had better be fed an enriched diet right away to produce food." People in town usually call it "fertilizer," and country people call it "manure," or worse. Whatever its name, I hoped it would make all the garden, lawn, and plants grow big and strong. There had been a lot of it left in the old chicken pen, and I saved it all. Now I could add rabbit manure, and soon there would be cow patties.

My own produce department! Feeling reckless during a still-cool morning in late spring, I bought more packets of seed with vividly colored pictures of perfect vegetables on the covers. I hoed and raked off all the garden area's brush and weeds and took them to the back of the property, where there was a small gully. With a shovel and a rake, I spread out all the chicken and rabbit contributions and set a sprinkler to soften the soil so I could shovel the fertilizer under and mix it with the soil. The earth was rock-hard even in spring. Along with the bright Arizona sun and the water from our irrigation pipes, this fertilizer had to make every seed feel its muscles and grow in record time.

Fortunately, during those first months only a few people came to view my work. Usually, as in the case of Faye, the teacher's wife, I wished they hadn't come. The daily sprinkler on the manure covering the garden soil made First Farm as smelly as a feed lot. If only I could have posted in the entrance to the driveway a big sign: CLOSED FOR REPAIRS or CLOSED UNTIL FURTHER NOTICE.

Our first visitor, even before Faye called, was a service man who had to take a reading of the electric meter. I had watered early, wanting to shovel the soil and manure over by 8 AM, before the late-morning sun dried out the soil.

Almost trapped in the mud, the meter reader managed to lift his muddy shoes out of the stuff next to the steps. His first comment was, "Boy, oh boy! Lady, are you sure you should have bought this place? It's a malodorous mess!"

Very firmly, I replied, "Yes, I'm sure. Here, let me get you a knife and a rag to scrape off the mud." Where in the world had he learned those wonderful and whimsical words, "malodorous mess"? I'd never used the word "malodorous" in my life, but I've remembered it and often laugh about his next remarks. The fellow was flabbergasted by how deep his feet had sunk, and as he tried to scrape his shoes free of mud, he added, "Well, all I can say is, you're really getting your feet planted firmly in the ground here. Talk about cow, chick, and bunny power— whew! It's strong! Those feet of yours could grow in this fertilized stuff and be permanently affixed to the land."

One of our other visitors wasn't any fun at all, although I've remembered him, also, all these years. Sam was an oversized, roly-poly friend of Dan's. He had come from Los Angeles to Phoenix for some business meetings, and he'd had some free time one morning. He'd picked up a map and arrived unannounced except for the barking of Cindy and Heidi, who were my only doorbells.

In an accusing voice, Sam announced that no one was answering our phone. What he didn't see was that the garden and lawn were planted and that the sun-hot soil had sprouted seeds, even though the over-all look was still one of brown dirt. Since nothing appeared very green yet, there was little to see in the way of improvements or beauty. No amount of air freshener could hide the still-pervasive odor. Quite naturally, this urban escapee thought I should have been inside doing housework and on hand to hear the phone ring.

"Sorry, I didn't hear your call; the price of admittance today has to be putting up with fertilized soil. Would you like to come into my humongous house, though it's a bit messy today, or shall we sit here in the shade?" Fortunately, he opted for staying on the porch in the shade. Sam sat in the folding chair, I on the steps. In his front-row seat, Sam loosened and then removed his tie, and, with raised eyebrows, his eyes swept over the whole scene as he observed, "It's one scorcher of a day— how do you stand this temperature all summer?"

Darned if I didn't reply like a native. "It's not too bad because it's such dry heat." And then, I added to myself, as I always did, "So's the heat in the oven."

"Dan and I have a ranch spread of two whole acres here, but as you can see, we didn't buy it for social standing in Tolleson. We're making haste slowly."

Sam might have tried to visualize what the tight quarters inside the house were like, but he probably couldn't imagine how bad things really were. That day the stuffy house smelled of a chaotic mix of Vicks Vapo-Rub, Johnson's Baby Powder, shoe polish, diapers to be washed, and mashed crayons. Then there was the stench of some very ripe melons that had fallen off trucks along the road; some extrasoft ones were on the counter ready to take out and dig into the soil in the yard. In addition to the odors, the two rooms were dark and gloomy, since I pulled down the window blinds each morning to block out the heat. Turning on lights would have only showed rumpled laundry and an unmade bed.

"What do you see, Sam? Too much ostentation?"

Our friend rolled his eyes and looked around some more. He gesticulated, with his arms swinging wide to embrace the whole property.

"Nothing good! My God, what have you guys gotten yourselves into here? It's a bunch of malarkey. Dan's got a teaching job, hasn't he? And someone said he's teaching vet classes and writing for the Phoenix paper."

"Yeah, he is. It's amazing, Sam. You don't see the finer things in life here? I've been thinking about it, and I can say it all with solid, wonderful words like home, fields, sun, stars, dawn, sunsets, kids, and animals. It's a great life, believe it or not, and I love it all."

I continued to observe him. With his overbearing contempt and disbelief, he continued to glare and turn down his mouth at this slum-house-moved-to-the-country. I found myself seeing and smelling our house and farm from his point of view. Its redeeming feature was that it wasn't a longtime slum. Someone had started to make this place home, but had given up just as the house became livable. There was no buildup around the yard of old cars, tires, lumber, wire, or rusted-out washing machines—the sorts of things that adorn many rural places. And all the weeds were gone from the yard. It actually looked better already.

Sam gave me a reproachful and unfathoming look as I tried to explain, "This isn't all my fault; Dan's my collaborator in this great venture, and maybe because of this happy beginning he's even gotten his repertoire of old jokes back. This is the place where we should be at this time. I didn't just stumble onto this place; it took a lot of work with months of daily searching the whole west side of Phoenix. We've dreamt of country living for years. I'm merely self-employed—hiring myself out to work here. The main thing is not to drift or wait; even daily bits of hard work can add up to big results over time. See the garden plants sprouting over there? Well, when the seeds grow into big plants full of vegetables, I'll feel like cackling the way my hens do when they lay eggs—it'll be a miracle."

Sam didn't seem to be listening, only formulating his next intemperate comments as he sat heavily in the somewhat fragile folding chair. "It's probably way over a hundred here in the shade. It even tastes hot. The truth is, you guys would have been better off in Vermont than here. Or in California. Why aren't you back in California?"

"What did you expect? We were still in college until about this time last year, and now we have our own land, house, and two kids. Be realistic!

This is just the way it is, and you're right—the sun really brightens the corner where we are this morning." Why was he being so aggressive?

In June the Arizona heat can be sizzling, and Sam felt it. As he sat there, his round face and neck became deep pink. He kept running his hands through his hair, and soon he unbuttoned the top buttons of his shirt. There would be a luncheon and meetings soon after he got back to the hotel. Had he packed an extra shirt? I couldn't make the temperature plummet, and I wondered if even this friendship was wilting. I tried once more not to escalate the talk and just to explain.

"Sam, I don't believe I really know you, and you certainly don't know me. Give me a break! We're not zany, and I'm thrilled to have this little farm. I can try to explain its value, but I offer no apology, for we have no regrets. We didn't just blow here like leaves in a wind, you know. With no money, First Farm had to be something simple like this. We found it because a sign saying the place was for sale was affixed to that post beside your car. It was the only place in the whole Salt River Valley I could find that was affordable. Our philosophy is that he who hesitates is lost, and we're both optimists and mavericks, you know. What I don't have or don't do should mean nothing to you—it's not important.

"I'm not blind to what's here—I know it's primitive. But you're crashing an early and far-from-ready rehearsal on this stage. Dan and I laugh about that sign up by Van Buren that says this lane is a 'Dead End Street,' but at worst this is a sidetrack, and we've just begun; it's like a campsite on a long trail—our plans stretch out far ahead. In ten years we may be far away from here. Also, when we borrowed from our landlady down at the university to get through our senior year, Dan had to promise to teach in Arizona for at least two years. Want some iced tea? There's some in a pitcher in the refrigerator, and I baked some butter cookies early this morning."

Perhaps this conversation, more than the fierce heat, was what was making his face and neck flush. "Well," I thought, "they should flush"— he was chopping me down like a tree.

"No, I've got to get back in time for lunch. What was wrong with renting during your first year? Rents must be cheap. Doesn't that Podunk town of Tolleson have any cheap rentals?"

"Of course, but what's cheap can turn out costly. You can't get country living if you stay in town. Listen, Sam, don't you know what I mean? Keep an open mind, this is our home, and it's where our hearts are. Renting is like giving away money every month in order to be cooped up inside and make no savings. We're fighting to create equity on this treasured house and land, both with monthly payments and the improvements. How many people start out at the top of the mountain? Not that we even want to be at the top, but we aren't setting our ultimate goals here, silly. We'll have a bank account in the black after we sell, and in the meantime, I'm hooked on this land and our expanded family—in addition to the kids, it already harbors some wonderful animals. I prefer working outside to being cooped up inside any house, even when it's hot. These vast skies are much nicer than ceilings in a house...self-analysis is always risky, but if I had a dollar I'd bet you that we'll prevail. You come back in a year or two and you won't know this place. This is just the first scene of the first act. In maybe a year and a half, there'll be no stink; the house will be bigger, with a living room, a dining room area, and another bedroom; and this porch will be enclosed. I'll have a big picture window in back, a nice front door, and flowers against the walls of a cool, white house. All this yard you see will be a green, green carpet of lawn, and it will grow up to the edge of a new cement driveway there where your car's parked.

"You know, I had some friends in LA and they didn't believe in making their own luck or working like we do. They were busy looking up at their family tree and all they were going to inherit, never looking down at their own two hands and feet and seeing what they could be doing by themselves. While we're on the first step going up, they're probably still stalled and renting, making do with two so-so salaries. It's an attitude—not a bunch of 'don'ts,' but a lot of 'do's', and I don't mean the 'doos' that you're smelling...I won't even try telling you how much I love this extended family of wonderful animals and kids. I want even more—a whole menagerie of kids and critters. I need to be home for these children, and that new Holstein cow out there is star quality, my first big animal, and, more than looks, she's a constant milk-and-cream machine. The other animals are treasures with great personalities—not one of them is boring. Teaching those two calves to slurp milk out of a bucket was not only tricky, but fun for a town girl. Gads, why do you want to free the slave or peasant when the peasant's so darn happy? I see life as terribly short, with every minute important."

"OK, I give. Only this is not good work for any woman. Women are liberated now, you know. You could be teaching."

"So you think it's bad that I'm digging a ditch and that I'm a part-time field hand or a country bumpkin?"

"No, I think it's bad not to use your education for something. Like the saying goes, don't just work harder but smarter. Hire someone to do this stuff." He sounded so blasted condescending.

"There's nothing good or bad, but thinking makes it so. With your beliefs I doubt if you'll ever know where we're coming from or where we want to go."

Suddenly I began to laugh and decided, to heck with praising my castle or defending myself. Why not shock this officious guy further?

"Sam, I surrender. In one respect you're right—it's worse than it looks with something you can't see. There's a famine on this land, and we're almost hitting bottom. It's not even a subsistence farm yet, and right now Dan and I are going hungry. Our mortgage is for the total price of this farm because we had no down payment funds and it includes some of our school loan as well. At the same time, we've had to buy the animals, their feed, a deep-freeze, a washing machine, and other stuff. New babies don't come cheap—the kids get the food, and Dan and I are barely surviving. Some days I'm not even boiling beans." He shook his head and got up to leave.

"Come on, Sam. It's your rules, not mine, that you believe I'm break-ing. It's too late to make me over. I'm more liberated that you are. We're mainly risking time and work, but I have choice and great expectations. You're tied tighter than a hog-tied calf by 'do's' and 'don'ts'—by what's 'proper.' There's no gender considered in choosing our jobs: Dan can change a diaper and I can dig a ditch. What's wrong with that? You stay in your habitat with those nice black shoes, and I'll stay in mine wear-ing these filthy tennis shoes. Yet, I believe in hunches, and mine are that we'll work our way out of being hungry. If you truly believe something good will come and you work long and hard enough, it often happens. Come back and see us in two years, and we'll buy you lunch in Phoenix at a restaurant of your choosing.

As he drove away, I suddenly realized he hadn't even shaken my hand when saying goodbye, nor had he so much as touched one of the kids or the dogs. In this setting he had seemed a stranger. Maybe he had always been one.

Thumbing my nose at his black car as it reached Van Buren, I changed Danny's diaper, got us all some cold water to drink, and walked back to my ditch beside the neighbors' fence. There, buried in the tall weeds a few yards away, was a perfectly usable partial roll of black tar-paper—I had been wrong, there was a little bit of clutter here. I picked it up and carried it back to the chicken coop. It would make good temporary roofing for the shed. Book learning hadn't been half as fun as this load of learn-by-doing. It's hands-on experience in the creation of a farm, that's all.

Chapter 13

Shoestring Living

The amount of water we were using from the dairyman's well was a far greater quantity than our farm was supposed to receive. We and several neighbors had only a verbal agreement with the dairyman about getting the water. The sellers of this parcel hadn't bothered to irrigate or grow anything, but I was determined the farm had to become a green oasis. When the dairyman dropped by one day to remind me that I was paying for water for household and animal use—not irrigation—I realized that we had to find a way to access the county land water. This meant, in the end, that I would need to finish digging an adequate irrigation ditch around the property.

Sam had pumped up not only my wrath, but also my resolve. Gritting my teeth and holding on to a somewhat unthinking and lunatic belief that a shovel and pick could suffice to achieve success, I shoveled faster and faster all afternoon, and soon I was as hot as I'd been when Sam had arrived. Fuming and full of philosophical thoughts, I was wild to make progress. Why had he come before the lawn and garden were green? This ditch I was building would let us receive our allotment of the district's canal water, and we would occasionally be able to thoroughly soak the entire lot. While digging the ditch, I was also creating a berm around the perimeter to keep the water on our property. Dan would have to spray the tough weeds with diesel fuel to help me keep the ditches from filling up with Johnson grass and thistle. Once more, things to buy—a large sprayer and a large milk can to store the oil.

Anxious to tell Dan about Sam and to sort out more of my thoughts in the process, I began talking the second Dan came into the kitchen that evening. "I want to proudly present to you this cast gracing our home...this is Barefoot Boy with Cheeks of Tan. Here's Nancy with the Golden Brown Hair. Meet Heidi of Lassie Beauty, and the Cat Made in Heaven. Hmmm...I don't see the Little Curly Black Spaniel."

A zany wife today, but he gamely said, "All right. How do you do, pretty stars? What's this all about?"

"You have to admit that the members of this family here are wonderful works of art? Yes? And this humble abode isn't too, too peculiar? Do I look like a poor-little-me type? OK...well, your old friend Sam from LA came to call today. He's in Phoenix on business, and just showed up with no warning at all. I was shoveling, sweaty, and a mess. I was wearing those jeans that I bought in high school, the ones that have the holes you tease me about, and I was wearing filthy tennis shoes, no socks, and the yellow blouse that I wear when it's hot—the one that has safety pins for two of the buttons. As you can see, my hair is horrible, and my nose is in its red and peeling mode. Danny was asleep in his playpen beside the house and needed changing. In fact, in the worst way, the kids and I needed Lifebuoy soap, showers, and changing...maybe Sam was just having a bad day, but he did not beat around the bush. He was boiling over the entire time, and obviously he thinks I'm dowdy and that it stinks that I'm doing unlady-like work and am mired down living like this. He was a pain in the neck. With his jaundiced eyes, he kept staring at the kids, the dogs, the yard, and our beautiful castle's stoop. I was left wondering the whole time whether that folding chair would collapse under his weight, and for some obscure reason, Heidi kept trying to lick his hand, and Nancy kept informing him she was getting a horse and showed him some little rocks and a very alive beetle in her dirty little hands. She wanted him to hold it. Sam is not fond of live beetles! Nancy looked as bad as I did and had a big splash of dried Mercurochrome on both her knees, where she hurt herself when she fell down out in the field the other day. She'd have looked better unshod than in those worn-out sandals. I'll tell you more later. If Sam hadn't had a luncheon date, he might still be sitting out there, fanning his face and sermonizing."

With the kids asleep, I finished my story. "The man crinkled his nose as he glared at me, thinking, no doubt, that I'm totally crazy or eccentric. He criticized everything in such a wimpy, patronizing manner. I'm sure neither he nor his wife would ever dig a ditch, and I can almost hear his report to her when he's safely home and relaxing with a cocktail—our life and farm will be packaged like a horror story. He thinks the world is passing me by, and he kept lambasting me for the work I was doing. He wouldn't be caught dead living here, but why did he have to fret so rudely over our living standards? Why should he fly off the handle over our life? He's not the one living it!

"Actually, I think I kept my cool pretty well, but ever since he left I've kept thinking of things I could have said better. Isn't it women, not men, who worry about having fashionable clothes, model homes, and ladylike jobs? I've heard that how a person looks says a lot about who they are, so I guess in my case I'm a ditchdigger now, and Sam read me that way. However, clothes can't spill the beans if no one sees me, and how did I know he'd show up? Sam does have a point about the house: it's undeniably a hovel. Not even the Fuller Brush salesman has put me on his route. And I've wondered about another thing—do you suppose living in two rooms like this will affect the kids? Their behavior or their psyches? They can't dash out to buy ice-cream cones when they hear the bell of an ice-cream truck, the way town kids can, and they can't wander into a nearby store to agonize happily over which candy sticks to buy with their pennies or nickels. They can't play hopscotch or trade stamps with other children whenever they want to, and, worse yet, they can't giggle and tell secrets to a best friend, at least not until they start going to school. Our kids can't even spend time with indulgent grandmas and grandpas, or run around the block to play with a friend who has a more solicitous mother. Childhood memories will be of a world of cats, dogs, rabbits, chickens, cows, and bugs! Is this so far outside the boundaries of normal life that they'll miss the boat later on?"

Dan laughed and answered with good words, "Naw, this won't hurt us or the kids—only people like Sam who come to see us. Maybe he thinks this is all we aspire to—just getting by. Real friends take us the way we are and stay tolerant, even if they don't quite understand. Sam doesn't matter. Don't try to overanalyze." Hearing Dan's words, I felt better.

Still, we both proceeded to overanalyze, and rehash goals, dreams, assets, work—everything we could think of. There was a paradox about this nondescript land and my valuing it like gold. I continued, "As I told Sam, this particular gosh-awful place was a coincidence, a lucky charm waiting to be found. You gotta go with what shows up and build from there! Little things can mean a lot. Even if our diet is still unbalanced and sparse, the future seems bright, doesn't it? Or does it?...Do you think we were wrong to uproot from that duplex in Goodyear and buy this place? We can't even talk normally now—we have to whisper, with Nancy sleeping so close to our bed. I'm glad Sam didn't come into the house or ask to use the john, but at least we don't have an outhouse. And it's not as though we have an earthen floor, though even that would be all right if we were all together and making progress toward our goals. Shucks, at some point all our early ancestors lived primitively. Who knows, when all the iron ore, oil, lumber, and other natural resources are used up or polluted, maybe people will have to go back to a simple life like this."

"Well, hon," Dan reflected, "Sam did have one thing right. This place doesn't make highest and best use of your degree and talent. Want to get a sitter and get a job? Like he said, you could teach in Phoenix. Perhaps Tolleson is a bit like those towns Mr. Drewes described in our high school civics class when he talked about Podunk places, but still, it's a nice farming area of good people."

"No teaching jobs for me right now," I answered. "This is right for me; it's a package deal. Call it an investment in being here for the kids. That's nebulous, but good. I do admit I'd be more efficient with a roto-tiller, a power lawn mower, and maybe a little more equipment in the kitchen, but it's working. I learned one great phrase in econ class—'discretionary income.' Those are delicious words; I admit I would gladly have some of that discretionary stuff."

"Did you tell Sam I'm starting on a Master's in a few weeks?

"Uh-uh. He wasn't here very long—it just seemed long. He did ask what was in all those trunks on the porch. I told him I used them to threaten the kids with—that I tell them I'll lock them in the trunks if they don't behave. I was really frustrated at that point, but then I relented and explained that all five trunks were mostly full of books. That was funny, too, because I'm not sure he believed me. I never noticed it before, but I'm not sure that Sam gets a joke, much less tells one. I threw at him some colorful bits about the joy of working on the ditch, getting the calf to drink out of a bucket, and other stuff foreign to him. Talk about not reaching my audience! He saw a tragedy, and I saw a happy comedy. Like lots of people, his self-esteem comes too much from fancy cars, houses, and clothes. Aren't you lucky I love this whole enchilada? In fact, it's rather fun to be a bit eccentric." With a slight smile, Dan took my hand and didn't try to answer.

"No, really, I love the challenge and the work, and we're not going to reroute; Sam really hardened my determination to work my head off all afternoon. As you say, only others think we're crazy, and he hadn't a clue. What in the world is his life like—who is he really? Oh well, we work as a good team, and, what the heck, we're becoming jacks-of-all-trades. That fires my imagination."

With a slight smile, Dan shook his head. "You're not saying that out of desperation, are you?"

"Only a little, I guess. We're planners, parents, co-ranch managers, real estate buyers, preschool teachers, ag writers for the paper, professors, photographers, milkers, gardeners, ditchdiggers, and sellers of words, eggs, and milk—you name it! Next we're going to become general building contractors for the house remodel and hire ourselves as cement workers, bricklayers, tilers, and roofers. Being hungry sure has a way of sharpening my resolve and makes all this just a bunch of variety acts.

"If he'd just come next year, we would probably have the new living room and bedroom, green lawns, and shoes with real shoelaces…it's sort of like I said to Sam, though I didn't want to hit him too close to home. The Big Depression scared us, and this is an opportunity. We're hardly a vanishing breed; ever so many are working like this since the war…those who won't even borrow for a house probably had parents who lost land, businesses, homes, and farms. Of course they don't have our Mrs. Marshall for a role model. We'll borrow for real estate but for nothing else. Well, a car and a camera to get a job was OK, and the washing machine—with four of us to keep clean, it was worth making a few payments. Either way, we'd better get some sleep. Dan, you be my cheerleader and I'll be yours; we'll have only happy faces around here."

He murmured something and immediately started snoring.

There was one other strange outcome of Sam's visit, in spite of my brave words about not caring and being individualistic. The next morning I broke the news: "There are few in the audience for my show here, but please, I've decided that my hair matters." Actually, short curly hair should have been at the bottom of a list that included only desperately needed things, like food. My hair was baby-fine, stringy, and straight, and I was the only barber for it.

The only mirror in the house was on an extrasmall metal medicine cabinet screwed to the wall above the sink in the bathroom. The mirror was cloudy, rather yellow, and had but one lightbulb hanging overhead. All this to say, it made my looks only a somewhat horrifying spectacle— a looking glass best to be avoided.

"Dan, would you cut my hair and give me a home permanent? I'll slave for you and for this place, come hell or high water, but I've got to have curly hair, even for just the daily show here."

Dan was taken off guard. "I think your hair and you look just fine. In fact, beautiful. I don't know how to fix hair."

"Please? I'll show you how, and help you. Store-bought perms cost almost nothing. You'll mainly have to help me roll up little bits of hair at a time and put pins in the roller to hold it in place. I'll put the solution on and do the rest. It's not hard, and if you save your slave, she'll bake you a cherry pie."

Thus it happened that, for the first and last time ever, Dan became a hairdresser and gave me a permanent. His fingers were clumsy as he tried to roll my hair onto the rollers. It was almost impossible for him to spread the pin and insert it in the roller while holding the rolled-up hair in the other hand. It took forever, as precious hours of a weekend were lost, and a thousand outside jobs waited while he humored my cockamamie demand. He often hummed a nameless tune when things became difficult...there was a lot of humming that day. Still, he created a curly-headed, contented slave with a smile on her face.

"Well, actually, there is one other thing, and I'll feel complete. No more demands ever," I added. "I must have lipstick. I promise—no other cosmetics: no eye shadow, no mascara, no powder, and no good clothes, pretty underwear, or decent shoes. Just some lip gloss in a nice coral or red. You know, animals do much better than I. They don't wonder if they need lipstick and curly hair to look better. They're beautiful just because they exist and are so unique. But may I buy lipstick?"

Dan nodded and laughed. "Buy all you want, silly."

With curly hair, bright red lipstick, and my faded old shirts and shorts, I finished digging the ditch and building up the berms. There would be no going back or changing horses in midstream, no matter what Sam had advised. I wasn't a country bumpkin, or if I was one it didn't matter.

We spent our time betting on horses, but not in the same sense that Sam did. We were wagering all of our hard work on the prospect of one day seeing our own horses trotting around in a nearby field. It was a long shot, but that did not matter. In the meantime I decided that a farm might be a great place to be flexible, to change course if some things didn't work out. If I didn't find a better market for rabbits, maybe I could sell more eggs and fryers or plant a pumpkin patch. There was always some way to keep traveling on down the trail.

Chapter 14

Slow and Fast Food Diner

In some ways the food I served my clan was fast food, given that we lived on milk, fryers, and eggs that the working hens produced daily. It was hard to believe that those scatterbrained chickens and the cow were saving our lives. I fried, scrambled, poached, and offered omelets with surprising fillings of refrigerator leftovers. Several nonlaying hens were made into chicken stews and soups. Most women could have done better—I was neither inventive nor creative with seasonings, and our early-bird suppers were never a buffet of choices.

Almost as prevalent as the eggs in our meals were the many melons that fell off the trucks on their way to the melon-packing shed at the end of Fowler Lane. So much for the innocent-looking country lane that I had judged to have little traffic! A stream of big, uncovered trucks overflowing with melons rattled past, leaving billowing clouds of dust that blanketed the inside and outside of the house. The melons which dropped from the trucks made the whole countryside smell like overripe cantaloupes. These melons were instant desserts, even when, by the end of a long summer, we had gotten sick of their cloyingly sweet smell and taste.

Breakfasts became an assembly-line job, in large part due to the advice of a pediatrician. When I took Nancy to see a doctor about an eye

infection she'd developed he told me that her eye was not the only problem—she looked far too thin. The doctor looked over at little Danny
and then at me, both of us just as skinny, and in a sergeantlike, com-
manding voice, he laid down the law: "From this day on, and that's every
day of the year, this girl, and the rest of your family also, must be served
breakfasts that include a bowl of cereal with milk, one or two eggs, one
slice of bacon, one glass of orange juice, a piece of toast, and a full glass
of milk. That's the prescription I give you. Here, I'll write it out."

And from that day on, all our lives—until the last kid left home for
college—that menu became a commitment and a law for me to follow.
We ate that breakfast, even if I had to get up at 3 AM to cook it before a
kid left on a camping trip, even if we were running out of time, or even
if lunch was in an hour or two.

Despite these efforts, all my clan continued to look malnourished.
Huge meals never made us fat. At least there was no clamoring for junk
food—after one of these big breakfasts, no one could swallow another bite.

Lunches were easier, and delilike. Dan took to work mostly sandwiches, plus a carrot or an apple, several cookies, and a thermos of coffee or milk. We ate much the same at home. Sandwiches were made
with whatever was on hand—leftover chicken or cheese, and, on rare
occasions, a can of tuna fish with mayonnaise.

Hors d'oeuvres were nonexistent or superfast. "Have a cracker if
you're hungry," or "Here, have a slice of apple," or, worse yet, "No, there's
nothing to eat until dinnertime." My game plan was to delay, improvise, substitute, or, if need be, refuse. "How could you be hungry when
it's only three o'clock?"

My supper express never had even a tinge of haute cuisine, but, eventually, we became less hungry and there was a surplus of milk, cream,
butter, chicken, rabbit, and vegetables. There were all the eggs we could
eat, and I put them into cakes, pancakes, cookies, sandwiches, and any
other food I could think of.

I didn't know the word "savory." Except for butter, salt, and pepper, everything I served was bland, low in flavor and aroma. No tangy,
spicy, zesty herbs, lemon juice, or marinades to enhance the taste of
anything.

I never mastered casseroles, except a brainless one of chicken and vegetables covered with canned mushroom soup. My Fannie Farmer Cookbook featured some casseroles, but since I planned most meals at the last minute and almost always lacked a key ingredient or two, I gave up on them. Food markets were far away, and I rarely had the car at my disposal for shopping or errands.

A balanced diet? Although I'm not sure I knew the term, from my own childhood I remembered soups and salads, meat, potatoes, and vegetables. Still, in my ignorance I would probably have guessed that "high fiber" was a reference to some kind of cloth. The only fat I knew was the lard in the cakes and piecrusts, or potatoes fried in bacon grease. Cholesterol wasn't in my vocabulary. It was easy to plan menus because I was never slowed down worrying about calories and fat. Never once did I think about the fat calories in all the stews, gravies, eggs, whole milk, and cream. It's probably why my feet and hands are so cold now—my veins may be 99% clogged with all those early era fat globules.

Since the kitchen was crowded with kids and animals, this slowed down food preparation significantly and made results chancy at best. Did I add the baking powder or the salt? Was that three cups of hot water or four that I had just poured over the Jell-O? My audience's great enthusiasm for my simple meal preparations didn't include a very rich dialogue. Mostly, they begged for some "tasting." Sleepy-eyed Cindy and Heidi sprawled out on the cool linoleum floor, and their tails occasionally flopped up and down as they watched me cook. They became more interested when I began to prepare the meat. Stepping over and around the kitchen crowd and pushing the baby's crib toward the counter every time I needed to access the refrigerator also slowed down my efforts.

Some staples, like beans, took longer to prepare. I bought large bags of lima and kidney beans, and had to wash them and let them soak in water overnight. Then the beans had to be cooked for an eternity. Fortunately it helped my schedule to never have to buy or fix gourmet items like fresh lobster, fillets of sole in cream, or three-layer cakes. I shopped as seldom as possible to save time and funds, and we had to eat what was still on hand. Leftovers made return trips to the table until we finished them off.

Despite my preference for preparing fast and easy meals, much of the food we ate was, in a deeper sense, slow food—very, very slow. It took months to prepare the garden plot, plant the seed, wait for it to grow, weed the soil, pick the vegetables, and then clean, cook, and serve them.

Still, harvesting the produce and bringing the basket of vegetables into my nest somehow gave me great comfort and created a sorely needed variety and quantity in our meals. Soon I was able to cook up a mess of beet tops and then slice and pickle cooked beets in a little vinegar and serve them cold. Many other vegetables became groceries without my ever going to the market for them, and I continued replanting throughout the year in this region that never froze.

Finding the cow to buy had taken time, and after she arrived, it was a twice-a-day milking ritual for ten months each year. This wasn't like quickly buying a bottle or carton of milk or cream in a store—I couldn't serve milk, cream, or butter until Dan went out and milked the cow. Then, before anyone could use the milk, I had to strain the warm milk, put it in gallon-sized mayonnaise jars that Dan had brought home from the school cafeteria, and chill it in the refrigerator. I couldn't ladle the rich cream off the top of the milk until it had set quite awhile in the refrigerator, so there was another wait to whip cream or make butter. When neighbors bought milk from us, I filled jars for us and then for them and then put the last remaining milk back into a bucket for the recently purchased small calves to drink.

To make butter I took a big spoon, skimmed the cream off the top of the jars and bowls of milk, and shook the cream in a jar until some of it turned to butter and I could lift it out with a slotted spoon. Since this was a long, difficult process, it was a lot easier just to make whipped cream using our hand-driven eggbeater. Dan and the kids made a game of finding all the things they could top with whipped cream instead of with butter; soon mounds of whipped cream went on top of potatoes, vegetables, cereals, toast, pancakes, and a host of other foods.

Eventually, I found a simple butter churn at a ranch sale. The large glass jar had wooden paddles inside that were connected to a crank which we worked to churn the cream. After I turned the handle for a while the yellow butterfat separated from the buttermilk and floated to the top.

Then I lifted the butter out, put it into a bowl, ran some cold water over it, pressed it into a mound, and put it in the fridge. Most farm wives would put the butter in a cloth and squeeze out any remaining liquid, but this took additional time that I wasn't willing to give.

I bought an old hand-cranked ice-cream maker like the one I'd come to know well as a child. I'd forgotten the endless turning and only remembered some wonderfully rich and fresh-tasting peach ice-cream. With lots of extra cream, eggs, and a deep-freeze waiting to be filled, I cranked out a wide variety of ice-cream desserts. This was a slow-to-make treat, but it certainly became an easy and cheap dollop of pleasure in our austere lives.

The slowest foods of all were hamburgers, steaks, roasts, ribs, and other meat from the steers. That production schedule began when little calves arrived just a couple of days old. I taught them to drink milk from a pail and eventually fed them hay and grain. The steers were butchered when they were eight months to a year old. Beef dishes began to arrive on our table about a year after we bought the farm.

I quickly learned that fried or baked rabbit dishes could be produced faster than one might think: Momma Bunny had one bunch of bunnies after the other. I had to wait for Dan to butcher them, but, since the job upset him terribly, he did it as quickly as possible, and the large, horizontal freezer speeded things up because I could cook food ahead of time and freeze it.

Eventually, the fryers and older hens were gone, and it was time to order twenty-four baby chicks. We left the feed store with them crowded into a small cardboard box. On the way home I found a large empty box at a furniture store. I set it on the porch and rigged it up with an electric lightbulb at each end for warmth at night. The newly hatched chicks needed to be kept warm for several weeks before they could graduate to larger quarters.

The fragile chicks were endless work, and I counted the days until they were old enough to go into their pen by the chicken house. I put fresh newspapers in their cardboard box at least twice a day and kept chick feed and clean water in pie tins, which the chicks constantly walked in and spilled. I also had to buy grit for the chicks, something sort of like sand that aided their digestion. They chirped away happily, and only one of them died. They often entertained the kids, but they were slow to furnish us with eggs or meat, even when they seemed to grow bigger by the hour.

At least in our diner, the cook/server/waitress was always present and working and couldn't resign or quit. Putting a HELP WANTED sign in the kitchen window wouldn't have worked with the job specs: I had no pay, no tips, and no promotions, and certainly there wasn't the option of calling in sick, taking vacation time, or working just Monday through Friday.

I had two rules for mealtimes: everyone had to sit down and eat at the same time, and no one was allowed to criticize the bill of fare, no matter how bad it was. Everyone knew they had to eat the meal or wait for the next one without complaint. No one could send food back to the kitchen, for there were no other entrées, and we were already sitting in the kitchen. I dished out the food; they ate it. It helped that Dan and the kids rarely ate meals prepared by other cooks, so they had no way of comparing our fare to any other foods.

No matter what I served, one or two meals each month were a nightmare for me. Those were the ones served when we had to entertain guests. Most of our friends came from the agricultural community of the valley. The men were frequently teachers, farm machinery store owners, farmers, or ranchers. Often they had wives who had majored in Home Economics in college. On occasion we were invited to have dinner with one or another of these families, and all too soon the time came to return their hospitality. I desperately studied my cookbook until I could have passed a doctoral exam on it, but I still couldn't decide on a menu, much less cook it right. Despite my good intentions, not once did I ever cook even one of those recipes: no home-baked rolls or bread, no tasty sauces, no fancy appetizers. I served fried chicken or steak, baked potatoes with butter, vegetables from the garden served with salt and pepper, and usually one of the few desserts I had finally mastered—apple, chocolate, or lemon meringue pie. On occasion I made ice-cream and oatmeal-raisin cookies.

Since having any food at all seemed such an achievement, I forgot all about the love I long ago had for a host of exciting foods: shrimp cocktails, fresh raspberries, salmon, almond macaroons, dried apricots, artichokes, and asparagus, to name a few. Instead of these delicacies, by the end of that first year on our farm, even a box of graham crackers was a big thrill!

Each day, as the fierce summer sun went down, the kitchen remained baking-hot far into the evening. There was no respite from the heat of the kitchen short of building a campfire on the lawn and roasting our food there. I hoped to eventually do battle with the sun by getting a swamp-cooler for the house, but until that time I developed a new schedule for evenings when the kitchen was unbearably warm and Dan didn't need to return to school or a meeting. "Come on, you guys," I would say, "let's not sweat it; let's just wait a while before eating. Meanwhile we can go out and talk to the animals."

On one of those hot nights, I taught Nancy the custom of making a wish when seeing a shooting star. She took the idea quite seriously and was silent for a long while. When she finally saw a shooting star one evening she leapt up and shouted, "I wish to get on Toast and ride him!" Burnt Toast was our name for the neighbor's dark bay horse.

The part I remember most about those hauntingly lovely, warm evenings was Nancy (and even little Danny as he grew older) whispering good night to each and every one of those critters before going in to supper or bed. Maybe it was better than a barbecue, and part of the reason for being out there on the desert land. Little things can mean a lot.

Chapter 15

No Singing in the Rain

Dan came in from school to observe, "If cleanliness is next to godliness, you've got two heathens, completely coated with mud and as happy as mud hens. They're still out by the driveway, so I guess I shouldn't ask you how your day went."

Still talking through clenched teeth, I mumbled, "Oh, I was just mucking around here, I guess. How can you tell?"

"Well, the kids asked me if I wanted mud pie for dinner. Nancy also mentioned, 'Mom's not cooking tonight' and something about Chicken Little and the sky falling, falling, like Chicken Little said. I see you're cooking, but I've never seen your hair dripping wet at suppertime, and I believe that's a bathrobe you're wearing, not a dress?"

"Hon, it's not a very big story to tell. It's God's fault, not mine—He opened storm waters on the kids and me. Isn't this great Sonoran Desert called 'the land of little rain'? It just so happens that I had two loads of wash on the line when that storm blew in. I knew it could rain in the summer here, but it blew in so darn fast. At first it even caught the sun by surprise, and there were sun and rain at the same time. It just poured here, and the sheets and clothes got far too wet to iron dry; both loads are sitting back in the washing machine until tomorrow. By the time I'd gathered the laundry and put it back in the washer, I was soaking wet, but I still needed to get that new tarp over the hay. It seems we buy stuff and then wait to use it until there's an emergency and it may be too late. I wrestled the flopping thing around and around in the rain and wind and kept loading more things on top of it to try and secure it on top of Maude's precious hay. The unused fence posts are up there, as well as the hammer, the axe, Nancy's scooter, the wagon, and everything else I could find. The tarp finally stayed in place, but it's a weird sight out there. We need rope to fasten the tarp down before the next rain. You mean you didn't see it?"

"No, I was taking in the mud-babies' conversation about Chicken Little."

"Well, since I was soaking and muddy, I decided I might as well do the evening feeding, so I fed the chickens, rabbits, and ducks. Then, as I tried to feed the calves and Maude, I slipped and fell forward into the mud that's all mixed up with manure out there where Maude stands waiting for her hay. You've got real vaudeville acts here. Maude didn't even move or show any appreciation for my performance on our outdoor stage...then the sun came out, and my hair and clothes started steaming, and so did my temper. When Nancy asked if she and Danny could go outside, I just said, 'Sure, why not?' I told them the pouring rain had been like Chicken Little's warning that the sky was falling. It really seemed like the whole damn sky had been falling. I can now visualize how cars and people sometimes get washed away in flash floods down those desert ravines. Actually, I'm sorry about the kids. Guess it doesn't always pay to follow my impulses. I'll owe you one if you'll bathe and feed the kids; I'll read them a story later. Supper's all cooked and on the stove...why are you grinning? What's so damn funny?"

Dan, still laughing, only managed to say, "I'm very sorry. It's just that I've never heard you say 'damn' before. Never. It sounds so funny to hear you say it, and you've repeated it about ten times. Sure, I'll get the kids and clean them up and take over for a bit." Of course, Dan had surely whispered or choked on many a "damn" since marrying me, but we both had agreed to avoid such words in our marriage.

I had never thought that diamonds were a girl's best friend—I had always preferred the thought of owning land—but that evening I wasn't so sure. This wasn't "soil" out there on First Farm; it was mud! Mud in the house, and mud that didn't just touch the kids, it embraced them. Most nights their shower water ran off them a rich chocolate brown and lingered as a muddy pond around the sluggish shower drain. Tonight Dan would have to help it even drain at all.

However, as the children headed through the door toward the shower I finally began to laugh. "Thanks, Dan. This is all beginning to seem funny. However, if I play comedian to an audience of cows, kids, and dogs, why can't they be fans and take notice?"

In time, like the natives of the Salt River Valley, I got so I could usually predict the late summer storms that arrived quickly and swept over the wide valley. The began with a stillness and heaviness to the air, even on a sweltering day with the sun still shining. Maude would suddenly wander in from the far end of the pasture, the dogs would come to sit on the porch near the kitchen door, and the birds and animals would become quiet. Off on the horizon, I would notice puffy clouds beginning to pile up in the sky. Then a warm wind would start blowing, and dark clouds would roll in and blot out the sun. The kitchen door would slam shut, and the roofs of the chicken coops and the rabbit hutches would rattle. As the chickens clustered in the back of their shed, thunder would boom a faraway warning, and lightning would flash across the mesas. At that point, the horses in the next field liked to stampede in real fright and race to the far ends of their field and back, their heads high and their tails flying out behind them. The first big drops came ever so quickly, and it often turned into a Chicken Little downpour.

When there seemed to be no thunder or lightning, the children and I would hurry out barefoot in just shorts and shirts to savor the cool rain falling on our heads. The saying "When it rains, it pours" might have been penned in Arizona, even though the average total rainfall for Phoenix is only seven inches a year. I grew to long for those short heavy rains that swept over the Valley, washing my world clean and fresh, if only for a very, very short time.

Chapter 16

Attitude and Adjustments

One Monday morning, Dan phoned from school almost as soon as he got there to report that his department head, Dr. Cline, was driving up from Tucson with a new practice teacher and that they were coming to our house for lunch. Tolleson didn't have a real restaurant at that time, and driving to Phoenix for lunch would have made them late for his after-lunch classes. I saw no way to plead helplessness: I believed that if I said, even once, that I couldn't do something, it might be the beginning of a downward spiral to total helplessness.

There was no meat in the new deep-freeze, which had been delivered a few weeks earlier, and Dan had taken our only car to drive to school. "Sure, honey," I heard myself saying, "bring them here. I'll have lunch ready."

That was some wake-up call, and in those next few hours, I gained a different perspective on my role as a farmwife. The farm and I would have to cooperate and provide the meal. At least it was early in the month, and I'd gone shopping a few days earlier. I put a pail of water on to boil and yelled to Nancy to come in.

"It's panic time, Nancy. Completely pick up all your clothes and hide the toys under the bed—way under. Stack up my books on the night-stand and lay out your best dress and Danny's good clothes on the bed."

Talk about being put to the test! The only meal I could furnish would have to be homegrown fried chicken and the last vegetables from a dwindling garden. I found several yellow and green squashes, some tomatoes, and the last two cucumbers. Store potatoes were in a bag on the porch. I would have to make an apple pie for desert.

I found the hatchet and chased the flock of squawking birds until I was able to grab one of the big Rhode Island fryers. I'd seen Dan do this job only once before, and I had scant know-how. I held the bird up-side down by his legs and tried to keep his head against a small stump with my left hand. My right hand held the hatchet ready to perform the grisly job of beheading. It took two swings with the hatchet—that's all I'll say about that. Farmwives can't faint.

I carried the fryer by his feet into the kitchen and submerged him in almost-boiling water to loosen his brownish red feathers and then tossed him in the sink to pluck. Hot, wet feathers have a horrid odor, and they stick to everything—fingers, clothes, the sink, the floor. Some-how I managed the chore without making too much extra mess. After the initial de-feathering I held the fryer over a burner on the stove to singe off the remaining, extra-small feathers. Finally, I cut up the car-cass and set the pieces aside on a plate in the fridge. Not much time to age the meat for this meal.

Happy day! In the cedar chest, waiting for such an occasion, were clean and ironed napkins and a white linen tablecloth that had survived my dad's garage sale years earlier. I had to fold the tablecloth twice to make it small enough for the card table, but the men would hardly notice.

Somewhere I had gotten the feeling that I could keep some of the rough edges of this place from taking over if I ironed everything in sight—pajamas, sheets, pillowcases, and even dishtowels. Every meal was served on a small, pressed tablecloth covering the card table. There were five or six sturdy table covers for everyday use which, over the years, must have been laundered and ironed a thousand times or more. This was one time I was grateful for my obsessive ironing.

In fast order, I made the pie and stuck it in the oven, picked the greens, squash, and tomatoes, cut up potatoes, and started picking up the clutter in the house. Nancy, Danny, and I all took one-minute showers, and I fed the kids before the guests arrived. When they had eaten, I hid Danny's high chair in our clothes closet. We grown-ups would eat in the kitchen as the family did, around the card table and seated on the folding chairs.

The kids, momentarily clean and dressed in their only good starched outfits, got into the spirit of things by climbing on the bed with their shoes on and keeping their eyes peeled out the window for the arrival of such important people. "Here they come!" Nancy called. They then became very quiet and thoughtful. What kind of letdown was it for them to see their dad and two men dressed in dark suits get out of Dr. Cline's car? Three cats or even three beetles coming to lunch would have been far more exciting.

"Please be seated." Voilà! Everything was in readiness and the table was set with my starter set of Franciscan Rose plates and some of my mom's sterling silverware. Plates and bowls that I had lined up in a row on the kitchen counter contained crispy brown fried chicken, mashed potatoes and gravy, and a garden salad with my own tomatoes, cucumbers, squash, and bits of lettuce. And, believe it or not, the last thing on the counter was a golden brown apple pie, made with homemade butter, all ready to be topped with a spoon of whipped cream. The guests even had a choice of tea, coffee, or milk. Despite my feelings of guilt and horror over that fryer, I felt as though I had swum the English Channel or painted a Picasso—or maybe both.

We continued to raise animals for food, although the final stage in that process never became any easier for Dan or me. Except for that one traumatic day when I had to do the butchering, Dan always "took care of" the chickens, ducks, turkeys, and rabbits. Steers were slaughtered and packaged by others, but their disappearance from our pasture was always followed by our feelings of loss and sadness.

All I could think was, "Don't look too long into the big brown eyes of a calf, and don't put little bunnies in your arms very often. If you do, you'll probably become a vegetarian right then and there, or the meat on your plate will taste like tear-seasoned sawdust."

Each of the new additions to the farm started out with my observing or thinking, "One more chore to do each morning and night—feeding, watering, cleaning, and keeping the animal dry and warm, but not too warm." Each one started out as just a stranger, a critter who required more work.

Then, in a mysterious way, they all became family, making it terribly difficult for me to be with them all day and still maintain the role I had set up for myself. A thousand times I warned myself, "It's a package deal, kiddo, the whole enchilada. I've got to be a good farmer and partner to this new agriculture teacher and husband of mine, and I must play the role well. Farmers all over the world butcher rabbits, chickens, steers, and other animals for the dinner table."

I tried not to become attached to the animals, but I, as well as the children, soon loved them, hugged them, and talked and laughed with all of them. They were all hams, and continually astonished me with their behavior. The calf thought my laughing presence was great while he raced about on clumsy, wobbly legs, kicking up his heels or thrusting his nose into the pail of milk and almost spilling it. The cow nudged me to scratch her face, neck, and sides. While trying to find some single pieces of straw to eat, she often looked up at me, clearly saying, "How about just a little more alfalfa? I'm letting you see that there's not even a stem left to eat."

Dan had raised a few FFA animals and had helped his grandfather and father butcher animals a few times. He started off by helping kill some chickens and finally slaughtered a pig he'd raised. None of his memories were happy ones—they were more like nightmares to one who had been barely a teenager at the time. How had we ignored or forgotten this part of the business when we developed such a longing for a farm?

As I was growing up, the only food that I saw alive before it arrived on my plate was fish. When I had gone fishing with my father, I was told that fish don't have brains, that they don't think and feel (though I realize now that that was merely a ploy to prevent me from feeling guilty). Yet here I was with animal friends who clearly had brains as well as all kinds of feelings and thoughts. I knew them personally as part of the family, and those rabbits, hens, and calves were breaking my heart.

I talked sternly to Nancy, "You can give names to the dogs, the cat, the momma rabbit, and the cow. The rest of the animals will only stay with us for a while, so just call them chicks, or bunnies." That didn't make sense to a small child, so she named them all anyway.

It was hard to explain death to children, especially when I couldn't even explain it to myself. With tears in her eyes, Nancy came to me one morning with a soft little sparrow cupped in her hands. "What's wrong? Is it dead? Why?"

I tried to explain, "I'm sorry. It may have flown too fast into the glass of the window. It might not have seen the glass."

"But why did it have to die?" She couldn't or didn't want to understand. Her love seemed to pour out toward all living things, from a crushed flower to that dead sparrow.

Sighing, I suggested, "Maybe we can bury him out beside the hedge. He'd be near the flowers. Want to do that?"

I tried to keep the kids from seeing any butchering, but it was difficult. Chickens had to be cleaned, and rabbits had to be skinned. Once, men came in a truck to butcher a steer for us, and Nancy ran to the window just as the steer was shot. Even without watching TV or movies, or ever having seen a gun, she somehow knew what had happened and cried long and hard.

One large brown hen named Brownie let us hold her in our arms and stroke her, and would follow us about the yard. At such times, all of us knew life was fun and lovely on a clear sunny day, and there could be treats for all. The kids had mini-picnics with cold milk and a cookie; the rabbits and chickens got leaves from the garden, and the dogs ate small bits of table scraps. "Yes, you can cuddle Brownie if you sit down here on the grass and make a lap for her when I give her to you. Don't let her out of your arms." This hen had quit laying eggs and would not be around much longer. No matter how hard I tried to change my outlook, butchering was a nightmare. What would I tell Nancy when Brownie was no longer around?

I told myself firmly and often that death was just part of living, a natural reality. I was sure that countless other farm families grieved too, but somehow it was understood as part of the process of being born, of living, and of dying. At least that is what I kept saying. Farm children who grew up near animals learned early that death is forever and that it can be a time of great sadness, but they also saw the wonders of birth and felt the beauty and joy of living with animals.

Already there were happy times coming with some baby chicks, lots of bunnies, a new calf, spring greenery in the fields, a garden, and the kids growing and changing daily. Someday there would be horses, I was sure. There would be companionable dogs, cats, and a cow for many years. Eventually there would be the children's adult years when they would leave the nest and have children of their own.

My philosophy about those never-ending, great cycles of life came crashing down upon me when I had to kill the fryer. It was my baptism into the reality of a farmer's life. A plumber had asked me the week before, "Tell me, just what's all this ballyhoo about country living that you and some of my friends seem to want? I like living in Phoenix—it's a lot less work, great neighbors nearby, and it's handy to everything."

Maybe it's good that farm life isn't the goal of everyone—it wouldn't do to have twenty animals and three feet of manure around every house in the United States.

Chapter 17

It's a Life

If I'd ever gotten hold of a copy of Better Homes and Gardens magazine, I would have given up the first day on Fowler Lane. Inside the house, at all times day and night, the rooms were disorderly. But that word "disorderly" is too tame—the rooms were chaotic. Practice never made any of my housekeeping perfect, but then I didn't practice housekeeping any more than a bare minimum, and I always enjoyed getting sidetracked. There were too many people and animals running in and out for the floors to stay clean, even though the last thing I did every evening was sweep (and sometimes mop) the bathroom and kitchen floors.

After naps and during the very hottest part of the day the kids could pull out from under their beds four boxes of wonderful wooden blocks in many shapes and colors. In the small space between the beds the kids built bridges, castles, roads, and farms. Tears inevitably flowed when the creations toppled over, or when one of the kids destroyed something on purpose. "Mom, Danny's foot pushed it over."

"No, no, Nancy did it."

It was obviously time to enlarge the house. Our finances had improved, and for the last dinner of the month I finally had enough food on the table for all of us. The local bank agreed to extend us funds for remodeling. We planned to more than double the size of our castle by adding a large living/dining room, and a bedroom for the children, and enclosing the porch to make it part of the house.

As we planned the features to include in our additions, I reminded Dan that we also had to have a picture window. There's such joy in light, and a picture window would brighten the inside area at the back of the house next to the new dining and living room area. With the window in place we'd be able to view our green lawn, the open field, and the calves and Maude grazing.

I sketched floor plans on pieces of lined paper and planted wooden stakes in the ground at the corners where the foundation and cement floors would be; I then tied string to the stakes to show me where to dig the trenches. We sub-contracted the cement work for the foundation and the floors, and the company's cement workers brought metal rods to reinforce the walls, floors, and a cement driveway. Workers then came with a couple of big cement trucks to pour and smooth the concrete. Next, Dan and I rented a cement mixer and bought a leveler so that we could lay the brick walls up from the foundation, leaving openings where the window and front door would go.

As we mixed the mortar and laid the block walls, my constant refrain was, "Nancy, don't you dare get near that cement mixer, and never, ever put your hand near the machinery!" A few days later I must have blinked or looked away for a second because she poked her finger into the machine's turning belts and almost had it ripped off. This meant another emergency trip to the doctor's office, but her finger was saved.

After the walls were up, we hired woodworkers to frame the doors and windows, but it was Dan and I who roofed the whole house with new, tan asphalt shingles. Those final days of labor didn't seem like real work, but rather a time of delirious joy and celebration, especially when I brushed two coats of snowy white paint over all the outside walls.

As a child, I had roller-skated on a sidewalk that encircled the house of a neighbor. The memory of this made me determined that our children be able to do the same, since they had no trees to climb, no creeks to splash in, and no place to play hide and seek. I staked out a pathway around the house, dug down a few inches, and put up the wooden forms that would let us lay a cement sidewalk around the house. Dan and I mixed the cement, sand, and water in a wheelbarrow and then poured the heavy concrete.

After we poured the walkway we realized that this project was premature: Nancy and Danny were still too young to have heavy skates clamped onto their little high-topped leather shoes. I placed the skates we had bought for them back in their boxes and hid them in the back of the closet to gather dust for years.

At least with the concrete walkway as a barrier, Bermuda grass didn't spread to the flower beds, where sweet peas once again thrived and blossomed with profuse exuberance. I picked the flowers regularly and displayed them in jars all over the house. Like the rest of us, the flowers adapted and thrived. We'd created a little suburban renewal on Fowler Lane: our house had become a home.

With the kids sleeping in their new bedroom, we came alive in early morning waves. First, Dan got up to do the milking. I got up a few minutes later to cook breakfast. In time, Nancy, still in her pajamas, wandered into the kitchen. About the time we sat down to the big meal prescribed by the doctor, little Danny climbed out of his crib to come sit in his high-chair.

I placed an old piano in the living room and began to give ten-minute piano lessons to the kids each morning. No sooner had I placed a small bookcase near the piano than it began to overflow with books.

Seeing the house in its new incarnation, a fast-talking salesman had finally stopped to call. By mentioning the magic word "education" he talked me into buying a set of the Encyclopedia Britannica "for the kids." I paid full price, and the huge set replaced stacks of library books, USDA Yearbooks, and countless agriculture bulletins. I didn't really buy the encyclopedia directly for the kids' use, but for me to read when trying to answer Nancy's nonstop questions: Do beetles have a home? Can a beetle hear me when I talk to him? Do they talk to each other?

Why aren't there any baby beetles? Where does the sun go when it goes down over there? Does this grasshopper eat grass? How can he fly? I don't see any wings. Where are the stars in the daytime?

It remained impossible to quickly find simple, satisfying answers to such questions. By the time I did the research and found some sort of an answer, Nancy had lost interest and thought of six or more questions in place of each of her original ones. Dan and I sometimes looked up something in the encyclopedia for one of his articles, but gradually, the fine reference books joined a free-standing, desk-model sewing machine to gather coats of dust.

The sewing machine had been given to me by Grace, a family friend, but my sewing turned out much like my bread-making—a disaster. Unwittingly, I had chosen one of the most difficult patterns possible for the first dress I tried to make. It took months to finish it, and when it was completed it looked as if it had been designed and put together by a committee.

Dan laughed and said, "I think you did a pretty good job, but I wouldn't sew another thing if I were you. There are better things to do that you enjoy. Read a book or dig another ditch." With his easygoing philosophy, I felt relieved and off the hook, and the sewing machine began its long decorative life.

In addition to the encyclopedias, I'd felt a growing duty to subscribe to Time magazine in order to not become a complete hayseed. That magazine didn't turn out to be much better for me than the sewing machine or the encyclopedias. Time made the whole world seem like a terribly hard place—even harder than life on First Farm. Obviously, bad news sold best.

Another salesman came to sell insurance on the house. I pointed out, "Look, in this first minute, you've already wasted your time. All the walls and floors here are concrete, and I don't even own a heater or light a candle for Christmas dinner. I'll just trust that my stove and hot water heater won't burn the house down for a few years."

The salesman immediately switched and suggested life insurance. I politely grinned and asked, "Would you really want to bet on a long life for this family in this environment? We're too impoverished to die."

Halfheartedly, he picked up his briefcase and gave a final pitch for a policy for the kids' education. While opening the door to encourage his departure, I shook my head and laughed. "Thanks, but no, I don't even know if they'll ever read at this point."

The farmstead continued to be a dangerous place for the kids. Nancy had to improvise her play since I was always gardening, digging ditches, and doing wash. Thus she decided that the old baby buggy, stored outside next to the house, could become a baby buggy and that brother Danny could be the baby. She rolled the carriage up against the side of the porch to dump him in, then wheeled him around the yard. Fortunately, I looked the carriage over fairly often. One day, I found two huge black widow spiders in it. There was a female in a corner of the hood, with a large white egg in her web. The other spider was under the buggy, and equally healthy looking. On this land, so recently fenced and somewhat developed, where did such dangerous spiders come from? I quickly gave the buggy away and bought a little red wagon from a secondhand store.

Black widows were an unwelcome presence, but where were the other creatures that I'd read about in books as a child? No cottontails hopped across our land, no Gila monsters or scorpions wandered in, no coyote howled to his mate, and no rattlesnakes coiled up in the field. Unless there were recluse spiders, which I wouldn't have recognized, those black widows seemed the deadliest creatures on our minuscule part of the Sonoran Desert.

The nicest wild beings, besides the birds, were little fence lizards. They created a small diversion for Nancy, who learned from me how to carefully catch one with a slip noose made from a stem of green oats, and then how to pet the lizard while holding it in her hand. She agreed to set the little guy back on a post as soon as she grew tired of keeping it in her hand.

Wild birds seemed to adapt to the changes we made in their territory. House sparrows, hardy and gregarious, stopped by and chirped while they hunted for food throughout the yard and field. Sometimes there were quail roaming the lane, and, loveliest of all, a few mourning doves crooning their soft, soothing songs. After the first year, robin redbreasts came to the lawn in the spring, and humming birds found my flowers.

In spite of my sense of time rushing by—so many sunrises and sunsets and so much work to be done—I tried both to create a variety of activities for the kids and to give each child attention, with hugs, small treats, or a book reading before nap time.

Animal life came to a standstill while the sun was blazing overhead. The rabbits took long siestas in their underground quarters. The chickens quit dithering about their close social contacts in the new pens and shed and huddled in the area with the most shade, often going inside near or on top of their nesting boxes. Maude remained a big hunk of placid contentment, watching us and chewing her cud. She no longer seemed to be missing the herd she'd left, and certainly not the jostling with the other cows for her share of hay. She could surely smell the alfalfa fragrance from the bales nearby, and she and the calves tried to rest in the shade beside the fenced-off haystack.

On some days I would open all the windows to get a breeze through the house, then call the kids in, saying "Come, Nancy and Danny, help me create the miracle of a cake." When they were settled in the kitchen, I'd continue, "Nancy, I'll let you break the eggs. Danny, you can pour this cup of sugar in the bowl with the butter and maybe try to stir it. I'll put this baking powder in with the flour and cocoa and sift it. Now you can dump the dry ingredients into the big bowl for stirring. Nancy, take your fingers and rub this butter all over the cake pans. See how gooey this batter is? Why do you think it will rise and come out of the oven as yummy cake?"

I needed to go with gentleness, to go with the flow whenever possible. I tried to use discipline sparingly, in order to make days as fun as possible. Would the fact that the kids had colored in a library book really matter ten years thence? Would anyone remember or care how dirty they got? It was easier to appear blind and deaf when the kids didn't share together, or when they refused to pick up toys at the end of the day; my working outside helped me ignore small infractions.

On a few points I scolded and reminded them, "Be kind and caring, tell the truth, and don't cry or yell in public, especially at Farm Bureau potlucks or when eating with our friends!" Concerning these few rules, there was little democracy; at their young age, I demanded and expected performance: "You'll do it because I say so!"

Trying to give praise helped: "My, you're sitting up so straight, and don't tell me you ate everything on your plate!" or "You've brushed your teeth really clean, so we just might go to town later on." It was excessive praise, and disgustingly sweet, but it seemed to work and it kept brother and sister peaceful some of the time.

I had a friend on Fowler Lane named Mary—always cheerful and positive, and always welcome. She lived close by down the lane, and in both our lives there were both fun times and some desperate times. These were years when most people figured out and dealt with their own bad or good luck and still found time to help others who had problems. Mary came often to buy milk, and sometimes eggs and a fryer. She saw life as I did, so of course I considered her very perceptive. We were each tackling a situation that we considered important as a beginning to something more, finding that hard work was the only way to our dreams.

Mary endeared herself to me by being positive and always voicing new and vivid thoughts about our somewhat stark life on the desert. She'd say things like, "I love my land right up to the barbed wire, just like you do. It's everything—the seeing, hearing, smelling, and just the feeling of being here." At other times she became enthusiastic over the billowing clouds, saying to Nancy, "Can you believe there are those wonderful white clouds up there in such a blue, blue sky? Nancy, in that big, puffy cloud over there I make out a horse running. Can you see it? See its mane and tail flying in the breeze? Do you know that these huge clouds usually come up on the wind from the Gulf of Mexico? Get your mom to show you on a map." Even on our isolated little lane, Mary felt high drama and few enclosing boundaries. This precious friend, always with a smile, brought mental sustenance at a time when I needed it desperately. Mary could put into words so many of my vague and tentative thoughts.

This irrepressible gal would always be an observant, can-do type, and would never complain, or grouch, or think of herself as a victim, even when faced with handicaps or setbacks. Mary was thoughtful and kind at all times, and she once suggested, "We must never complain and never give up, or it will make us bitchy. These lean times will just seem funny someday." Oh, the joy of positive, kind, and cheerful friends!

Before leaving, Mary usually stooped to pull some weeds in my garden alongside the driveway, while chatting several minutes longer. Her visits were always brief, for she, too, felt the presence of an imaginary labor boss who demanded, "Keep moving!" and she had a similar small farm where living wasn't easy.

One morning, noticing that I was wilting from a morning of work, she commented, "You and I can't worry or daydream about tomorrow when we have so much to do today; but if things pile up too high, you should go sit in your pasture beside Maude while she chews her cud, and you should do like Maude, chew on a piece of straw for a few minutes—you can't keep your motor running all the time. Of course that's the moment a friend, other than I, will arrive and think you a bit daffy." Prone to easy laughter, she chuckled and waved her arms in a big circle that included my derelict farm. "Still, we're so lucky to have all this. People content with what they have are the richest. I have a hunch we're both already beginning to get in the chips."

I hollered at her as she walked away, "Come back a second! Your thought about being lucky is wrong: Luck here is not something from on high. You and I are growing it—slaving daily is what's making good luck. Your big garden, like mine, now has our counters overflowing with fresh produce of all kinds. Agreed?" She grinned, raised her hand to tip a phantom hat in agreement, and left.

"Come on, kids, it's time for lunch and some shut-eye." Both children would take naps every day until they started school. Since I got up at 5:30 and went top speed until lunch I saw no reason that they, too, weren't exhausted by all my work. In that house Mom knew best: naps were in the Important Rule category.

Nancy was beginning to feign sleep at nap time. Sometimes I'd notice the fragrance of bubble-gum drifting from the kids' room, or maybe the edge of a book sticking out behind her pillow. Eyes that couldn't quite remain closed sometimes quivered before chancing a quick peek to see if I'd gone.

Some siesta breaks were spent with the Sears Roebuck Catalogue, a wish book full of wonderful colored pictures of things the kids and I had never seen, even in stores. The catalogue pages were always dog-eared, and they tended to get torn or to fall out due to constant use by tiny hands and sticky fingers. As for so many other folks after the war, this catalogue was our window-shopping. Whatever we ordered from it seemed fresh and wonderful, since we had almost nothing. We were so poor that the kids sometimes chose to receive new clothes as gifts, though it was really an Indian or cowboy outfit that Danny craved, and a cowgirl outfit that Nancy fancied. From the catalogue, I picked one gift for each child after they told me a number of things they just "had to have."

Christmas and holidays were matters of outwitting the bank account. "No, pumpkin, there can't be a horse for a long while yet, but Dad and I are working on it, and Santa knows you want one. What was your favorite wish in the Sears catalogue?"

Our New Year's celebrations were usually creating a party with oatmeal cookies, hot cider, and the singing of "Auld Lang Syne" around the piano at 7 PM before going to bed.

For five summers in a row, Dan drove down to Tucson to take classes at the University of Arizona and work on getting his Master's degree. From Phoenix to Tucson was a distance of about 110 miles. Dan left about 5 AM. Monday mornings, with a sack of provisions for five days—apples, oranges, canned baby food, cold cereal, and bottled juices and Cokes. He came home on Friday evenings with a pillowcase bag of dirty wash, usually just in time to milk the cow and eat dinner.

Dan lived rent-free in the laundry shed that sat under the oak tree in Mrs. Marshall's backyard close to our former barn apartment. The corrugated-tin shed had no air-conditioning, no shower, no stove, and no refrigerator. There was only an old laundry tub for a sink, and a toilet placed in a corner of the room. The furniture consisted of one table, one chair, and a metal-framed single bed. Dan hammered a few nails into the shed's wooden studs to create clothes hangers. No wonder he studied in the library as late as it remained open and left for classes early each morning after a simple breakfast of shredded wheat or corn flakes with water and an apple or some canned baby food. He took showers in the university gym or at a friend's apartment. Dreams could come true only if we really prepared, we kept telling each other, yet we wondered if just a Master's degree would be enough for Dan to get a job with a better salary.

From Monday morning until Friday afternoon I was the one who had to milk Maude the cow. Awkward and inexperienced at being a milkmaid, I fed Maude lots and lots of hay and straight lines of talk about how she should behave: "Stand still, will ya? Come on, be a buddy or I'll be out here all night!"

Maude let down her milk slowly, oh so slowly, while doing things like tipping over the bucket or swishing her tail constantly in my face. One time, she pushed hard against me in such a way that I fell backward off the wooden box that was my milking stool. At that point, with her mouth full of alfalfa hay, and munching away, she turned her head slowly around to gaze at me with her large brown eyes and gave me a look that said, "What's wrong with you? Why aren't you milking me?"

My reaction was not funny at all. I began to babble, "Cut it out! Quit giving me the eye and just eat your hay! Oh, dear God, how can I finish? My fingers hurt so much I can't squeeze out another drop, my arms ache, and the blasted pail is only half full!" Maybe I should have kept in practice throughout the year. The one thing I dreaded most about life on that funny farm was milking Maude each summer for those five weeks that Dan was away.

Chapter 18

Mystique

Soon after our precious cat Sage died, a wacky but wonderfully sweet cat named Mystique joined our cast of characters for ten months while her owners were abroad on a college program. This was not Mystique's first time being farmed out to a foster home.

This cat had huge, yellowish green eyes, and weighed even more than Sage had. She wore an all-black, medium-length coat that was sleek and soft to the touch. Sporting a green harness, she walked through our front door on a leash. Arriving with her were boxes of belongings designed to both comfort her and assure her that this had to be her home for a spell. There were baby-sized blankets, a comb and brush, water and food bowls, and a large collection of toys. One box was filled to the top with various canned foods like tuna and chicken, "in case she becomes finicky about always having the same menu."

Brooding, with only a sighing meow, she probably thought to herself, "I'm being abandoned one more time to a new family that includes those two dogs outside the door. The dogs will need putting in their place, which means staying at least three feet away from me." She quickly toured her new home with the kids following close behind.

Mystique's owners insisted there would be no trouble about her living with our dogs, so I called Heidi and Cindy into the kitchen without letting the cat get out through the door. Mystique didn't have enough time to jump to the kitchen counter, so she handled the dogs as Sage had. Standing where she was, she arched her back, puffed up her hair, and swished her tail back and forth while she growled and hissed at the dogs. After giving her a quick look, neither dog paid any attention to her—the cat was just another critter among so many that they weren't allowed to chase or hurt.

At first this black cat slept on the end of the kitchen counter below the wall-mounted phone. Soon she began to prefer the newly finished living room and always jumped from the piano bench to the bookcase to the top of the piano where she snoozed and dreamt her cat dreams for much of the day.

Even when Mystique went outside during the day she only wanted to roam for short periods, and then she stayed on top of the trunks, the chicken shed, or the hay. Cats are incredibly agile, and she probably liked the challenge of these lofty places, as well as the safety and privacy of being pretty much out of sight.

Inside the house the wacky cat took charge of as much of her life as she could, toying with everything she could move with her paws. She never broke anything, but just carefully pushed around a hairbrush, a comb, a piece of silverware, or an empty grocery bag.

After the first month or two, Mystique began to sleep on our bed some of the time and often sat there and watched the passing scene through the two windows over the bed. It wasn't a very exciting view, with only a few cars and pedestrians passing by each day, but she intently watched every move made by the birds who came to perch on the limbs of my new oleander hedge.

One of her less catlike habits was to jump onto the kitchen counter and sit beside the phone when it rang, or to race to the front door when someone rang the bell. Perhaps these were things she had done in her real home.

When Mystique's owners came to take her away, she gave no sign of recognition or welcome and remained aloof and disinterested when called from her perch on the bed. She must have remembered her owners and developed complicated feelings about where her home really was. To me, she seemed aptly named. I suspected this lovely cat wanted to control her life and make her own decisions, especially when her owners kept disappearing for so long. More and more, I felt that our animals were very much like human beings, with a wide variety of personalities and characteristics—including Mystique's light, good-natured, so-be-it philosophy.

Chapter 19

Want to Go Out, Girl?

I'd been satisfied just to make daily progress with the work on the farm and with the changes in the house. With the new rooms finished, I had been thinking about a wonderful word—serendipity. I'd recently heard it for the first time, and after I'd learned its meaning I thought, "Surely, this life now has a lot more serendipity." I still stumbled over the dogs, the cat, and the kids in the kitchen, but I found fun and laughter in so many very simple things. Plus there was a certain mood, a certain spirit to the land; the farm was becoming my own little community with the animals and humans getting to know each other well. Still, Dan and I were both working hundred-hour weeks.

One summer evening, while I finished mopping up the kitchen floor after supper, Dan asked, "Want to go out, girl?"

I replied with a big fervent "Yes!" but then realized he was talking to Cindy, the dog, as he held the door partially open for her.

We both laughed at my "Yes!" and then thoughts came tumbling out that must have been lying dormant and submerged under the daily routine. "Yeah, I guess some 'going out' is in order, a little more balance between work and play," I speculated. "Maybe I miss the camaraderie of student days. Something needs to be added on the nonfarm side. I'll keep working the same hours you do, and I'll even continue to find it fun, but the kids and I need to hear some other human voices and have some kind of change of pace and place. Most of my monologues have no audience except for the land, the plants, the critters, and the kids; I'm so darn boring, I even bore myself…for weeks I've been noticing in the paper that the Encanto Drive-In Theatre shows three movies on Fridays, and the price is only a dollar per car. How about that?"

Dan, who was reading the paper, mumbled absent-mindedly, "Sure, why not?"

Thus began years of going to Friday's Family Night films at the drive-in. Back then the movies we saw really reflected family values, including the Ten Commandments and no bad language. We took our supper with us—popcorn topped with my homemade butter, as well as chips, candy bars, and a large jar of juice or bottles of Coke. Equipped with pillows, blankets, and pajamas for the kids—who often fell asleep early—we drove off on our movie dates.

Before the show began, recorded organ music filled the warm summer nights. Nancy and Danny played on swings and slides down in front of the huge screen and then crowded into the car when the previews began. We all ate the popcorn and drank the Cokes. About a half hour later, both children would need to use the restrooms. Then, just when the first of the movies began to get interesting, they would decide to put on their pajamas, and it was only my rear end that saw the rest of that movie while I helped them change clothes and settle the fight over who'd get which blanket and pillow. Finally, if they didn't go to sleep promptly, Dan or I would accompany them to the restrooms for a second time. Still, those evenings were a good change of pace and place.

With our success at setting up the movie dates, I decided that there might be a way to add still a few more hours of "vacation" time to our lives. "If we could manage to get a backlog of an extra article by doing two articles and pictures on one weekend, life could open up a bit and I could phone friends and plan a day at the lake." I reminded Dan that he'd said there were a couple of lakes not too far from us. "The kids could learn to swim," I continued, "and we could all play in the water and have a picnic. Even Cindy and Heidi could go—dogs love picnics! It wouldn't be making whoopee, whatever that is, but maybe it would be better."

We found the time in our schedules, invited another family to go with us, and headed for one of the lakes. We tied the four corners of a bedspread and a sheet to the top branches of young willow trees or manzanita bushes, spread other old sheets on the ground, and had our picnics of cold fried chicken, potato salad, fruit, cookies, and lemonade or iced tea.

The kids learned to dog-paddle, while Cindy swam and swam in circles, splashing in delight. She was in cocker spaniel/poodle heaven. Heidi waded or stayed on our spread in the shade. We all relaxed and got tans darker than toast—at that time, sunbathing was still considered healthy. These primitive outings weren't trips to Europe, but they probably gave us almost as much fun.

With that success, I tried for a really big event—an overnight vacation. "Dan, tomorrow we'll be ahead a week on articles and I've read that one of the dams is almost dry. Let's go camp overnight at that lake. We have four big reasons to go—you, me, and the two kids. There will still be plenty of water to swim in and you could take pictures of the dam and the low water level and sell them to the paper to pay for the trip. Maude doesn't need milking right now, and Mary would feed the animals for us."

Dan looked up from writing his current column with its still-missing good lead sentence. He seemed to reflect long enough to get my idea, and then agreed, "Yeah, I think you're saying I've got to get these articles turned in right away. Sure, the pictures of the dam might sell for a few dollars. I'll look at the map. Maybe I could get a regular interview for a column on the way up there."

The plan worked and gave us the miracle of a tiny vacation. Again I tried to teach the children to swim but made no progress when they discovered they could hold their breath and swim under water. They thought that was a hilarious stunt.

After a day of swimming we ate a large picnic dinner and listened to a distant coyote sing in the warm, heavy air of the Arizona night. It seemed nothing could be finer than lying on granite-hard ground far from other human beings and marveling at the vast sky full of stars and a half moon shining on that man-made lake—even with its low water level. To top it off, the newspaper used two of Dan's photos of the dam.

I have a friend whose memories of living in Arizona are as different from mine as night and day. My friend Elizabeth shopped at Korrick's or Goldwater's wearing high heels, a black dress, and often diamonds or pearls. She dined in expensive restaurants and danced in swanky night-clubs. She regularly went to plays at the Phoenix Little Theatre, to performances of the Phoenix Symphony, and to other cultural events. While we had our own music and off-Broadway scenes, my curtain time came with the colors of dawn and the play lasted all day under puffy white clouds. The curtains closed with wonderful sunsets and dark nights full of stars. For our family, the best and worst shows of the season were on two acres with our own cast and over-budget scenes.

Elizabeth's sports were playing golf and tennis, while mine were wrestling with the calves as I taught them to drink milk from pails and digging the irrigation ditch that would bring water to our garden. Without doing the trendy sports, I got plenty of trendy body complaints, such as tennis elbow, golfer's back pain, swimmer's earaches, jogger's muscle cramps, and skier's shin splints.

Still, there was the magic of love for the hard life on my very own land, the love of a partner, our kids, and the critters, and the satisfaction of pursuing our far-off goals. Maybe life or progress didn't have to be complicated, the past was gone, simple hard work was at hand, and the future was hidden from sight.

Chapter 20

Create Rituals? You Better Believe It

As I look back at our years of farm living, I think about the lessons that I learned and that I would like to pass on. This chapter contains some of what I would say.

Don't try for perfection because you'll never achieve it, and don't try alibis for your inaction. Until First Farm I had been a take-it-or-leave-it casual housekeeper at best. There never seemed to be a great reason to keep working all day every day just to have a party-clean home, and those thoughts made a fine excuse to procrastinate. I would wait until company was coming, then clean the house, hide the messes, and polish like crazy the day before guests came. Also, I believed that one shouldn't "sweat the small stuff," that it was important to keep the big picture in mind and, sometimes, to relax. If I saw something wrong, too often I shrugged my shoulders and told myself, "Something must be done about that before long." Dan and I were both do-it-yourselfers, yet we had few skills with which to "do it." Just how much damage could I do on two barren acres with only a pick, a rake, a shovel, and a hoe? It didn't take long to learn that a farm was a different world. If you're yearning for a rural life, here's some lowdown that may help:

Procrastination brings penalties that are costly, embarrassing, and sometimes comical; the unexpected has a way of happening on a farm. Forevermore, the watchword has to become "Now." You can't just sit there, for little details matter both inside and outside. All our machinery and tools had to be kept clean, in working order, and in their appointed places. Procrastination is not an option; on the other hand, doing things in too much haste might end up in having to redo the job.

To make matters worse, there weren't many shortcuts, and I certainly couldn't fake it. Every day, every critter and family member had to have fresh water, healthy food, and clean living quarters. The plants and garden needed constant weeding, watering, picking, replanting, fertilizing, insect control, and other chores of loving care.

I had a fine teacher called Firsthand Experience. Eventually, I became an immaculate-farm keeper outside and even a little bit organized inside. Somehow I had failed to realize that a large number of old wise sayings applied to me: Do it today, for tomorrow never comes; sooner started, sooner done; there's no time like the present; an ounce of prevention is better than a pound of cure. Rituals and routines became important; these cautions represent a little of what I learned those years. Others come to mind.

Always do some investigation before you buy a place. Find out whether the fireplace draws and the heater heats. Don't buy land to build a house on unless you know how much water there is, and don't buy a house unless the water comes reliably out of the faucets at all seasons of the year (we squeaked by on that one). On the other hand, don't buy if the land becomes a lake or a river when the rains come.

Clean the shovel before putting it away—get the globs of mud off it before the sun bakes them on like cement.

Turn hoes and rakes with the tines or sharp side facing the wall, or install racks to hang your tools on the wall of a shed or barn. Stepping on the metal part of a rake may send the handle flying against your head and break your nose or give you a black eye or a sudden headache. Stubbing a toe may lead to a sudden fall on your face. Vaudeville is still alive, and if you ignore this rule all you'll need is an appreciative audience and some first aid.

Put small valuables, like trowels, hand clippers, screwdrivers, hammers, and pliers, back on the shelf or in a toolbox after using them. Searching two acres of high weeds for a pair of wire cutters is no picnic, and it may ruin your day.

Mow the lawn before it's knee-high. If you've ever pushed a lawn-mower that didn't come with a motor, you'll know what I mean. For the same reason, don't fertilize or water the grass too often—grass that's just a little sickly or dry can save hours of hard mowing!

Fix gate latches immediately, patch all holes in fences while they are still little holes, and ride or walk the fences and gates frequently to check for escape possibilities before the herd or flock is gone.

Anticipate. I got a garbage can for the chicken and rabbit pellets, but only after the young steer had scattered and eaten a whole bag of rabbit feed. If the bags had been larger, the steer would have had a gigantic tummy ache.

If something's not broken or hurting, leave it alone. Don't try to fix an imagined problem, because the attempted solution may goof things up even more.

Follow the rituals and rules of planting; heed the advice of experts on the time for planting, rather than deciding, "Oh, what a beautiful day to be outside! It's surely warm enough to plant." Also, if the vividly colored little packets of seeds say to bury carrot seeds one-fourth of an inch deep, and squash seeds one inch deep, that's a law and you'd better believe it! Having nary a seed sprout is terrible for the spirit. (All of this, of course, assumes that you have well prepared beds for planting.)

Never let Mother Nature sneak up and take over. Johnson grass in the ditches had to be sprayed before the grass completely closed off my new irrigation ditch. Brush and weeds in the pasture had to be dug out or sprayed before they became the main crop. Former wilderness can return quickly if the land is left alone.

In the house, keep track of available supplies. Gauging supplies so that we had enough food and animal feed for the whole week was something that I never did learn to do very well. Having no bread meant not being able to make sandwiches, and Dan was never enthusiastic about the leftover stew I would put in his lunch thermos. As den mother and provider of meals to more and more family, and with no car during the week, I learned to write out lists for the family's menus and to inventory the sacks of pellets and other food for the chickens, rabbits, cat, and dogs. Still, too often I had to make emergency trips for food and feed.

Have some supplies on hand for the unexpected. Keep a box or part of a drawer filled with items for the times unexpected guests come to dine—an ironed tablecloth, good silverware, dishes, napkins, shakers that actually produce salt and pepper, candles longer than one inch, and a couple of candleholders. Don't forget to have matches in the house for those candles.

Make sure there are bandages and first-aid antiseptics handy. Constant scrapes and cuts on the kids seem to literally come with the territory.

Keep money in the Crisco can, if not the bank, for the inevitable financial emergencies.

Store baling wire in at least three places, since farm existence seems to "go haywire" constantly. Keep a piece in the car. You may need it, as I did, to keep the muffler from dragging on the pavement. Keep lots of wire stored outside, or in the shed, for repairing fences and gates, and even for holding up drooping tomato vines. And lastly, keep wire inside the house. I used it to retrieve toys, clothes, and magazines from behind or under appliances and furniture, and even to fasten a side of the crib and keep it from falling off. Extra rope is also handy.

Use labels to date stored foods that might become too old to eat. Also use labels to date medicines, both for humans and for livestock.

Do not procrastinate. It seemed to be in my very genes to put things off, but farming cured me of some mañana ways. I hated to admit it, but eventually it felt better not to put things off.

Handle all trash and leftovers promptly. If you live in the country and have no garbage service, trash can grow into a disgusting mountain in a hurry. I used to squash the few empty soup or fruit cans and bury them in a small culvert that needed filling. Paper, cardboard, and anything else that would burn went in a big metal barrel, since there were no laws at the time against burning such things. I saved table scraps in a garbage can and then shoveled them under for mulch. Other scraps went to the rabbits, chickens, dogs, or cat.

Be careful about saying, "While I'm at it, I might as well do this, too," or "Before it gets dark, I'll try to come back and finish this." If you fall into that pattern, you'll never finish anything, and you'll have ten jobs started and none of them done. It's better to say, "While I'm at it, I'll finish this project."

It's better to buy than to borrow, and especially don't make a habit of borrowing from neighbors. If I didn't have an item, neighbors probably didn't have it either. If they did have it, they probably used it daily. When I broke a shovel, I couldn't ask to borrow one because all of the farmers around us were all using their shovels. Avoiding breaking a shovel is a much better approach. Remember that you will break tools more easily as your muscles grow bigger and stronger.

If you're not mechanical, think twice about being a farmer. Know that you will need to be able to fix anything that has moving parts. Save all directions that come with equipment, because at some critical moment, that equipment will get out of whack.

Finally, one last rule to follow: devise some rituals for having fun and creating a change of pace. Find a swimming hole, make a picnic, see a movie, call a friend, or take a nap. Reading this advice, you might say, "Look who's talking!" But we really did try!

Maybe this whole idea of rituals and rules could be summed up in one sentence: take more time now, and later you'll save time, suffer less guilt, sleep more peacefully, and live happily ever after on your farm. I must have been a slow learner—only rarely did I sleep peacefully.

Chapter 21

Let's Go Home, Edgar

At school, Dan and one of his fellow teachers decided that their two wives should become acquainted. Susie, the teacher's wife, was almost hysterically afraid of animals, especially of those who tried to be her friends. I had not been warned of her fears. As a result of the husbands' planning, Susie ended up coming out to First Farm for a visit. She brought along her young son Edgar, who was anxious to play with Nancy and Danny.

I watched the mom and son as they got out of their car, while the dogs barked a halfhearted welcome. Susie began pulling her son along as fast as possible. Both of them were all gussied up, with the boy in ironed blue shorts and a white shirt and Susie in a light pink and white dress and little hat. Both wore white leather shoes. Susie's skin was as delicately pale as mine was toasty brown, and her hair had been curled that day, while mine undoubtedly looked like it had been through a tornado. I immediately supposed that Susie must stay inside most days to polish her house, sew, crochet, exchange recipes with neighbors, and perhaps play bridge. What could we possibly talk about besides the children and maybe a few mutual friends?

Darned if they didn't walk toward the kitchen's rusty and torn screen door instead of my fine new front entrance. I ran to greet the two of them, and as soon as I opened the door, I knew there was a problem, a big problem. I understood then why Susie had quickly headed for the nearest door.

Susie was deathly afraid of Heidi. Cindy never got up to greet them beyond her first few woofs, Mystique stood up from sleeping on the steps and padded over to Susie, and friendly, beautiful Heidi ambled over to the porch from the side of the house. Susie certainly knew we lived in the country, but she must have assumed, somehow, that all the animals on a farm would be caged, fenced off from the yard and house, or tied up. Maybe her husband had been instructed to tell Dan of her fears and had forgotten to tell him.

It was apparent that little Edgar had been around friends' animals in town; he immediately took off with Nancy and Danny to explore the farm. I gave up on the idea of seating Susie on the new redwood picnic chairs on the lawn. Instead, I asked her whether she would like to be inside or out.

"Oh yes, please, inside will be fine. Do the dogs bite?" By then she was actually standing in the kitchen. She turned to call Edgar through the screen door and tried to get the children to return and follow her to the living room.

Edgar called back and pleaded, "No, Mom! First, I've got to see the rabbits and the chickens and the black-and-white cow." His mother walked through the kitchen to sit in the living room, probably just to avoid a scene.

I offered her lemonade or iced tea and some cookies. She struggled to keep up a conversation, but her mind was clearly on Edgar, out there with all those vicious beasts, and she kept consulting her watch. I wondered how she had managed to avoid dogs and cats all her life. Her friends must have always locked their pets away before she came to call. I recalled my mother's friend Ada, who had feared all our dogs while I was growing up. Now Susie and I tried to keep up a conversation about mutual friends and about places we had lived. She had lived in Los Angeles some years before I had gone to UCLA, but this didn't exactly make for exciting conversation.

Susie intrigued me. I had known people who were afraid of dogs, cats, snakes, or spiders, but Susie seemed unable to tolerate any animal, even the bunny rabbits. In her mind, germs were a colossal threat and lived everywhere. Had Edgar ever picked up a spider or a bug in a jar to show her? Might she at least like birds or goldfish? Then a funnier thought came to mind: as she'd walked through the kitchen, had she seen the row of jars along the back of the counter and windowsill—all those jars had nail holes in their lids, because the jars contained living spiders, moths, beetles, a bumblebee, and other horrors. I decided to make darn sure that Susie left by the front door.

Eventually, the children came in asking for lemonade, with Edgar carrying Mystique in his arms. Susie jumped up and whispered hoarsely, "Son! Put that cat down! He'll scratch you. He doesn't know you." It was hard for me not to smile when Edgar set the cat down, not on the floor but on the couch beside his mother. She quickly stood up as the cat moved toward her lap.

"Shoo, shoo! Look, I've suddenly remembered, John has to eat early tonight, and I forgot to take the meat out of the freezer. This has been lovely. We'll be seeing you soon."

I had Mystique in my arms by then, and assured Susie we could put the cat outside. "No, I really must go. But would you show Edgar to the washroom? He should soap his hands before we leave." Then, with a quick wave of her hand, they were gone.

The boy must have spent much of his life washing his hands, and I wondered later to Dan, "Do you suppose this mom's equating hugging or petting an animal with the immediate need of fierce washing with soap and water will destroy the deep feelings of caring and love that her child felt for the animals? He obviously had fun at our petting zoo, not only with the dogs and cat, but with the rabbits and Nancy's pet hen. Nancy said she even convinced the boy to pet Maude by letting him hand the cow some hay. Surely children raised without a pet or who aren't permitted to get grubby or dirty now and then miss a whale of a lot in life." Later I tried not to laugh when I learned Nancy had persuaded Edgar to kneel down and take a lick of Maude's salt block when he wouldn't believe it was really "salt for a cow."

The lovely new living room with its picture window, the sweet peas blooming beside the new front door, and my other wondrous improvements—such as the newly installed swamp cooler—somehow didn't cut the mustard for Susie: I lived in a wild and dangerous zoo, a zoo containing everything from billions of unseen germs to big, gentle Maude.

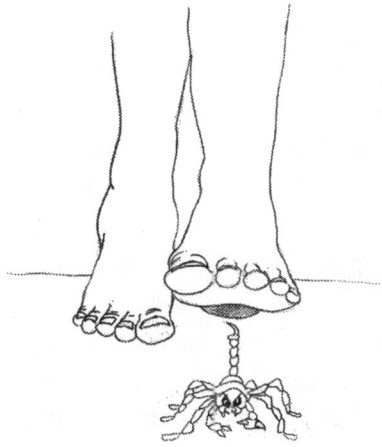

Chapter 22

What Are We Waiting For?

In the fifth year of his Tolleson teaching job, Dan was offered the position of professor and head of the Agricultural Economics Department at Arizona State College in the nearby town of Tempe. Though it would likely mean eventually having to get a doctoral degree, the position would be a new and rewarding challenge. The job was to start in the fall of the new school year, and Dan planned to leave the Tolleson job after the semester ended that fifth spring, though it was still too early to inform the school. His contract didn't actually end until August, so he would teach or do farm visitations until then. It had been a rewarding and fun job. He loved his students, and they had all become outstanding young men. In addition to teaching units of farm mechanics, crops, animal husbandry, marketing, and such, he provided his students with snippets of philosophy and ideas for their lives beyond school—such as having a good lifetime partner, choosing a career they could enjoy, and staying in school beyond high school—things that other teachers seldom bothered to discuss.

In addition to winning dozens of honors for their FFA projects at the Maricopa County Fair for five years running, Dan's students took

first place in the state runoffs for best public speaker and best parliamentary team for four years in a row. Dan had also served as president
of the Arizona Vocational Teachers' Association and president of the
local Lions Club, and we had made lifelong friends with many of the
faculty and students and some of their parents.

"Let's sell First Farm after Christmas and try to get closer to Tempe," Dan decided. "I can drive out to Tolleson for the spring term and
until my contract is up in August." And so, it quickly became checkout
time at First Farm.

Change came faster than I had imagined: my little outpost was
bought the day the ad came out in the paper. We may have set the
price too low, but the buyers had cash, and in my mind we were already
packed and moving, moving along that trail of dreams, dim though it
still was.

The buyers wanted to move in as soon as escrow closed, and they
wanted the rabbit hutches, the adult rabbits, the hens, and the cow to
remain with the property. I had only a few days to try to find a place for
us near Tempe and the college. We wanted another farm, for our love
of land had grown rather than lessened, but I had no luck at all, and we
decided we would have to rent for a while.

I settled for a new tract house between Fowler Lane and Phoenix.
Fortunately, there wasn't much time to say goodbye to our first farm.
I was now a pretty tough gal who could work all day with a shovel,
pick, hoe, or mower. I'd changed a lot from the bone-weary college co-
ed who had first glimpsed the place four and a half years earlier. I had
gone from plain skinny to strong-and-wiry skinny, and from being ignorant about agriculture and farming to raising gardens and animals
while caring for kids.

Our meals were still peasantlike, but I could cook food to the appropriate point of heat and doneness, and I could finally create a number of desserts, including lemon-meringue pies and chocolate cakes
made from scratch.

Experience had involved many mistakes and failures, yet First Farm
was no longer the pitiful place it was when we bought it. The house was
twice as large, with the new bedroom, an enclosed back porch/laun-

dry room, and a living room with a dining area. There was a large front door, and the house wore nice coats of white paint.

This land never became a Monet garden full of lush shades of green, winding paths, graceful trees, and little ponds; but in the flower beds, colorful sweet peas grew six feet high and geraniums and cactus succulents framed the walls along the other three sides. There were an orderly and productive vegetable garden, a large green lawn on two sides of the house, a cement driveway, and a cement sidewalk all around the house. The oleander hedge was growing thick, with pink and white flowers bordering the road and the north boundary. Several small trees would soon be tall enough to shade the house somewhat. Though it lacked glitz and glamour, the house had become my castle. All the kids had become aware of the need for us to all work together and take good care of the animals. They knew where the food on the table came from and what work it took to get milk and garden vegetables to the table. They had seen baby chickens and rabbits grow, and had felt the loss of the ones that died. All of us seemed to have become more perceptive about the land and living creatures—their many needs and vulnerabilities and values.

Nancy cried as she said goodbye to the mares across the fence; she had spent the morning finding the last bits of loose hay and carrots from the garden to hand-feed them. She would begin school in the fall, so the timing of our move was ideal. I tried to explain, "Nan, never feel condemned to live or work in one place forever; there may be need for more changes before we all reach our dreams, but each move should be worth it. Dad and I also have goals and dreams; some are the same ones you have."

Knowing we had to move to a tract house for a while didn't help my spirits or those of the rest of the family. It was especially hard to leave the cow, the momma bunny, and the hens. They were like close friends and family. I prayed that the new owners would take good care of them. The family seemed nice, and they promised to treat the animals well, but they had never kept animals in the heat of Arizona's summer days, and they seemed to tire of my repeatedly stressing the need for always having fresh water available for all the animals. Maude's watering trough was an old bathtub—they'd find it easy to keep it full of water, and the salt block, partially hollowed out from her licking, would remind them to buy a new one soon. We also left a partial stack of baled hay.

Several of Dan's students helped load and move the piano, the deep-freeze, the trunks, and the washing machine. I called our new place "Hyphen House." Hopefully, it would be a brief bridge between farms, but it was a dramatic change—not in distance, but in the more citified living. Dan would drive out Van Buren Boulevard several miles farther west to teach. The good part was that the house was large, with three bedrooms and the nice feel and fragrance of wooden floors, fresh paint, and newness.

Although our plan was to be there a few short months, I quickly hoed and raked the yard and got some lawn growing both in both the front and the back. When I wasn't working in the yard, the kids had to share my ongoing search of the outskirts of Phoenix, Tempe, and Scottsdale as I looked for that next little farm. Finding no small places with three to ten acres for sale anywhere near Tempe or Scottsdale, I began to look in the area north of Phoenix.

Our dog Heidi, meanwhile, became pregnant soon after we moved to Hyphen House. She must have fallen for a stray wandering through the neighborhood, since her puppies looked nothing like the few dogs living nearby. One neighbor owned a dachshund, and a couple of blocks away were two more dogs, a Scottie and a terrier.

Having decided the kids might as well see how puppies are born, I placed a folded sheet on the floor in the bathroom where Heidi could give birth, and the children and I crowded in almost beside her. If Heidi could give some instruction on delivering puppies in this home classroom, perhaps I'd never be tempted to mention stories about storks bringing babies. Heidi didn't get me off the hook—Momma Dog remained indifferent and casual as the puppies arrived ever so fast and easily, and in such a manner that the kids saw nothing. Neither child cared or even noticed how the puppies came into the world; both of them just wanted to run back outside and play with a new swing set. They asked no questions at all. This was a puzzlement to me ever after.

Heidi didn't seem to care that she had produced a family, and continued to be an unprotective and casual mom. Instinct at least told her to let the puppies nurse, and she washed their coats, faces, and ears now and then. That was all. She never slept with them. Fortunately, the nights were warm, and the puppies were fine on newspapers and a folded sheet. When the pups were seven or eight weeks old, I easily found homes for them by placing a sign on the front lawn. That was fortunate, because by the time the puppies left, Heidi was snarling and curling her lips at them as they climbed over her or tried to nurse. She failed to care, or even to notice, as her babies disappeared one by one.

I also remember Hyphen House for a certain sound. For hours, every day, the lady next door sat in a rocking chair on her front porch and rocked and hummed. Not a soft hum, but a loud hum of some song or tune I didn't know—about six bars of something. She crocheted, rocked, and hummed continuously. The yarn she used was always shades of pink and purple. At first, as I planted the lawn, hung out the wash, and took care of the kids, it seemed rather funny. Then it seemed sad. I tried to talk to her, but she would say "Hello" and then look back down. I suppose the crocheting was an outlet of some kind for her, or maybe a soothing backdrop for daydreaming. She gave me two pink potholders one day, but still she shied away from conversation.

Our last memory of the house is of the night Nancy stepped on a scorpion. We were still driving to the movies at Encanto Park on Friday nights, and we had just returned from a movie. Nancy ran barefoot ahead of us into the dark living room as Dan unlocked the door and pulled it open. A second or two later, Nancy screamed at the top of her lungs and hopped back toward us. As we turned on the lights, we saw a scorpion on the floor, still very much alive, and ready for battle with his tail in the air.

All those years of my carefully checking in corners, under sinks and furniture, and standing the legs of the crib and playpen in little jars of water, and still one of us had been stung. Dan scooped the scorpion into a jar to take with us, and we drove to the hospital's emergency room back in Phoenix.

We were lucky. The staff helped us monitor Nancy for about an hour or so, and the doctor decided that little or no poison had gotten into her foot. It probably helped that the soles of her feet were like shoe leather from going barefoot much of the time. Perhaps that scorpion, or a family of them, felt as uprooted as we felt on this land that had been a bare tract of desert a year or two earlier. However, I kept wondering where the scorpion's family and all his relatives and friends lived. Could he be a member of a big clan living under the kitchen sink or somewhere else inside or outside the house?

Those thoughts were quite an incentive to find us a farm, and I redoubled my days of searching. It meant driving Dan to school every morning and picking him up at the end of each school day. The problem was, I couldn't find any darn farm. The Tempe area was growing with farmers, students, and teachers from the college, and there were no small farming parcels for sale. Some of the most desirable land was out in the boonies north of town, but all that land, including Scottsdale, was mostly made up of large ranches and farms, with sleek cattle and horses grazing, or alfalfa and melon fields surrounded by strong, straight fencing. Other mostly flat lands had been developed with giant machinery for agribusiness ventures or the planting of new suburbs creeping out from Phoenix to these neighboring towns.

The growth of Phoenix and the intensive agriculture of the whole Salt River Valley was made possible by a number of dams which ensured a year-round water supply. The dams, like Roosevelt, Coolidge, and Hoover, had been built by the federal government and had spawned a large, complex system of irrigation canals, for the Salt River alone couldn't begin to furnish water for all who came to live in the valley. Because of the dams, the desert had become green with all kinds of crops, and the Phoenix population had begun to grow. Yet Phoenix was still a baby city then, with most of the large, uncontrolled growth still to come. Back then people did not have to worry about the spreading smog and diminishing water supplies that residents of this still fast-growing capital city face today.

Scottsdale, at the time I was searching, was known as a tiny, very western town that had begun to grow after World War II. Even there, I couldn't find a small plot of land that was a minifarm with a house on it. It's hard to believe how few houses were there at that time, compared to the present Scottsdale of sprawling shopping centers, resorts, golf courses, and far-reaching housing developments. Today it seems almost a part of Phoenix.

On Glendale Avenue, in the north part of Phoenix, I finally found a sign that said, "FOR SALE BY OWNER, 3 ACRES AND HOUSE." The parcel was well fenced, and the house was a white, craftsman/bungalow style, with a sturdy brown wood-shingled roof and a brick chimney. Dan's drive to Tolleson would be longer, but this was a lovely place except for the busy street out front, and the price was right. Using the funds from the sale of the Fowler Lane house, we bought the farm and moved again. Like First Farm, Glendale Avenue Farm would never lay us a "nest egg," but it gave us some aspects of the rural way of life we craved.

Again, I was free to do good or bad with the house and land. Dan often came home to say, "Farmer Chase, you done good today." He was tolerant when I bought our first mixed-period furniture pieces from Joe's Good-As-New store, adding them to the dining room table and chairs. Company could now sit on a couch or on matching chairs. There were even two end-tables with lamps. No plush, newly brocaded or velvet-upholstered pieces, and no Persian rugs under a crystal chandelier, but wonder of wonders I had seats in front of my first-ever fireplace: a cozy, comfy, but not lazy, home.

I'd long dreamt of the colors, aromas, and warmth of the orange, yellow, and rose glow of a fireplace—even in the desert. Just the thought of fragrant wisps of smoke escaping into a room seemed special. After we'd burned the logs that had been left behind in the garage by the sellers, I continued making as many fires as possible by using cardboard boxes, paper, and dead branches for fuel, while Dan brought boxes of scrap lumber from houses still going up in the Hyphen-House area we'd left. We sharpened the tips of small limbs from trees on the property into points and toasted marshmallows over the fire for an after-dinner snack.

"Kids, pretend that we're all sitting companionably around a real campfire of hot coals, and that we'll soon be crawling into warm sleeping bags under a canopy of tall pine trees. When you're older, we'll all camp up in the high mountains, perhaps the Sierras, and we'll build ourselves a fire like this."

The next fall, a couple of months later, little Nancy, our cowgirl-without-a-horse, started first grade. There had been no prenursery school, no nursery school, and no kindergarten for her in the Tolleson area. Nancy and I went to the school to meet her teacher and look over the classroom, but when the first day of school came I couldn't suffer the trauma of walking her up to the schoolroom door for a teary mother-daughter goodbye. Instead, she walked down the driveway carrying a green lunch pail and climbed into a mile-long yellow school bus. She didn't know another child on the bus or at school, but at least she rejoiced in already knowing how to read and do some math. I finally relaxed when she reported that there were two girls who wanted to come over to see the white rabbits, and that the boy seated behind her pulled her pigtails each day and chased her at recess. I asked her if she'd like me to cut the braids off, but she knew that the boy who tugged on her hair and chased after her liked her. She kept her long hair, and usually came home with a smile in place.

Today's Glendale Avenue and North Central Avenue, with their rivers of cars, seem an affront to what was then a peaceful area of orange and grapefruit groves, small pastures, and homes. North Phoenix has changed to "a higher and better use," with apartment buildings and commercial complexes sprawling across the once-fertile pastures. Our old California-style bungalow, rows of historical homes, and the once-expansive grapefruit and orange groves are now gone. The Heritage Square Foundation managed to save one square block and a few old Victorian homes, but the rest is now city.

Dan's offer from Arizona State College was contingent upon his completing his MS degree in the summer—a fifth summer of staying in the oven-hot tin washroom behind Mrs. Marshall's house in Tucson. Dr. Cline made Dan redo the wording of his thesis again and again. Usually it was just a change of one or two words on a page. If it hadn't been so important that Dan finish that summer, it might have been rather funny. At one point, Dr. Cline started to change words back to the way they had been in the beginning, from "the" to "a" and then back again to "the."

"Isn't that what I wrote in the first place?" Dan chuckled.

Dr. Cline only gave a thin smile and continued to poise his pen above the pages as he pursued elusive errors.

The kids and I accompanied Dan when he went to these short thesis review sessions. I sat in the backseat with the typewriter on my lap and lots of extra paper, changing words and phrases according to the department head's latest revisions. Typing in a moving car was only part of the problem. The two-door sedan had no air-conditioning, and as temperatures rose well into the triple digits it became increasingly difficult not to smudge the pages with my sticky fingers and dripping face. Toward the end of August, when time was growing frighteningly short, lo and behold, Dan's thesis was finally accepted and he received his MS sheepskin! He would have the Arizona State College job in September.

Chapter 23

Floods and a Gopher-Warrior

Three acres of good soil and a nice double-walled house were encouraging steps along our trail. There was a friendly sweetness about the property. The house was nestled under huge sycamores, oaks, and cottonwoods, and I suddenly realized how much I'd missed trees. Out front, a mature orchard of healthy-appearing grapefruit trees screened the house from busy Glendale Avenue, which went from Phoenix out to the town of Glendale. The driveway went past the orchard and house to a sturdy single-car garage in back. Behind the garage was the pastureland. Neighbors on both sides of our land had orange groves.

"Look at this, will you, kids? All these trees! Dad will make you a tree-swing in that sycamore. How about that!" Except for the one straggly oak tree we'd had beside our Tucson apartment, these trees would be the first we had lived under or beside in Arizona.

Glendale Farm would be an easier life than before, but once again, I knew it might be a temporary home. Still, I was so delighted by the gigantic trees that I continually found some excuse to go out and sit on a picnic table bench and envision their leaves growing hourly. It was a quiet and private place where the trees enveloped me in their shade, and

I began to do my letters and check-writing there. Soon we used the picnic table for early weekend luncheons and suppers.

In addition to trees, there were other things I hadn't had time to miss before. Now I could feel cozy and warm just knowing I had both a wonderful brick fireplace and a floor furnace that heated the whole house in minutes. In the still rather cold nights, this was a wonderful thought.

The kitchen was on the back side of the house. From there, I would be able to watch the children playing and animals grazing in our field beyond the fence. Best of all, there would be no more melon trucks blowing clouds of dust throughout the house much of the harvest season.

From a rancher that Dan had interviewed for an article, he discovered a source to buy weaned calves. We would have to do something about the lack of feed in the pasture, though—gophers had eaten nearly everything. We bought three calves and a small load of hay, and began a gopher battle.

Gophers can wreak havoc upon anything, from lawns and flower gardens to huge farms, fields, pastures, and orchards. Not only had these cute, soft as velvet, cuddly gophers eaten everything growing on our pasture land, they had also ruined the canal-based irrigation system. These little critters didn't know about fences, property lines, ditches, furrows, or berms; their tunnel roads could create underground canals that submerged part of the land under several feet of water and left the rest of the land bone-dry. Something simply had to be done.

My first attempt at eliminating the gophers and their gopher suburban housing tract was with traps. Right away, though, I discovered that traps could be a full-time job and they still wouldn't destroy enough gophers to save the land. Poison seemed even crueler, and my lesson with Sage and the grasshoppers also made me wary of such endeavors. That field contained far more gopher mounds than green alfalfa, and from a distance the pushed-up gopher diggings made the whole area look brown.

I asked Dan, "What would happen if the fields were deeply flooded again? Maybe a couple of times. Would the gophers drown?" I asked Dan.

"Sure, some might. It's worth a try."

Again we bought water from the irrigation district, and again we found it could be scheduled to be turned into our ditch at any time of the day or night. At 4 AM the zanjero turned water into our ditch and the flooding began.

Dan, followed by a tail-wagging Cindy, went out to observe the coming of the water and plug the places where the water was seeping through into the wrong areas. The field had raised berms that divided it into thirds, with another berm around the perimeter. We wanted to flood each part of the field between the berms, and eventually the lawns and the front orchard.

As the water deepened, the Glendale Farm "residents" pushed up through the center of their wet mounds of dirt to the surface, then crawled or swam out, their coats soaking wet and their eyes blinking in the early morning sunlight. They tried to walk and paddle through the water to the raised earthen berms, but even the berms became mushy mud, and the hundreds of gopher holes gurgled as the water filled the tunnels and prevented any safe escape. Some of the gophers probably drowned.

Others met their fate in the form of a valiant and wonderful gopher-warrior in the guise of a dog. Quickly, and with obvious joy, Cindy waged full-scale warfare. I had long puzzled over the personality of our little cocker spaniel/poodle-or-whatever mix, but I hadn't thought about her having a bloodline going back in history to a hunting breed. As the rodents popped out of their holes, Cindy splashed and raced back and forth all over the field, and, with one quick bite, dispatched each critter to gopher heaven. She never tried to eat them; rather, she just left them on the battlefield. Dan also dispatched a few of the critters with the back of his shovel when they got within his reach. He continued to repair, as best he could, the holes and tunnels in the berms around the perimeter of our land and the two berms across the field.

In the following weeks, each time the irrigation water flowed onto our pasture, Cindy took on her go-fer-gopher tasks and repeated her patrol, looking out over the field or peering down into the water like a fisherman on a boat as he looks down into the depths for a school of fish.

When the land was dry, Cindy was still a gophering-dog, but then she hunted more like a cat. She sat silently and motionlessly for long periods, hunched over or beside a mound or hole, and, when the gopher decided to come up and nibble a little alfalfa for supper, or push up more dirt from one of his tunnels, she was there waiting. Gradually, the back field lost its crop of gopher mounds, and finally it once again became a field of tall grasses and dark green alfalfa for the calves to enjoy.

Cindy found being a hunter challenging work, and she came in exhausted each evening. With no interest in anything but food, this dog had remained a freeloader until her gophering days. Now she more than earned her keep. After her dinner, she lay dreaming beside the fire or at our feet, while her body twitched in happy dreams of vanquishing our enemies. Her whole attitude of chronic unease and dissatisfaction with life changed for the better, and she quit slouching around, grumpy and grumbling. This little dog had been born to hunt, and the daily challenge, the exhilarating pursuit, made her almost happy.

The floodwaters of our irrigation system also provided an exciting episode for me and for our new family of rabbits. As on First Farm, I had bought a snowy white doe before any hutches were built. Consequently, the doe had to stay in the bathroom during the day, and at night she slept on a bed of straw in the laundry tub, with a piece of chicken wire, weighted down by boards, across the top.

As before, we built three hutches, with a ramp to underground rooms where rabbit families could stay cool during summer months. This time, it would be even easier for the rabbits to stay cool, since we put the rabbit pens under a big oak tree. Before long, there was a large number of baby rabbits, and, soon after that, the irrigation waters came again.

Under moonlight so bright that our shadows followed us, Dan and I trudged out to the far end of the back field to let the valuable water flow onto the land. After breakfast, Dan left for school, and I went out to see whether the extra water had reached the lawn around the house only to find the whole rabbit area completely under water. The partially wet momma rabbit was upstairs, but her babies were nowhere in sight. I quickly removed the sheets of roofing covering their basement quarters. There crouched all but one of the bunnies, huddled together on top of a thick mat of floating straw. All alive. The one baby was in water up to her neck, but still was held up somewhat by a buoyant bed of straw under her chin and front paws. I ran for a box, gathered all the babies up, and took them into the kitchen. They were ever so cold, and quite wet.

Bake the bunnies? The only way I could think of to get them all dried and warmed quickly was to set them in a small cardboard box and to place the box in the oven. With the oven barely on and the oven door left open, I heated the bunnies until they were dry. Every one of them survived, and there weren't even any sniffling noses. Momma Rabbit got her oven-dried babies back in a little over an hour, while I blocked the ramp to the rabbits' basement room and put a layer of straw over their upstairs floor for the day so the babies would remain warm and their little paws wouldn't get caught in the wire mesh flooring.

Irrigation water also flooded the grapefruit orchard. The Bermuda grass under the trees flourished and began to use the tree trunks as lattices and ladders to grow up to the highest limbs. This wasn't pretty, and it didn't do the fruit trees any good. My days were busy, but I fretted about that Bermuda grass every time I looked at the orchard.

"Dan, if you weren't going for another degree anytime soon, I think several sheep might be the answer for the runaway Bermuda grass in front." By the beginning of our second year on Glendale Avenue, Dan had decided he would need another academic degree if he intended to stay in a college-teaching career, and I knew there was no sense in purchasing sheep if we would be moving soon.

"Well, I'll have to get the coursework in stages," Dan reminded me. "I've been thinking about trying to get a couple of courses this summer at Texas A and M because of their big agricultural offerings. Then, if Tempe would give me credit for all my graduate courses, and if we liked it there, I could get a doctorate at Tempe…Before we get bogged down with sheep and a cow this coming fall, would you and the kids want to go with me to College Station, Texas, for the summer session? Maybe you'd also like to take a course or two?"

I nodded and decided, "I'd love to go along, but I'm not ready yet to take any classes. Maybe later I'll go for a master's degree, when you go back to school full-time. But if the kids and I go along with you this summer, what about Cindy, Heidi, the rabbits, the calves, and the watering here?"

He had an answer for that. Recalling a couple new to Phoenix, people he'd met several times, he suggested "I'm almost sure Helen and her new hubby would take care of things here if they could stay here rent-free.

That would give them more time to house hunt, and Helen's as besot-
tedly crazy about animals as you are, though we don't know her partner
well...the main hang-up is that Tempe wants me back on the job a full
week before the end of the courses that I'm thinking about taking."

As it turned out, Arizona State was happy to give Dan another week
off, as long as it was for graduate course work. Like a horse jumping over
high and varied obstacles in a series of horse shows, Dan registered for
ag credit and marketing-type courses, and we moved into graduate-stu-
dent housing on the Texas A & M campus—housing that at an earlier
time had probably been army barracks.

The kids and I spent a lot of time swimming in the big campus swimming pool, while Dan attended classes and studied. I soon wished I had
never dipped a toe in the water, as Dan's concentrated courses didn't
end up being the only challenge on the agenda. Suddenly, I became an
arthritic cripple. My pain became intense, but Dan was taking final
exams and was already on borrowed time from Arizona State, so there
was no time to find a doctor. As I packed up before we headed back to
Phoenix, I mostly just threw things loose into the trunk of the car.

I mentioned my "painful arthritis" to the veterinary science student
who lived on the second floor above us, and he suggested that some
horse liniment he had upstairs might help me on our drive home. He
encouraged me to try the liniment, saying, "Lots of farm people use
horse liniment and other animal medicines for human ailments like
aches, sprains, and bruises. Some of us even use creosote as a quick and
handy antiseptic for our cuts when we're working with livestock. Let
me get you the bottle of liniment. It won't hurt you, and it might help.
Please let me give you the bottle."

Early the next morning, Dan coated me with a thick, messy ap-
plication of the horse liniment, tore up a sheet to wrap and safety-pin
around my greasy, aching body, before we took off for Phoenix. In a car
without air-conditioning and with the outside temperature going well
over one hundred degrees, I stretched out as best I could on the backseat, while the kids sat with Dan on the front seat.

We all shared one towel to mop our brows, and one cup for drinking
water. Although I vaguely knew my illness might not be arthritis, I hurt

too much to think clearly about the possibility of passing my germs to the other family members. Except for brief stops for meals, restrooms, and gas, Dan drove straight through to Tempe. The kids somehow knew I was really ill. They slept some, and suffered long hours together beside Dan on the front seat, scarcely complaining. Dan built up the space for their bare feet with two cardboard boxes. This made the stretching-out space wider when they tried to lie down.

Once home, I soon felt somewhat better, and I began to clean some kitchen cupboards. Immediately, my legs and back stiffened up and hurt. A doctor confirmed what I'd begun to suspect, telling me, "I'm quite certain that you've had a case of polio. Several of my other polio patients were enjoying public swimming pools before they became ill, and you have many of the same complaints. You won't get well without a month or two in the hospital; you need lots of rest, along with hot, moist heat, and limbering-up therapy."

Polio, or "poliomyelitis" by its longer name, was a greatly feared and widespread disease at that time; many polio patients ended up crippled or in "iron lungs." Some died. In my room in the special polio ward of the hospital, there were a number of tragic cases. A pretty girl next to me had been on her honeymoon when she became ill; this was her third year in the hospital, and she was still unable to move more than her head and eyes. Her husband had recently left her. I kept in touch with her after I recovered, but she later died.

Each day the hospital staff heated moistened blankets in a drumlike contraption on wheels, and then applied them, as hot as I could stand, to my aching muscles. The blankets were wrapped around me several times a day, and a therapist spent time stretching my arms, legs, neck, and back.

In the acute stage of the disease, had we, perhaps, done even better than any hospital could have? I had had strong, hot, horse liniment applied around my body; I was tightly wrapped in the sheets, and the temperature inside the car must have been one hundred and fifteen degrees or more during a major part of the long trip back to Tempe.

After my hospital stay, the doctors ordered another couple of months of bed rest and exercises at home before I was allowed up. My nurses and cooks at home were Dan, before he left each morning for his new job, and then Nancy and Danny the rest of the day until their dad got home. Fortunately, Nancy already knew most of the material that was being covered in school that fall, and she and I reviewed her work. Nancy served me lots of Jell-O and toast, and small portions of canned soup that Dan left on the stove for Nancy to heat. Dan also bought lots of fruit, cookies, and milk for snacks, and then cooked a complete dinner every night.

The house became dirty, and even our dishes were not always completely clean, but, luckily, my outlook stayed broad-gauged. As usual, I wasn't too concerned about details or perfection in lifestyle. However, as I lay in bed beside the open windows, there was plenty of time for me to observe the Bermuda grass growing higher and higher into all the grapefruit trees, and thus began the story of the sheep.

Chapter 24

Sheep and the Ruby Red Grapefruit

When I was back on my feet and mostly over the effects of polio, the idea of sheep still seemed a happy and logical solution. "How about getting some sheep to be my mowing machines for the Bermuda grass? They'd be safe and fun farm animals for Danny and Nancy." Abracadabra! I could then have a lawn in the orchard throughout spring, summer, and fall, and the grass would be neatly trimmed. Sheep would fertilize the soil, and eventually there would be lamb chops and roasts on the dinner table. Or maybe I could knit wool sweaters, or we could sell the wool. Perhaps little lambs to frolic and play...what could be better? Lamb chops, roast leg of lamb, and rack of lamb were fond but distant memories from my childhood, when lamb must have been far less expensive. Dan had no students whose parents raised sheep, so what he knew about sheep was from classes and books. Our knowledge was not enough, for buying sheep then seemed a perfect solution to the problem of the Bermuda grass.

The orchard of Ruby Red grapefruit had been planted at the front of the property, between the house and the street. Following a power mower around and under each of the thirty-five huge trees, with their skirts of fruit, limbs, and leaves down to ground level, was a "No-you-do-it" sort of job, especially after mowing the other extensive lawns around the house. Moreover, I was fighting a losing battle—with all the irrigation water, the Bermuda grass had become exuberantly strong and healthy. Not only had it climbed into the top branches of the trees, but it had wound around and around the trunks and branches, while its roots probably went several feet down into the ground.

City and country were in close proximity here, and Glendale was not the place to be insensitive to the neat front lawns of our neighbors. Maybe a lot more importantly, it was not good for the grapefruit trees to have to share water, nutrients, and sunshine with the weedlike Bermuda grass.

I didn't know any more than "Little Bo Peep" did about sheep, and Dan didn't know much either. After checking the pictures of different breeds of sheep in a USDA Yearbook, we decided that we liked the large Suffolk breed with the fine black faces and black legs. In anticipation of the ewes' arrival, Dan and I quickly fenced the orchard with woven wire. And after hearing some gruesome stories about what stray dogs can do to sheep, we added two ugly strands of barbed wire a little above the three-foot woven fence.

True to form, I bought the sheep before their new home was completely ready. A breeder of Suffolks had three young ewes he would sell for such a worthy cause, but he suggested that the ewes not be bred and that I should "just try them for a season first." Upon reflection many months later, I realized he knew very well what would happen. Anyone who raised sheep, or even goats or cattle, could have told me.

As the sheep arrived, they mutually agreed, with anxious "bah-bah-bahs," that this was a weird and scary place to be. I assured them that Bermuda grass was delicious, and an old laundry tub could be a perfectly acceptable watering trough. Yes, I certainly would place a salt-lick near their watering trough. And yes, they could supervise their new shepherds in the construction of a roofed shelter that would be built the following weekend.

The next morning the bah-bah-bah cacophony had not ceased. "If you're doing all this bleating to complain about not having a leader any more, you can jolly well figure it out!" That, I immediately knew, is not what one should tell sheep.

Soon these young ewes moseyed around the orchard and munched away most of the day, but languidly lay in the shade of the trees and chewed their cuds when the bright autumn sun was hottest. The grass began to have a nice mowed look.

Sheep conversation was hard to understand but fun to hear, rather sweet and musical. With bribes of sheep-pellet feed or hay, the ewes learned to let me pet them, and they came racing up when they saw me with three pails of sheep feed.

I decided not to let the children name the ewes yet, just in case our lawn-mower venture didn't work out and we had to make lamb chops of them. "Nancy, why not wait until you can tell one sheep from the others before you give them names?"

All was going as planned, but in farming, this is often best left unsaid. I watched the ewes beginning to spend a lot of time dancing around on their back hooves, or bracing themselves on a limb with their front feet while picking off the grapefruit leaves and all the lower limbs and stems. Being a slow learner and working in the kitchen at the back side of the house most of the day, I didn't realize right away what was actually transpiring, but it was a growing problem—no, make that a nongrowing problem!

The gorgeous trees, adorned with a heavy load of sweet, ever so big, ruby red fruit, were changed from dowagers with full, floor-length, ballroom gowns of leaves, into whole Folies Bergère chorus lines of very short-skirted, skinny-legged-girl trees. At the lower levels, every single limb and leaf, and much of the mostly ripe grapefruit disappeared—right up to the full height of the sheep as they stood tiptoed on their hind legs and stretched their considerably long necks and heads to the sky to pick and munch. Why hadn't I searched out the tiniest, shortest breed, instead of falling for these large critters? Notice, I no longer called them lambs or ewes. Where was my vision of sheep with heads bowed over neatly cropped grass? These girls were programmed to be more creative than that, and they continued to eat and toe-dance around every tree in the orchard.

Do things, good or bad, often come in threes? I hoped not, for strike number two with the sheep happened next. The sheep got out and disappeared. The gate was completely open. Believing that sheep aren't the brainiest of beasts, I had just a hook-and-screw type of fastener on the gate, and one of the sheep had likely pushed up the fastener with her nose. Maybe the ewes thought they would go find their former home, or locate the source of those yummy sheep treats I fed them, if they thought at all. Mind you, the roads around us were busy ones, with Glendale Avenue running east and west in front of the house, and other arteries running north and south. In fact, just barely eight blocks east was Central Avenue, one of the busiest thoroughfares in Phoenix. We would have to drive the roads in a car to find the sheep. While I waited for Dan to come home with the car, all I could do was visualize those sheep, in their heavy, winter, wool coats, running erratically down Central Avenue in late-afternoon traffic.

As soon as Dan got home, we took the backseat out of the car, loaded a pail of feed, some alfalfa hay, ropes, and halters, and took off to search the surrounding yards, driveways, streets, and orange groves. Eventually, we found the very subdued and weary girls about two miles north of home. Fortunately, they had turned onto a side street and were too tired to move very fast. When we found them, they were in the front yard of a nicely landscaped house. Two of the ewes were just wandering aimlessly around on the lawn, and the third sat in the center of a bed of geraniums.

Getting ropes around them was easier than I had imagined. They were exhausted, and perhaps they recognized us or remembered that sheep pellets come in pails. To them, alfalfa hay and sheep feed were preferable to flowers, lawns, and pyracantha hedges.

Standing at the back door of the car on the opposite side from the sheep, I spread alfalfa on the floor of the car and rattled the pellets in the pail. Dan got a rope on one of the ewes, stood behind her, and shoved her up to the car. Straddling her as best he could, he pushed again, and she jumped into the car to see what was in the pail. Abracadabra! Being follow-the-leader animals and smelling the feed, the second and third ewes followed the first one into the car's backseat area, with just a bit of persuasion from behind. It looked as if sheep weren't so dumb after all.

On the way home, two of the sheep hung their heads out the side windows. The third one, wedged in between the other two, faced the rear window, with her tail hanging over the front seat, where Dan and I, of course, had to sit. This created an immediate new worry—that of what the sheep might "doo" while in the car, especially the middle sheep, with her tail practically over my shoulder. Their manure would be unpleasant, but the thought of their urine, which seemed to come with the force of a fire hydrant, made Dan streak for home. What other drivers must have thought of this speeding car full of bleating sheep and frantic people, made us laugh uncontrollably loud, but it may also have played a part in the Big Decision we reached later that night. With the ewes calling out their bah-bah-bahs at the top of their lungs throughout the adventure, we got them back in the orchard by driving across the lawn to their open gate.

Late that night, after much serious thinking, the Big Decision was finalized. It won't be a nutty vision, we agreed. We'll go with our instincts and make some big changes once again; maybe we'll go back five moves to make six ahead. We'll sell the farm, travel to Pennsylvania, and go completely broke still one more time while studying for sheepskins of another sort. Dan's Doctoral degree and my Master's degree would surely be the tickets to get us back to California, and maybe with fewer sheep in our car. Perchance, taking this roundabout route might someday lead to our dream of a real farm, with barns, white fences, a bigger house, and, best of all, horses instead of sheep.

To make the move financially feasible, the gigantic deep-freeze would travel east with us, and in it would be lots of lamb and mutton, all in four-person servings in packages of double-wrapped freezer paper, labeled with words like Lamb-Chops, Stew, Leg-of-Lamb, and Rack-of-Lamb. The three sheep would join our steers as butchered and packaged meals for our table in Pennsylvania. Until we actually left Arizona, I rented some extra freezer space in town. There would also be seventy cartons of Ruby Red grapefruit, picked, of course, from the higher branches of the trees, and all cut up in sectioned pieces with a sprinkling of sugar on top. Sometimes happenings in life do occur in threes. Might there be a chance that this faraway destination and return trip would be a home run to California?

Chapter 25

I Must Buy It by Noon

On the steep and twisting trail, once more it was time to move. This had been a fun time in spite of wandering sheep and severely pruned citrus trees. Nancy liked her school and classmates, and Dan enjoyed college teaching, the staff, and the students. Still, as his second year of teaching at Arizona State continued, the commuting time seemed to grow longer, and he realized he couldn't advance very far in college work without a doctorate.

More importantly, we decided that our eventual goal would be the wonderful central Californian town of San Luis Obispo. SLO, as the locals called it, was situated in an area of oak trees, high mountains, gentle hills, and valleys. The town was the perfect size, and it was the only place we knew about that was small and rural yet had a college with a strong agricultural department. The climate was warm, and nearby was the wonderful Pacific Ocean with long, sandy beaches. We'd acquired quite a wish list, and that town was the one place that had everything we wanted.

California State Polytechnic College, as it was called then, was one of the California state colleges with a major emphasis in agriculture. We had visited the campus and some of the faculty members several years before, but a master's degree hadn't been enough to open the door to a professorship. The Dean of Agriculture had advised Dan, "We need more doctoral degrees, even though we have a strong philosophy here of 'Learn by Doing.' Come back with that degree and there should be a position for you." Therefore, the only thing that would make our move possible was a sheepskin with "Doctor" written on it.

I ventured to suggest, "With some goals, you just need to be patient. San Luis Obispo will just have to wait while we go back to the books. Maybe I'll get a master's at the same time you get your degree. How about that? There must be some kind of small part-time jobs that we can take to help finance our stay once we're back in school."

"Hon, you've got to get your master's," Dan replied. "I'm not getting another degree alone—we'll bag two of 'em."

Arizona State was willing to give Dan a leave of absence without pay, allowing him to obtain a degree while maintaining job security. While Dan continued to teach at Tempe, his inquiries, records, and letters flew off to several schools with good graduate programs in agriculture. We might have preferred Cornell University, but Pennsylvania State University's offer of campus housing and a graduate scholarship came through a week or two sooner than the one from Cornell. Dan had accepted the first offer right away and didn't think he should cancel it just a short time later when Cornell matched the first offer. Meanwhile, I also sent my transcripts off to Penn State and was accepted. There was nothing more that stood between us and our sheepskin hunting in Pennsylvania—except that we had to sell our farm to finance most of it.

One more time I suggested, "It'll probably take many months to sell this farm. I'll start by placing an ad and keeping the place more attractive." Very early several mornings later, I trimmed all the shrubs around the house, and then used a power sprayer to hose off the entire house, including the roof and the front side of the garage. Then I took a mop and soaped and rinsed the foundation boards until all of them were white and shiny. Next, I carefully raked up the thick carpet of leaves from the back, front, and side lawns, and mowed the grass. With so many golden sycamore leaves still floating down from the trees, the grass would look tidy for about an hour. I hosed off the picnic table, benches, and lawn chairs. Finally, I raked the driveway and sprinkled it down to settle the dust. The whole place sparkled and looked inviting under the late autumn sun.

At that very moment, a young man in a dark business suit drove up the lane, got out of his shiny black car, and asked "Is this the property for sale?" When I informed him that it was, he took a silent walk around the outside areas for about five minutes. I finally broke the silence and offered to show him the inside of the house, but he said it wasn't necessary.

"I want to buy your property; I'll meet your price and pay all cash. Is your husband at work? Well, go phone him and tell him to meet us for an escrow. Where does he work? I've got to buy your house by early afternoon and take a plane out of town by 5 PM. You'd better phone an escrow company, too, and tell them to expect us. Your husband can meet us there. Any escrow company will do."

He didn't ask, "Would you phone?" or "Would your husband be able to get away this morning?" He was plenty cocky, with his statement that he was buying the farm at the selling price. Fortunately, Dan had an office hour followed by a lunch hour, so he could come home, pick up Danny and me, and meet the man at the escrow company to sign away the farm.

In that hasty manner, Glendale Farm was sold, and, one more time, we probably sold the property for less than it was worth (and certainly in far less time than we had planned). Once again, too, it had been a lot of little things, like washing the house and cleaning up the yard that just might have made big things happen.

Dan always said, "Don't sweat the little stuff," but it was in my genes to sweat the little stuff. In this case, at least, it may have helped—fussing over the dusty house and leafy yard may have inspired the sale.

Over half a year remained before we could travel east. "Dan, we'll need to have a house to hold all our farm and house belongings, both now and while we're away. It seems to make sense to buy a house in the town of Tempe right away, because, ready or not, we have to vacate and move in less than forty-five days. We can make our purchase contingent upon the final sale of this Glendale place."

The house I found, almost immediately, was on a large lot near Arizona State in Tempe. The down payment was low, and we'd be able to rent it mostly furnished with our belongings when we headed east. The rest of the funds from the Glendale Farm sale would have to tide us through the time of no regular salary until we completed our degrees.

Both children were confused and uneasy. Nancy insisted, "I want my sheep, and I want to stay right here. Why does Daddy have to have another sheepskin?"

"Hon, we're getting closer to getting horses. This isn't a good place to ride. There are no trails or dirt roads, and we don't have enough money. Your only hope of getting a horse depends on Daddy and me going to school some more. We have to go far away in the east before we can go west, to California. Maybe, after we find a farm in California, we won't have to move again."

Turning to Danny, I tried to be reassuring, "You'll love playing in real snow in Pennsylvania, and you'll slide down hills on a sled and maybe build a snowman."

The kids didn't know it, but I, too, wondered about the stress-filled rigmarole of me and Dan getting more degrees. "Dan, one should be careful about detours, and this is a whopper. I sure hope we're not just tumbleweeds on the move again, rolling east so far, and maybe for nothing. There's a good chance both time and money will run out before we can pull the degree stuff off. Instant and crazy decisions in the past didn't involve such great distances and so much cost."

"Naw," said Dan. "We'll be rolling east, all right, but then we're gonna roll all the way back to California like it's downhill and we'll dip our toes in the Pacific. We'll come back to really arrive."

Chapter 26

A Covered Wagon Rolled East

In an exuberant, booming voice, the salesman at the trailer and truck rental lot in Phoenix tried to assure us. "Would ya just look at this big baby! It's brand new, completely new, and has never been used, not even once. Of course it won't leak! Sure, you can pull it with a bumper hitch; the hitch is included in the rental price. Having four wheels instead of two will make it a lot easier to load and balance it right—just don't put too much of its weight on your bumper. It's so much better than a two-wheeled one; you'll be just fine." The muscular and deeply tanned owner-salesman demonstrated how to hook and unhook the trailer to the bumper hitch (which he put on the car for us), and in a flash we were pulling the monster home.

I was spooked every time I carried loads of boxes out to this version of a big covered wagon parked in the driveway. I could stand up straight inside it, and it measured twelve feet in length. Since we would be charged by the number of days we used the trailer, we hurriedly packed it with reference books, our typewriter, bedding for snowy nights, linens, dishes, pots and pans, a complete twin bedroom set of furniture for the kids, and the large deep-freeze stuffed to the top. Our rations would be so tight that the frozen food just might make the difference between success and failure.

Although Dan's leave from his college job was without pay, there was a time limit on how long he could be away. The school wanted him back the following year in September when classes began. He hired tutors to help him study for the two foreign language requirements, and taught days while studying French and German most evenings until midnight.

Our kind friends John and Bess Dutton agreed to give a good home to beautiful but not-so-smart Heidi. Poor little Cindy had been killed by a car while we lived in the Tempe house.

I found tenants who would rent our house until we returned, and they promised to water the row of bare-root fruit trees and the large lawn I'd planted in the backyard. I gave the trees and yard a final heavy soaking overnight with hoses and sprinklers.

After packing paper plates full of prepared dinners for each night on the road, I wrapped the plates in foil and stuffed them on top of the other fully packed frozen foods in the deep-freeze and forced the lid down until it closed.

"Dan, each night we should try to plug the freezer into a motel outlet, so let's buy a long, heavy-duty electric cord. I'll take the hot-plate in the car; we can then heat cans of soup or make hot cocoa and coffee in motel rooms. Breakfasts will have to be cold cereals with powdered milk and fruit, and I'm taking a dozen hard-boiled eggs. These foods can go in the trunk of the car."

Eastward ho! In predawn darkness, on a day that would be well over a hundred in the Salt River Valley, we started out toward the first light in the east with an overloaded car and trailer, driving through long stretches of desert and little Arizona towns. We would be a long time away from farm settings, and with nary an animal to hug.

The only part of me that could swivel around to monitor the kids in the backseat was my neck. On the passenger side of the front seat, I was stuffed between the lunch sack, bottles of Coke, and two boxes full of things we had almost forgotten until we all walked out the door for the last time. These included my precious alarm clock, Danny's baseball cap and binoculars, Nancy's four library books on horses (which would be returned over a year late), Dan's three flashlights to change any flat tires in the dark, the current and not-so-current magazines from his nightstand, and the latest huge USDA Yearbook. Regional and national U.S. maps already lay on the dashboard.

Danny and Nancy, with limited attention spans and little patience, were confined to the backseat, where they fidgeted and squabbled. They had a mess of crayons, coloring books, puzzles, and storybooks, but these were of little assistance. In my purse were pages of Reader's Digest vocabulary lists that I insisted we all had to learn as we drove along.

"Knock it off, you two. You're going to count all the cows and horses you can see, and the first one to see each animal gets a point. I'll keep count on my pad, and the winner gets a double ice-cream cone instead of a single one this afternoon." Games helped settle down our troops, but the real highlight that defused their arguments and restlessness for a while was a small horned toad (which is actually in the lizard family) that the kids picked up in a field behind a gas station. They begged and begged to keep him, and I finally agreed they could hold and pet him for a half-hour of driving time. "We can't take him out of his natural desert habitat. He'd never live in snowy Pennsylvania, and he'd miss his horned toad family and the desert insects to eat."

After we left the toad by the side of another gas station, and the kids began to grumble again, I gave them a pep talk, saying, "Remember, kids, this move will hopefully open the gate to California, to live where there can be a horse and a bicycle. Another secret to happiness is to think about fun things: you've lived in desert country. Now you're traveling across the country to five-oh-two Elm Street, State College, Pennsylvania, where you'll meet new friends and play in lots of snow."

Then Dan chimed in, "Let's be an upbeat and happy bunch. This is the key to living in California."

After we'd crossed Arizona and New Mexico, there was a new pastime for the squirrelly kids that was much better than counting critters. In sets of six, one after the other alongside the highways, little red Burma Shave signs showed up, touting a brushless shaving cream. Thousands and thousands of these slapstick and humorous signs were planted along the main highways of much of the country from the 1930s into the early '60s. However, the company had never put them up in Arizona and

New Mexico because these were still sparsely populated states. There was always enough distance between each sign to let the message sink in. Nancy shouted most of the words:

TRAIN APPROACHING
WHISTLE SQUEALING
PAUSE!
AVOID THAT
RUNDOWN FEELING!
BURMA-SHAVE

——————————————————

SHE EYED
HIS BEARD
AND SAID NO DICE,—
THE WEDDING'S OFF—
I'LL COOK THE RICE!
BURMA-SHAVE

Most of the verses needed explaining to the children, but somehow the kids decided the messages were hilarious even without really understanding them.

Luck followed us: each night we were able to find a motel where the car and trailer could be parked close to our room. It took lots of backing up and going forward again to position the trailer up close to the motel room door or window. Gradually we caught on that when backing up with a trailer, you turn the wheels on the car in the opposite direction from what you would do without the trailer.

Motel owners or staff laughed heartily at my request to plug in a deep-freeze. Everyone thought it was extremely funny that what we were taking to school included, along with two little kids, a monstrous freezer full of food. None of the desk clerks let us pay for the electricity we used each night. Their kindness saved us from the potentially serious predicament of the freezer food's thawing.

There were two scary times, however. We were pulling the gigantic load with Rover, our Chevy sedan. For the fun of it, we pulled off the road at a truck weigh-in station somewhere in New Mexico to weigh the trailer. It weighed four thousand two hundred pounds, which was more than the car weighed empty, and the car was stuffed with kids, us, and all the last-minute sacks and boxes. Could we sit any lighter for the rest of the trip? We tried.

The second scare also came because of that heavy load. Somehow, our southern route missed all steep mountains and hills, but when we were just a few hundred miles from our destination, we encountered one hill with a traffic light at its crest. The light turned red, Dan braked, and the car and trailer started to roll back down the hill.

Somehow, the sun kept shining on our parade. By using the brakes and, almost at the same time, by gunning the motor while the car was in low gear, Dan got the car jerking and roaring forward through the stoplight. While he drove the car and trailer through the intersection on a red light, I reached over and continuously honked the horn.

With no flat tires, no blown transmission, and no running out of gas, we arrived at 502 Elm Street, State College, Pennsylvania, our home-to-be for the next year. Graduate school housing was in ugly Quonset huts that had been converted into duplexes and scattered around on a grass-covered hillside on the campus. The car and trailer's parking space was on the street, down a steep grassy slope from our two-bedroom apartment. Dan found the first students he talked to more than happy to help us unload and carry everything up the hill, except for the full deep-freeze, which a moving company moved in for us.

Just as the final boxes and the freezer were moved into the house, dark, thick clouds rolled across the sky and covered the sun, with thunder and lightning announcing the arrival of a storm. It quickly began to pour. To make sure the trailer was empty, I ran back down the hill and took one last look inside the massive trailer. When I looked inside, rain was streaming in around every bolt in the roof—and there were a lot of bolts! Almost everything in there would have been ruined if it had rained during the days we were driving east. Like some prairie schooner from an earlier era, we had gotten through the passes with our wagon and belongings safe and dry. It was a good beginning. We turned the rental trailer in the next morning.

Although we had arrived safely, many miles still lay ahead, and much work was to be done! Once more our dreams were deferred—dreams of a wide valley and rolling California hills and mountains, a ranch house, perhaps two more children, a large barn with horses, and warm summer evenings with a gathering of family on a porch while someone strummed a guitar and sang verses of cowboy music—a beautiful image we held of our far-off paradise. While our dreams lay in the west, we were in snow country far to the east, using up all our savings and everything we could borrow.

Chapter 27

Studies and Salamanders

With the trailer unloaded just before the storm arrived, I helped set up the kids' beds, unpacked until the rain stopped, and then suggested, "It might be smart to go to town immediately and shop for more secondhand furniture before other summer-school students arrive. It would also be nice to have something other than the floor to sleep on, a table, some chairs, and something for the living room like a lamp and sofa. We need to hurry because the most inexpensive stuff will go first."

At that time, the town of State College had few shopping options, but the sun was out and shone on our parade again. Lo and behold, the secondhand store had a fine upright piano for the kids to use; there were dining chairs and a table; a matching couch and chair; and a wonderful, solid wood, antique dresser with a matching bed that had an intricately carved headboard of solid wood. And, at the last minute, I couldn't resist buying two fine etchings of farm scenes in nice frames for a dollar. Everything seemed to be at bargain prices. Maybe it was because we arrived in early June instead of September. The store manager agreed to deliver the furnishings at no cost. What a nice small-town courtesy!

Dan continued to worry about those two foreign-languages tests he had to pass before starting on his doctorate, so he again hired tutors and studied long hours. We both enrolled in summer classes and found part-time jobs in the school library. Dan also began to work in the ag ed department as part of his graduate scholarship responsibilities.

Summer schedules were somewhat involved, because my classes had to be at times when Dan could be home with Nancy and Danny. Since much of Dan's time was spent at home learning the foreign languages, it worked out. I found a piano teacher for the kids, and Nancy joined a Campfire group whose members were girls who would be her classmates in the fall.

Almost-ripe wild blackberries grew everywhere alongside roads not far from town, and there seemed plenty for all who wanted to pick them. With a summer sun and white clouds drifting lazily overhead, and carrying makeshift containers along with all our pots and pans, we happily scratched our arms and legs to harvest the ripe berries for me to freeze. "This isn't a bad way to be doing our one-step-back and two-steps-forward, is it?" I shouted to anyone who was near enough to hear. Foraging for the berries was fun for the children, but, although pleasurable, it was deadly earnest work for me.

During evening hours, fireflies, or lightning bugs, as they are sometimes called, delighted the kids. None of us had ever seen these nocturnal flying beetles before. Some got in the house and ended up in glass jars after the kids danced around on the beds to catch them in their hands. A neighboring student said this was the fireflies' mating season and explained that the male and female fireflies were signaling each other with their neon blinking.

Our main recreation was going to a small lake called Whipple Dam. It was nearby, and there was enough water to swim. Salamanders at the water's edge were an added attraction for the kids. These delicate small amphibians were easy for the kids to catch with their hands. The kids would hold them and contemplate their strangeness—they looked rather like pale lizards. Some other parents, lying nearby on the sand, explained to the children that these creatures don't have scales to cover their bodies so they need to stay where it's damp or wet. "Don't hold them too long, and then set them down carefully where the sand is wet," they advised. Sometimes I wonder if that little lake and the salamanders have survived the many decades since and are still there to delight future generations.

I tried not to let the kids know how concerned Dan and I were when he failed to pass one part of the language requirement the first time he took the exam. In translating from French to English some pages of a research article in his field of agriculture, he had made two or three small mistakes, such as saying something was "little" instead of "minute." But it was only one section of the French test, and the second time, he passed. Before we arrived in Pennsylvania, Dan had started to study German as his second foreign language, but the school decided that Spanish should be Dan's second required language, since "we would soon be living in the west." Spanish is more like French than German, so it seemed like a good choice. Dan hired a Spanish-language tutor and concentrated on learning to read Spanish research magazines and reports. When he passed his exam on the second try, we both slept better and longer—there was no way we could've spent an extra year in graduate school.

Juggling so many different jobs and school in Arizona had prepared us well; after the language exams were out of the way, the school year seemed easy for both of us. For the first time since Dan and I were married, we attended university football games, gymnastic competitions, and basketball games.

Christmas during a snowstorm was exciting, and I bought two used sleds for the campus slopes. Both Dan and I felt some guilt over uprooting the kids so many times, so Danny's intense desire for a Lionel train set for Christmas was fulfilled, and he received a used bicycle for his birthday. Nancy received new dresses and gifts with horse motifs.

Danny and his bicycle had a rough beginning. "Son, you've got pedal power now, but you need brain power, too, so think about potholes, gravel on the road down in front, and cars—especially cars! You must stay on Elm Lane at all times."

The second day Danny went out riding, he was brought back home bloody and tear-stained by a student who lived down at the end of the street; the student's handkerchief was soaked in blood. Danny had tried to turn around in the gravel at full speed.

Time passed quickly, and in late spring all of us drove to a hotel in Washington, DC to meet a dean from Cal Poly and talk with him about a job opening there. Over lunch in the hotel, Dan and the dean discussed the position the school had waiting for him. Dan now had college teaching at Arizona State University to his credit, and soon he would have that doctorate to fatten his resume. These were the proper passports: Cal Poly had a fine position waiting, back in the town where we most wanted to live.

Giddy with delight and relief, we both suddenly looked at each other and my words tumbled out, "Let's goof off and stay another night. Nancy and Danny, we'll take you to see the White House, where the President lives, and if there's time, maybe the place where they make the money in a town not far away. We'll even go where President George Washington lived." Stress, uncertainty, and worry floated away during those wonderful two days. Maybe we wouldn't be aimless tumbleweeds after all.

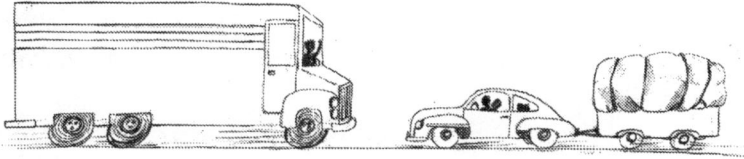

Chapter 28

Hit the Trail

It was time to leave. At the advanced ages of thirty-four and thirty-three, Dan and I finally possessed the official certificates of our new degrees. Dan's was the key to open the door to California. I wasn't sure we'd learned much, but the degrees made possible all that followed.

After placing a short ad in the local paper, I was dumbfounded to be overrun with buyers for our student-priced furniture. The piano, dining room and living room sets, and the double bed all went for much more than we had paid for them when we had arrived. Well-used snow-country clothing—boots, rubbers, wooly caps, warm jackets, and coats—all went for almost-new prices. Everything sold within a couple of days.

Once again, we found a huge, long, rental trailer to hook up to the bumper hitch of the car, but this trailer had no roof at all. We filled the empty deep-freeze with clothes and books, in case rain got under the new canvas tarp; then, we packed some of the State College treasures acquired during this short period. Danny was allowed to pack his new Lionel train and tracks plus his secondhand bike, and I packed two lovely etchings of farm country I'd found in the back corner of a used furniture store. As usual, whether needed or not, we filled many boxes with all the textbooks we'd studied.

The trailer, when it was finally loaded, really looked somewhat like pictures of the horse-powered wagons that rolled west in pioneering days. Our big wagon was covered with heavy-duty, cream-colored canvas. The load was much higher than the sides of the trailer, and the canvas cover had to be thoroughly tied down with lots of rope over the load. It was a cumbersome Conestoga wagon in size; but this was freight, not for the frontier, but for a still rather small college town in California. I just hoped it weighed less and would be pulled more easily than our eastbound trailer.

"Dan, we're making a circle, and you know what happens to people who go in circles." It all seemed a bit odd, geographically. To get to California, not far from where our trail had begun, we were completing a circle around much of the country.

I marked maps in red and showed the one of the whole country to the kids. Danny immediately disliked the route, or pretended to. "Why can't we go on a straight road? The sun goes straight, and you said we are going from where the sun comes up out to where the sun goes down." I explained about towns growing up along rivers, how roads connect towns, and that cars can't go straight up over high mountains.

Nancy wanted a horse the day we would arrive. "No, kiddo, we can't get a horse right away. Dad and I will have to rent a house for us in town at first; then we have to sell our house in Tempe. After that, you can help me find a little farm that's fenced for a horse."

Well before dawn, with the gigantic trailer hitched behind us, we pulled out and headed out toward our vision of valleys, mountains beside the ocean, and a new farm with horses. Again, it was my job to read the maps, especially when we were in towns and cities. I kept close tabs on the gas tank and tried to spot filling stations for rest stops and gas. Since the freezer was full of clothes and books, I had only packed sandwiches for one day and one dinner, but we stayed in motels where I could serve fruit, cold cereal, and cookies, and heat canned food. Choosing the right motel was difficult because motels weren't as plentiful in those early years as now. I had to aim for places that were clean, cheap, and had room for a trailer. As soon after 3 PM as we found these conditions, we stopped and checked in.

In San Luis Obispo, the college personnel officer had found a new house for us to rent, one that had recently been purchased by a faculty member as an investment. "What wonderful luck to have a house waiting," Dan and I reminded each other over and over again. We unloaded our belongings quickly as soon as we arrived, because we had paid for the use of the big four-wheel trailer for only three more days, and we still needed to make a long trip to Tempe Arizona and back. With no funds left to live on, every penny counted.

After several hours of sleep, we locked the door to the house in San Luis Obispo at about 3 AM and headed back to Arizona with the trailer to get our houseful of furniture and to give a listing to a broker to sell the Tempe house. On the way, we drove Nancy and Danny to Lake Arrowhead to stay with our friends Grace and Fred.

It was well over a hundred in Tempe the day we were there, and neither the car nor our now unrented, empty house had an air-conditioning system. I had phoned a friend who lived next door to our house to ask her to find us a couple of students who would work with us and load the rest of our belongings—garden tools, a roll of fencing, the piano, the battered old furniture in the living room, dining room, and two of the three bedrooms, the kitchen appliances, and all the rest of the linens, dishes, pots, and pans, plus the five black trunks. There was no dog to reclaim, as the kind family who had adopted Heidi for the time we were away had not been able to save her when she'd had a stroke.

As the frantic packing and loading progressed in the burning heat, there was neither time nor energy to contemplate the many years we'd lived and worked on little patches of land in that Salt River Valley, the warm nights with a huge moon and a sea of stars, the days with so many animals, the earlier years at the University of Arizona, and all the rest. The next "gig" would begin the next day in the different world of Central California. Cool mist and fog would roll in on many evenings, and there would be wonderful winter rains to make the land green. I hoped the children would develop the same love we held for the nearby mountains, valleys, seashore, and ocean.

Still with no sleep, we covered the gigantic load with the tarps, tied it down with many feet of clothesline rope, and headed back to San Bernardino, where we stopped to try and sleep in a motel. Totally spent and aching all over, we did not have time to sleep, and time on the use of the trailer was running out. We left the loaded trailer beside the office of the motel, drove up to the north shore of Lake Arrowhead, picked up the still dazed and weary kids, and went back down the mountain to hitch up the trailer.

It was way after midnight. While the kids slept, Dan and I kept on going—all the way through Los Angeles and up Highway 101. I watched Dan's driving every second through scratchy, burning eyes that kept trying to close. That effort saved our lives. Near the town of Santa Maria, a big semitruck barreled down the highway toward us, and Dan, even with his eyes open, sitting up very straight, and with both hands on the steering wheel, started crossing over the center line just as we approached the semi. I yelled and started to grab the wheel, but in an instant he was awake and focused, and he turned the station wagon and our mammoth load back to the right-side lane just in the nick of time. The deep blast of the truck's horn, coming too late to have helped, and the terrible closeness of the rig's long side, seemed to push wind and the echoing sound of the truck's horn against our car, even for a second or two after the truck had hurtled past. It was a nightmarish scene I'll never forget.

When we reached the new house, it was too close to dawn for us to go to bed, and, moreover, none of the beds were put together or made up. With no gas or electricity on yet, I prepared a cold breakfast, and some Cal Poly students arrived to help us unload this second mountain of belongings. We were a couple of hours late in returning the trailer, but there was no extra charge. Rushing so frantically to meet that turn-in deadline and to avoid further charges on the trailer was probably the most penny-wise and pound-foolish thing we had ever done.

Chapter 29

Are We There Yet?

After laboring and yearning for so many years to reach this exact destination, I was almost too tired to rejoice. Still, it seemed like old times: we were back in California just about as far west as we could go, with the Pacific Ocean about ten miles away, and, even in a tract rental house, I felt it was home. Only a block or two away from the house was Terrace Hill, with its fall coat of yellow oats, grasses, weeds, and brush growing wild. Other mountains and hills were close by and within hiking distance for the children.

The central coast of California, halfway between Los Angeles and San Francisco, is bisected by the Santa Lucia Mountains going north and south at the eastern edge of the town of San Luis Obispo. Highway 101 goes through town, then climbs steeply up Cuesta Grade and over the crest of those mountains to what is called the North County. Over the grade, days are often warmer and nights colder. North County towns like Paso Robles with its County Fair grounds, and Atascadero

and Santa Margarita with their small lakes and fenced-in range and pasture lands were still very western in appearance, and were surrounded
by cattle ranches, grain crops, and fields of alfalfa near the Salinas river-
bed. The county had a huge and diverse amount of agriculture (although
vineyards have become increasingly prevalent in recent years). Both in
the coastal areas and the inland valleys, many people worked on farms,
ranches, and in agricultural businesses. The college also reflected this
emphasis with its many agricultural departments.

Also over the mountains and going more or less from north to south
in the county is the famous San Andreas Fault, a much-studied large
earthquake fault that runs for seven hundred miles through the state.

On the other side of the still delightfully small college town of San
Luis Obispo, strung out one after the other like beads on a necklace, are
the Morros—nine large volcanic plugs, the last one being Morro Rock,
northwest at the town of Morro Bay. Our rented house in town was not far
from the most southerly peak, called Islay Hill, and we would buy our first
farm just a couple of fields away from the third morro in the chain, called
Bishop's Peak. Like several of the other morros, Bishop's Peak was laced
with trails made by town youngsters, rather than by cattle or deer; these
trails would be good but not too difficult climbing for Nancy and Danny.

Near the volcanic peaks are several valleys, with names such as the
Edna Valley, the Chorro Valley, and the Los Osos Valley. Just a few miles
farther west are eighty-five miles of county coastline beside the mighty
Pacific Ocean. Sprinkled about the county are some two dozen wonderful small towns. When we arrived, there was little urban sprawl, and
each of these small towns was quite unique, with lots of charm.

The ocean was always special, whether placid as a lake under a summer sun, or with white caps and booming waves under the heavy clouds
of a winter rainstorm. Somewhat to the southwest was Avila Beach,
which quickly became our most frequent destination. It was a pictur-
esque seaside village with two piers and a headland to the west that made
a somewhat sheltered harbor for boats and also protected the swimming
beach from some of the ocean breezes.

Other coastal towns were also special and received many tourists,
along with seasonal renters and full-time owners. On the North Coast

was the town of Morro Bay with its Morro Rock, as already mentioned, and beyond it Cambria, with its many artists and galleries. Up the coast, near San Simeon, was Hearst Castle, one of the biggest attractions, and perhaps the hugest and most ornate private home ever built in the country. The rooms and gardens were filled with art treasures from Europe: statues, paintings, furniture, tapestries, antiques, and carved ceilings and doors. Guides describe how the castle was built by William Randolph Hearst, and they tell about the famous movie stars and other celebrities who once visited it. The castle was part of a ranch of a quarter of a million acres, and it looks out over miles of coastline. In the years ahead, we sometimes took visitors from other parts of the country and world to visit the castle, with all its ostentatious beauty, art, gardens, pools, architecture, and views.

To the south of San Luis Obispo there was the small seaside town of Pismo Beach, with famous miles of sand dunes and the well known Pismo clams that were plentiful back then. A few miles farther south, Arroyo Grande spread out a few miles inland from the ocean. Once a stagecoach station, Arroyo Grande also had a western feel, with a big feed store on the main road through town. Farther inland, Lopez Lake was a popular vacation destination.

The local college, affectionately called "Cal Poly," had also become well known, due to its special methods of education. Now called California State Polytechnic University, it began in 1902 as a small vocational school, with the goal of "teaching the hand as well as the head," or of having the students "learn by doing." It gradually grew to be somewhat like a junior college, and then became a four-year college on a spread of six thousand acres. Later on, graduate programs were added. The school became co-ed in 1956.

The early emphasis at Cal Poly was on agriculture. The School of Agriculture had departments such as dairy, poultry, sheep, livestock, animal husbandry, a horse unit, crops, and horticulture. There was a rodeo arena, and there were specialty courses in horseshoeing. Over the years, the college expanded with other specialty departments and areas such as engineering, architecture, business, and computer science, and, with Dan's arrival, an Agriculture Business Management Department.

Decades later, the school now has a strong liberal arts program and is gradually losing some of the emphasis on having the students work with their hands, although there is still a strong component of practical experience mixed with general education.

I immediately had this whole glorious county to comb for the right area for us. Could I locate a farming area that would be a quick and easy drive to the campus, to the junior and senior high schools, the hospital, and the main shopping area? The farm would have to be, once again, in a slow-lane, rural area, with no imminent possibility of being engulfed by the town's expansion. There's a saying that "Money can't buy happiness." In our case, money would have helped. While I felt a gnawing impatience to buy a place, nothing could be purchased until the house in Tempe sold. Still, I began looking.

Chapter 30

No Slow SLO

San Luis Obispo was supposed to be populated with slow, relaxed people, people who savored good living, a mild climate, mountains, sea, trees, and a lack of big-city rush hours. Many abbreviated the town's name and lifestyle to "SLO" and pronounced it "Slow." I gathered these folk had time to play cards, hike, fish, golf, barbeque, and read books. They probably went to concerts, plays, lectures, and college ballgames. We arrived with no money and no slow.

Lack of money was a great incentive to find alternative and fast ways to feed us, because once again we were teetering on the brink of serious hunger and empty wallets. With Dan's teaching contract and the unsold Tempe house we had only owned for about two years, our only assets, we went together to our new bank, explained who we were, and asked for a loan. The bank squeezed out a small personal loan to us on the strength of Dan's job, but the rent, the utilities, the kids' school clothes, and a few bags of groceries gobbled those funds up in short order.

The clock was ticking; there was no time to savor the area and my new show. Gung-ho to make progress, my immediate pressing need, one more time, was for food—we would need to live off the land. Choosing a garden plot between our home and the house next door, I gathered up my pick, mattock, shovel, and hoe. As in Tucson, the earth was almost like cement. The road repair people talked about it as "red rock," while others called it "caliche." Next to our house, the soil was cream-colored, but it was still the caliche that was often mined and spread on the dirt roads of the county to make them harder and less muddy when it rained.

Without fertilizer and without much water, that non-loam, rocky soil grew beets, carrots, chard, lettuce, onions, and radishes unbelievably fast. A college psychology prof and his wife lived next door, and I'm not sure they ever understood their crazy neighbors, especially the pick-and-shovel lady who made vegetables grow in what looked like rock. That couple and their daughter came to see us the other day, and, many decades later, they still remember our way of life at that point as not only ludicrous, but also unbelievably poor. The wife claims she even left a bag of groceries at my back door at one point. Maybe she did.

But, like the hobos who sometimes hiked up a nearby hill from the train tracks near town, I was working for food. "Lady, I'll work for food," they'd tell me, and I understood. I was doing the same thing, and I had already done it in Arizona.

It was a time of Indian summer, a period of summerlike heat that comes during the fall. This kind of weather came often in the central part of California. I loved those words, "Indian summer." Putting off winter always seemed a good idea, even here, where rains usually arrived in the winter months, and the average rainfall was only about twenty inches. Most years, the land needed all the rain it could get.

On those special fall days, the kids went to school nearby in short sleeves and left their sweaters at home. Several weekends we went to swim or fish from the public piers at Avila and Pismo Beach. Nights turned cooler, but the sun shone hot and bright, and there was more of a quiet, waiting feel to the land than there had been in the Salt River Valley, where short, heavy rains might arrive suddenly in late summer.

By Christmas day, I managed to serve a dinner of canned creamed tuna on toast, as the main course, with a hodgepodge of vegetables from my side-of-the-house garden, along with a homemade apple pie. Only the kids received gifts: a horse currycomb, horse brush, horse rope, and rope halter for Nancy, and a bicycle basket and a bedside radio for Danny.

While others were worrying about the country's overall cost of living and the inflation rate, we had our own version of increasing expenses.

I took the two courses I needed to get a secondary school teaching certificate in California, but then I was informed that I lacked one unit of student-teaching credit. When the State Department of Education insisted I'd have to do my student teaching all over again just to get that one unit, it suddenly seemed to make more sense for us if I raised the kids and Dan brought home the bacon.

Things were looking up, though; the Tempe house sold in Arizona, and some friends wanted us to take their dog. An animal! The kids wanted a TV, but I wanted a dog.

"Give us a break, Mom. Everyone in this whole neighborhood has a TV. Everyone but us. We'll still practice the piano and do homework. Please? There's nothing to do around here."

And I replied, "It's not 'nothing' outside or inside the house—the whole neighborhood, the nearby hills, and you and your new friends all are full of thousands of things to do. Figure it out."

It was a good thing we were the last family in the block, or even the whole subdivision, to get a TV. When Dan and I finally gave in a year later and bought a secondhand floor-model TV, I learned those sets sell "gimmes," "got-to-gets," and a whole new diet of "yummies" in all sizes, shapes, and flavors, triple-wrapped and boxed. The commercials intrigued our deprived kids more than the programs did, and their heads filled with endless want-lists. I held a strong suspicion that the more they got, the more they'd want. How would I ever manage them when they became teenagers, even in a time of relative prosperity in our house? "Kids, you'll have to have real money in your piggy banks if you order that stuff. How much have you saved?"

For Christmas that year, Nancy got only a cheap Mexican saddle, with a blanket and a bridle. When we heard that we could buy a saddle and bridle for almost nothing if we went across the Mexican border, we decided to mix a shopping trip with an educational excursion for the children to see another country. We drove down to Ensenada, about sixty miles beyond the border town of Tijuana, and drove home the following day with the tack.

Back home, I located a sawhorse to drape the saddle over, and it stayed in the living room as long as we lived in the rental house. Nancy's horse fever rose higher and higher; she often got a school book and sat there in the saddle, reading and invariably looking up with a solemn and sad face every time I walked by, obviously hoping that I noticed she was still dreaming of a real live horse for that saddle. Not even Bud, a nearby neighbor who whistled or knocked at the door to see if she could play, took her mind off horses. I felt bad for her, and I felt even worse when she didn't object if I told Bud she still had to practice the piano or walk the dog.

Other times, Nancy did more than hint. "Mom, you said I could get a horse when we got here. Well, we're here, Here, HERE!"

"Sure, hon, but I did say we had to find a place in the country for it. The Tempe house had to sell first. It just closed escrow on Monday, so I can begin to look for property."

The Tempe house brought only enough money for a very small down payment on a farm, but it was high time to begin looking. As in Arizona, and like Nancy, I didn't make a career of patience. I was off and running. Some of our new friends seemed to be just drifting through their thirties, while I shuddered at the thought of being even one day older: birthdays weren't celebrations, they were horrible alarm bells. I dropped Dan off at the college most mornings, and, with Nancy and Danny safely in school, I combed the countryside, on the lookout for signs of farms for sale.

Chapter 31

Treve

"Want a great dog?" I didn't hear that question nearly as often as I heard, "Want a lovely cat?" Word had gotten around school and town that we were looking for a place in the country—out where pets could roam free, and any dog or cat, or even a hamster, would have a good home. I don't know if city life is more stressful, with more people moving, divorcing, dying, graduating, or getting landlords who won't allow pets, but those of us who lived rurally surely got more than our share of animals needing homes. Sport's owners were moving to another state and into an apartment that didn't take dogs, and they wanted us to take Sport.

This new dog, arriving before the horse or TV, would turn out to be a treasure. Since I usually acted first and thought things through later, I saw no reason not to take this beautiful ranch dog a few months—or even a year—early. Our backyard was fenced, and the family members voted unanimously to give this dog a home when his young owners brought him over to meet us. I didn't mention it, but the one thing that I would not give a home to was his name.

He seemed a mix of many breeds, but I guessed part collie and part golden retriever might describe him, or perhaps he had some German shepherd ancestry. His face was less thin than a collie's. He had floppy brown ears, bright, dark brown eyes, and a thick ruff of white hair around a happy face. Suffice it to say he was immediately accepted as a member of the family. It was so good to have a dog with us again.

I'd grown up with many dogs, and my dad had always said, "Mongrels are the best; they usually come with a more natural shape and have more brains, more vigor, and better health as a result of the crossbreeding." I had believed him. In fact, aren't people mongrels of various nationalities and races if their ancestry is traced back far enough? This collie/retriever was a prince among dogs, and the words "mutt" or "mongrel" didn't even come to mind as all of us met him at the door. He seemed to have great dignity, yet an equally great desire for fun and laughter. When I laughed the day we met, he seemed to almost grin back at me with pleasure.

Soon after the owners introduced Sport to us, the children wanted him to go out to play with them in the yard. Eagerly, the happy-go-lucky fellow followed them out to the lawn and retrieved balls, had a game of tug-of-war with a jump rope, and then seemed to ask, "What's next?" Of course, the dog didn't know that when the couple drove off without him he would have a new home.

A few more days of tennis ball games on the lawn, and we decided to name him Treve, shortened from "Retrieve." As our only pet that year while searching for a ranch home, Treve became a super dog, for, just like kids, pets need lots of attention, and they need to be taken to see the world, to hear lots of talk, and to be around people or other animals of their kind. They become smart in the process. However, Treve had a head start: his IQ was in the stratosphere compared to our Arizona dogs Cindy and Heidi (though Cindy to a lesser extent). And, after living with the earlier dogs, it was plain flattering to enjoy Treve's love and adoration as he seriously began to carefully guard the house and each of us in our mundane life.

While numerous dogs pine for former owners, and a few go long spells in a kennel or a new home refusing to eat and worrying about what could have happened to their previous families, others just seem to believe in living for the moment and, if given lots of fun and hugs, soon find happiness with new owners. The first week or two Treve often went to the screen door and looked out, obviously with some questions and worries in his mind about his former owners, but, at such times, I gave him a bite to eat and some hugs while telling him what a good home he had. Treve was about three years old, but we were told he had been part of at least two other families in his short life.

Somehow, Treve sized up his situation quickly and began to live with us like an old friend or family member. While I knew little about his former life, it didn't matter, for soon we were involved in a mutual love affair. After Dan and the kids left for school, it was easier to sit down with a steaming cup of coffee, and, with Treve at my feet, consider the dog's fine points. I assured him over and over again what a great pooch he was, but I still wondered if he missed his former home. I was expecting a third child—would Treve be good to a new baby?

Our subdivision certainly seemed a safe area for both dogs and kids, with neighbors who were friendly and a number who had children. Parents drove the streets slowly, keeping on the lookout for kids, dogs, and cats. Even the school, a few blocks away, had an informal, friendly, and supportive atmosphere.

On the day after the evening that Doug, our new baby, was born, Danny's and Nancy's teachers and a crowd of their students ran out to the car to ask about the baby when Dad drove the children to school. One teacher then wrote the statistics of Douglas Graham Chase's weight and time of delivery on a corner of the blackboard, while she had students draw pictures and write messages to Baby Doug and me. One teacher laughed and reported that Danny had written more about Treve, his new dog, than he had about his new baby brother. This wasn't a country school, but the feelings there were small-town and caring.

From the day the baby came home, Treve was extremely curious about him, and soon seemed to feel that Doug was really his puppy and in need of lots of attention. Because of their ancestry, dogs have a sense of being part of a pack, and having a lead or top dog. This dog seemed to show he'd accept Dan and me as co-leaders, but he obviously tried to be next in line to help me raise and keep track of all three kids.

Treve cocked his head and listened and watched for the kids to walk in the door from school. When the kids came home from school they were always happy and laughing to see a dog impatiently watching for them from a window. With his size and enthusiasm, Treve became a whole welcoming committee of one, acting as though the children had been away for months, and, barking excitedly, almost knocked them down with his rough-and-tumble antics. The dog also quickly figured out that the family wasn't complete until Dan's car turned into the carport in the evening. This was a talking dog, and by the second week he barked a greeting for each arrival.

Since the dog was allowed in the kitchen, he always came in to lie down on the floor in the late afternoons. There, he would listen, pant, and watch all of us with love and intense interest. Treve was a good teacher and made me realize that I, too, needed to take more time to let the kids see me really seeing them and listening to them.

The dog's mood also seemed to reflect the mood of the family. He recognized and believed in laughter and was quick to become lively and hope for some fun game. Not even the aroma of roasting meat brought him running to us faster than hearing some chuckles. Perhaps it signaled to him that all was right in his world.

At first I had no playpen or buggy for Baby Doug, so I placed him on a blanket on the living room carpet for part of the day. Treve remained near Doug after the rest of the family left for school, and often he would lick not only the baby's tears, but his whole face. Doggy-germs never seemed to cause any harm. Although Treve was a male, he soon became my assistant nanny and took to his post most willingly. Yet he was invariably relieved, wagging his tail and smiling, each time I came to check on the two of them.

The older children decided to teach Treve some tricks. Being kindly and wanting to please, he would have learned them, but I asked the kids, as I had asked them years before when we got a cat, "Would you want to roll over for a cracker or lie down and play dead every time I told you to? Would you want to shake my hand every time I said 'Shake'? Let's not insist our animals do such foolish things."

"Well, can we take him up to the top of Terrace Hill?"

To that, I gladly agreed. "Sure, he'd love to go. He wants to be a brother, a pal, and also keep you safe. But you have to keep him on a leash at first and keep him safe, too. Eventually, you can turn him loose up there." I had a feeling this dog knew a bit of what I was saying. At the least, he knew it involved him, and I was talking in terms that might involve fun or agreeable restraints. Later I asked, "Nancy, do you think he leads you on the hikes, or does he know you are taking him?"

Nancy stated firmly, "I'm the one taking Treve." I wasn't so sure, for he shared some of my claustrophobic feelings in the house, except when all the family was home. He was happiest out on Terrace Hill, with breezes blowing through his hair. Still, he was territorial and loyal to the family, so he almost always remained near the house except when he was out with the children.

Who let the dog out? Treve only disappeared probably half a dozen times while we lived on South Street, but it always scared me to death. This dog was a wanderer at heart and came to know every inch of Terrace Hill. Like most dogs, he had a keen sense of smell, and he tracked, with nose close to the ground, the trails of small critters through the tall and tangled maze of wild oats, the low weeds, and the brush. The hill eventually had countless trails where the oats had been flattened by Nancy, Danny, and other neighborhood kids taking weekend hikes up its face from their homes in the subdivision. Treve tried to go with them as soon as they stepped out the door; his main dilemmas were deciding which child to follow if they went in different directions and how to round them up when I rang a loud bell for them to come home.

Treve was also intent on giving paws-on-clean-clothes affection. There was often mud on Terrace Hill through the rainy season, and he usually came home dripping wet and muddy. I believe his muddy affection was his way of suggesting, "Isn't this water and mud great? Come out and play in it!" Anyone who has walked a dog near a lake, stream, or ocean has experienced his dog shaking water on him. When a pooch gets soaking wet, he wants you to enjoy it and to share his wetness. But mention a bath, or get out the bottle of dog shampoo, and a dog will cringe and flee, as though water through a hose or in a bathtub is unbearable torture.

Like neurotic Cindy and unemotional Heidi, Treve came free, but our luck had turned—he was the first of a number of healthy mutts, full of happiness or sadness, spirit, fun, love, and loyalty. He had common sense as well as intelligence, and somehow we seemed to communicate without speaking. His great qualities made me think that maybe people also needed a bit of mutt breeding, and maybe this was why so many Americans, being a little bit of this and a little bit of that, became a sturdy race in their country.

Giving love brought love, and, in all ways, Treve became part of the family. The kids had a dog that could love, teach, and change them. His adoring eyes and capacity to care for and to protect them seemed to remind them to be more patient and caring—thus I decided not to notice the cookies and bites of apple they gave him. Both children sensed his dependency upon them for food and fun, and they usually kept him with them whenever they played with friends in the neighborhood or on the hill.

Treve was also an ego-builder: his appreciation of the kids was unlimited and helpful when I was too busy to be with them. The kids often sat with him to talk over hurts and successes from a day in school. With their young arms around his shoulders, he stayed on the steps beside them, listening as they talked. Clearly, he was tactfully letting them know, "By Jove, you're completely right about that! I not only understand your feelings, but I love you no matter what happened in school today."

Love isn't love without honesty, and both children knew this dog was honest. With equal honesty, they felt the same about him. Might we all be as fine a being as this dog, who made the house more of a home and actually taught humanity to humans. Schooled by Treve, all of us learned more about caring, maintaining loyalty, being a true friend, and always carrying positive, happy thoughts.

Chapter 32

In the Valley of the Bears

As I had done in the past, without the help of a Realtor, I continued to search for a small, subsistence-type farm. I'm not sure why I avoided Realtors. Probably, I thought I could just read ads in the paper or find a homemade sign tacked to a stake on some mini-farm. This "dream farm" had to be near the college and the town, yet rural and affordable.

First Farm in California would also have to cost a very small nugget of California gold, because we'd paid very little down on the house in Tempe and had owned it such a short time. The new place couldn't be much better than the first one on Fowler Lane. Once again the possibility of finding one—especially one that could provide for a horse—seemed almost nonexistent.

Exhausted, I fretted and reported to Dan, "It's a puzzlement—this trail of our choosing is surely a zigzag process! I've gone back again and again to the few streets with small parcels and old houses, and there's not one FOR SALE sign."

"Yeah, I'm sorry it's so hard," Dan replied, "but someone will eventually want to move. If we'd gone in a straight line, we'd have gotten here too fast. Think of the sights and fun we'd have missed along the way."

As with the Arizona places, the farm also had to be chosen with a wary eye on the growth of San Luis Obispo. If I guessed wrong, the farm could disappear almost overnight and become surrounded by gas stations, warehouses, or tract houses—all in the name of consolidation or progress. I often recalled an elderly prof at UCLA who had been around the campus for many years and who remembered the beautiful fields of hay which had grown where the campus later developed. However, he seemed to regret lost chances for real estate wealth more than the loss of waving fields of grain.

Finally, on O'Connor Way, a seldom-used back road to the community junior college, I discovered a new homemade sign on a fencepost: FOR SALE—EIGHT ACRES. There was a phone number, and, written in smaller letters, the injunction, "Do Not Disturb Tenants!" There were only a few other small farms or houses on lots along the road, and it seemed as if the town probably wouldn't spread out to this part of the Los Osos Valley for years. I parked on the side of the road and tried to see all I could.

In the middle of a stark field of weeds sat a plain, alien-looking, wooden-framed house, with a green asphalt roof and small, push-up-and-down wooden windows. It appeared to be about a hundred years old, and it had obviously just been moved to the middle of this parcel of land. It didn't seem to be anchored there: no trees or shrubs to soften its appearance, and no long porch where I might kick back in a rocker or where all the family members might gather to chat on warm nights. The porch on this place was about a yard square, and made of concrete to match the steps.

The narrow house looked as though it had been built to squeeze between other houses on some small city lot. It would always miss its old neighborhood, where other houses snuggled up close on both sides, but some trees and shrubbery would make it look more inviting. Renovating another old house would also keep me fit—and, likely, in a fit. There was no garage, barn, corral, or even a clothesline in sight.

However, the whole property had good barbed wire fencing, mostly hidden in the tall brush and weeds around the boundaries, plus a one-car-wide, rutted dirt road leading back to the house. With no red-rock or caliche surface on that narrow lane, cars would sink in the mud when it rained; I would have to order at least two dump-truck loads of red-rock or gravel before winter.

Whoever had planted the house there must have feared floods, for it had been placed on a strangely high foundation, with several steep steps leading up to the front door. The house wouldn't flood, but it looked like it was prepared to move again, and it probably wanted to. A mover could just put rollers under it, with no lifting necessary, and go on down the road.

Since Baby Doug had to be with me on all my prospecting for a farm, he was the only audience for my thoughts, so I informed him, "What nice crawl space this house has for fixing broken pipes, frayed electrical wires, and rotten floors. You know what? I've just found your home, and once again this place at first will be a 'Why-in-the-world-land?' to others and a fine 'Wonderland' to me."

I rushed home to phone the owner, and later I reported to Dan, "Bingo! I've just discovered our next farm, though the price needs some hard negotiation. Mr. Johnson is really anxious to sell, and he can meet us at his home at six tonight. You'd better go see it before then—right now would be best."

When we drove up, Dan commented, "It's OK, I guess, and I admit it's perhaps a small step up from your first house, but I'd say you'll be starting off at the bottom all over again. A new beginning, with more Spartan living, huh? Can you take this kind of challenge another time, town girl?"

"Sure. In just these few hours, I've programmed myself to stay the course and see what happens next. It's no resort, but neither is it slum living when the house sits all alone in a sea of golden weeds. The sign is here, so we're predestined to move in. The chances are about one in a million that I can find another such place for sale, and certainly, there hasn't been any other one that can match this one for size, location, and, probably, price. Sure, it's exactly the same scenario as on Fowler Lane." Again, I thought, no storybook cottage, no trees, brooks, white fences, or barn, yet I acted as though the land would all go at a garage sale the next day if we didn't buy it that night. What do they say about great oaks growing from little acorns? I would plant some acorns!

The meeting with the seller was hard for all of us. The down payment Mr. Johnson wanted was more than we had. He was still upset, because he had bought the eight acres and had the house moved to the vacant land as a surprise wedding gift to his daughter and new son-in-law. Thinking that they would be thrilled at the chance to make a beginning there, he had not consulted them beforehand.

The young couple had turned down both this gift and his help. Some folks just aren't country people, and some think they have to start right out with white fences, big homes, beautiful barns, and green fields. Or perhaps the couple just wanted to start making their own decisions and do things their way. Whatever the young couple's reasons, Mr. Johnson was stuck with a property that he didn't want to keep.

Then, here we came, not reaching for the stars, but for land—unable to hide our love for the whole forlorn place, and thrilled at the thought of getting a farm-in-the-making—the passport to once again have animals and a rural life.

After we made it clear that we couldn't quite pay his asking price, and explained to him about our limited funds, Mr. Johnson did some hemming and hawing, looked us both over again and again, perhaps to be sure we sincerely wanted his white elephant, then completely changed his mind. He would sell the farm to us for the price we offered, and he would accept the low amount we had offered as a down payment. He even appeared to suddenly accept the sincerity of our passion for the land, and my desperate feelings about wanting to live there and improve the place. He actually tried to help us further by suggesting a generously long payment schedule and a low interest rate on the remaining balance.

Mr. Johnson explained that the house was rented to a family whose child was quite ill, so we couldn't go onto the property or into the house. He told us that the house had three bedrooms and a separate dining room, and that there was a hookup for a washer.

"That's all right," I said, "We'll go ahead and buy it. We don't need to drive up the lane or see inside the house. There's not even any need for us to go home to sleep on this decision. We can say we'll buy it right here and now." I did wonder to myself, how can there be three bedrooms, a dining room, a living room, and a back porch for a washer? All the rooms must be doll-size, because that looks like one very small house.

Bingo! In this manner, without ever stepping on the land or seeing inside the house before escrow closed, we moved in as soon as Mr. Johnson's renters moved out. The rooms were indeed small, but sensibly placed, and the house seemed solid. It would keep us warm with a fine gas floor furnace, and no valley wind would sneak in around the tightly made doors and windows. Still, I sensed that the house and land were keeping some secrets.

With not even a day to make inquiries about this acreage, we also saw no surveys or maps, and no percolation test results on the water supply. We hadn't even checked out the neighboring area, talked to any neighbors, or researched county documents about easements, restrictions, or plans for the future. We hadn't even turned on a faucet or stepped on the land until it was ours. The question of "When would another chance come?" dictated our haste. A go-ahead chance never seemed to come often or easily, but when one did, I tried to grab it with all my might and conviction, whether it was getting college degrees, buying ugly First Farm, having a third child after nine years without conceiving, or now, acquiring a new home and perhaps one last baby. Dreams still do come true if one never gives up or lets an opportunity float away, no matter how many rocks and turns on the trail.

From this property, it would be a drive of only eight to ten minutes for Dan to reach the college. In back of the house sat Bishop's Peak, one of the area's peaks or hills that were of volcanic origin. I had read that the name of this peak was chosen by the mission padres because the outline of the top of the hill seemed similar to the shape of a bishop's headdress.

Since the hill was only a short hike away, it would be fun for Treve and the kids to hike to the top and sit on the granite boulders to picnic and view their world. This peak is higher than the others, and on a clear day, from the top, we might see the Oceano dunes, Morro Rock, and even the pine-covered hills of Cambria. We were told that quarrying on our side of the peak had furnished rock for the local Presbyterian church, the breakwater at Avila Beach, and several private houses.

With the first trailer load of furniture parked out front, I rested on the front steps, laughing to myself about this new reality: a tiny house set in a big, primitive landscape, not on top of a hill or mountain, but in a fine valley, and with our own ranch spread of eight whole acres— all the way to the barbed wire fences! Would this be a permanent farm, or another stop on the way? Sure, the house had its faults, it needed work, and it came with a big mortgage, but I was certain of the changes I could make. The house could be enlarged and given a veranda. Surrounding the house could be plantings of trees, lawns, and a garden. A barn could be built out behind the house. In addition to the children, a big family of fat, happy animals could again be a part of our life. We would have a foothold, a clean slate to start over on, and Nancy could at last get a horse!

As Dan remarked, the house and the land were better than our pathetic First Farm in Arizona. The house was larger—instead of two rooms, this house had six. The mortgage was larger, too, and way over our budget. At first, we would barely keep our heads above water. Whereas in Arizona there had been just flat land stretching to the horizon, here there were the Irish Hills across the Los Osos Valley to the west, and beautiful Bishop's Peak not far behind the back fence line on the east side. However, like the first farmhouse in Arizona, it had only one bathroom and no barns or corrals. And, like in Arizona, there were no trees on this property. On the number of minutes required for Dan to get to work, I guessed the desolate First Farm was ahead by a half a mile. Probably, the water supply would once again be undependable and inadequate. Irrigation water had eventually come to our land in Arizona, but this place seemed destined to only be "dry-land farmed." My tools would still be only a shovel, hoe, rake, mattock, and paintbrush.

In the Los Osos Valley, even more than at our places in Arizona, I sensed ghosts of the past. "Los Osos" means "The Bears." Large numbers of huge, shaggy grizzly bears with long claws and powerful jaws full of teeth once roamed the Valley. Indians, too, were once numerous in this lovely area. For thousands of years, the Chumash had lived here, but they hadn't been farmers. When San Luis Obispo was settled in the late 1700s by Spanish missionaries, they brought in livestock and planted corn, beans, grapes, and grain, along with Christianity. Their missions developed vast herds of cattle and horses, but hay and feed weren't normally stored, and in the 1860s, there was a severe drought and the cattle starved. Many were shot for their hides, and the carcasses were left on the land where they were shot.

This valley, which had seen the passing of the bears, and of the Chumash, and then of the vast herds of mission cattle, seemed to still resonate with the memory of them. The very old but sturdy house, too, had a past, but one we'd probably never discover. Where did the house's first family go when they stepped out the front door for an evening in the little town of San Luis Obispo maybe a hundred years ago?

I began my chores that first morning after moving in, and immediately I got my first big shock. I rushed to phone Dan with the news: "You know the saying 'You never miss water 'til the well runs dry?' Well, there's a big problem. I'll joke and say the seller never told us the 'hole' truth, but it's no joking matter. I did the dishes, and I've spent the rest of the morning trying to get enough water to do my wash. The little well's no good!" On a farm, what a difference water can make! As the resident groundskeeper, I suddenly realized why the neighboring houses lacked green lawns, gardens, and large trees.

I hung a sign on the door to the bathroom reading, "TAKE TURNS—ONLY FLUSH WHEN FULL." After some quick and intense deliberations, we took what was often considered to be an ignorant and superstitious step—we hired a dowser, or water witcher. The well produced only about two gallons an hour, and we couldn't see why one spot could be better than another for water, since all the properties on the right side of the road, including ours, were almost flat, with only a slight rise in the direction of Bishop's Peak. Yet when I looked at the surrounding hills of brush, I had to conclude, "There has to be some runoff from the rain, and this valley is the basin for the runoff, even if the rainfall is only about seventeen to twenty inches each year. The junior college, just a mile or two northwest, has water from wells, and it should be somewhat similar to this land. Also, in the Los Osos Valley to the south a mile or two, there's a marshy area and the small Laguna Lake. These are all good omens, but would another spot bring forth a trickle or a flood? Would we be crazy to hire a water witcher?" I found a witcher's advertisement in the phone book and made the call.

The water-witching man arrived with a small forked branch. He held it in front of him with upturned hands as he walked up and down the eight acres searching for an underground vein or body of water. I carried a bunch of stakes and a hammer for him, and he pounded in a stake wherever the wand dipped down. Talking was allowed, so he told me about different wands or divining rods that are used. Some witchers use willow limbs, while others use branches from peach, pear, or other fruit trees. Still others use metal rods or just their bare hands. With a wry smile, the witcher told of many successful outcomes and assured me I was not alone in being embarrassed and skeptical about my phone call for his help. He said that some dowsing is done to find pipes, electric lines, and telephone cables. Plumbers sometimes use "pipe finders." The whole procedure seemed to have a bit more general credibility than I'd believed possible.

The witcher, or dowser, continued, "Since colonial times, thousands of witchers have found water all over the United States. Sure, many geologists shake their heads and say it's not possible, but we find water where geologists fail." I later read that it's the witcher's hands that move the limb or divining rod, and that perhaps some people are more sensitive to the earth's magnetic field, or to other intangible forces.

Soon there was one area of stakes fairly close together. We drilled the well there, and our supply of water mysteriously tripled, although it was still a very meager amount. I wasn't sure there would be enough water for much more than the house, my vegetable garden, and a small lawn. But the tripled amount was a great improvement. Nevertheless, this witching still seemed to be like planting by the phases of the moon, and Dan and I never mentioned to others that I had hired a witcher.

Besides having too little or too much water, living out in the boondocks may have other challenges that town folks don't often have to worry about. My second big shock arrived soon after the water well problems. The house's plumbing was hooked to a septic tank with leach fields. The septic tank, buried about fifteen or twenty feet out from the kitchen window, began to overflow. The only good outcome of this development was that we found out exactly where the septic tank was located.

Unlike the SLO folks in town, I was speedy, but there was one problem—I wasn't sure what direction I was speeding toward. Surely none of my goals and visions had been about having no water, or having raw sewage flowing out over the land from an extrasmall septic tank and a lack of enough drainage trenches (which are often made with perforated pipes on top of layers of stone and gravel). Inside the house, the kitchen sink, the clothes washer, and the tub drains gurgled sluggishly or not at all, and then the water in the toilet and in the sink began backing up.

When Mr. Johnson put the septic tank in, he must have decided to economize, thinking that two newlyweds wouldn't do many loads of wash or have stacks of dishes. Then we came along—two adults, three kids, and another one on the way.

Once again, I had to do punishing work with out-of-shape muscles and little stamina; recent years of being away from farm life had not done much for maintaining my strength. Being with child, I fleetingly wondered whether I could convince Dan to do this job, but he was so overloaded with other projects at school that I didn't ask, and it became my immediate fate every day and in every way to dig a new, longer, and deeper leach line as soon as the larger holding tank was installed.

While I dug the leach line, Dan did find time to unhook the drains to the kitchen sink, the bathtub, and the washing machine, and then attached garden hoses to them to use the water wherever it was most needed outside. The unplanted yard drank lots of soapy water from the hoses. As soon as the ditch was finished, I began the vegetable garden bed where the soil was sometimes soapy wet. Hadn't I always said one thing leads to another? I did wonder whether I would get a day off to have the baby. Meanwhile, until the new septic system was hooked up, the constant refrain from the bathroom was, "Mom, can I flush the toilet yet?"

Paved public roads and road crews are nice to have in the country: it's nice to have an easy drive to get home or to town. In spite of clouds of dust, we had managed all right when driving a dirt road down a lane to our first farm, but there was no severe weather except months of great heat in Arizona's Salt River Valley. Now I wondered, "What happens to other farms in this valley in times of floods, mudslides, or just heavy rainstorms?"

Not all country homes at the time had paved roads connecting them to the county roads in the valley, and we were no exception. However, we needed a more reliable connection from O'Connor Way to the house. We would have to improve it ourselves. To save costs, I ordered just two dump-truck loads of the gravel-like red-rock. The driver tried to unload it slowly as he drove forward down our lane, but he left me with the job of spreading the rock out evenly over all of the parking area and road.

Once you navigated your driveway or lane to the main road, you traveled over and over again through that wonderful countryside, full of space, to all that used to be nearby, such as schools, doctors, stores, car repair shops, shows, the bank, lumber yards, beauty salons, etc. Soon, using plastic curlers in your hair and staying home may seem easier than driving a half hour each way to reach a beauty salon, for already your kids have made you a taxi driver much of the day, and their schedules have a way of taking precedence over all else.

Refuse trucks don't usually come out to farms or ranches for your weekly garbage or yard clippings. Hey, you bury it, or you take it to the county dump. Fortunately, as faculty members, we could transport ours to the college dump on campus.

Bus strikes in town? They won't affect you, because, like the garbage trucks, the buses don't normally come to many rural ranches, even when they're not on strike.

Starting to feel lonely? Just wait for duck or deer season, and your spread may blossom with red-clad hunters all day long. Some are lost, and some think your land is a hunting preserve, even if it's not where the deer and the antelope play—the only wild beasts playing on our spread appeared to be unwanted rats, squirrels, gophers, and mice. Lost domesticated hunting dogs may arrive at your door, and are often claimed at the end of the day by those sportsmen. Even if you post KEEP OUT signs on your land, a few hunters, their dogs, or their bullets still stray. The first hunter I met knocked at the door to ask where there might be a good place to find deer. I pointed toward the main road and to the mountain or the other side of the valley saying, "Not on our property; we only hunt for Easter eggs."

A second man came to my door resting a rifle on his shoulder and asked, "Which way's town?" Just how long had he been there on the side of Bishop's Peak waiting for a deer to come by? It was midday and, since he had hiked from the eastern to the western side of the mountain, he wasn't sure where he'd parked his car, or where to find a cold beer.

Another hunter smirked at me in my pick-and-shovel attire and asked, "Where's your better half?" I glared, told him he was looking at her, and closed the door. These gate-crashing hunters weren't hunting for food, but for the enjoyment of killing beautiful, gentle animals who were just wandering, wild and free, around the hills and mountains.

If you're still lonely after the hunters leave your rural property, you can't just lean over a barbed wire fence and get the latest gossip from a neighbor, or run next door to borrow two cups of flour. You'll probably just change your dinner menu, because the neighbor lives a block or more away.

After you take several decades to make your lands fertile, plant fine fences all around it, and perhaps build a large barn and a beautiful house to lean back and enjoy, the biggest enemy may come in an official car, with an official-looking person or two inside. Backed up with a fistful of official-looking documents, a county planner may report any number of developments to a "higher use," such as a major highway that will come through the middle of your property, high-powered electric lines needing an easement across your land, a new development of a thousand houses that will sprout up nearby, a mile-long mall that will go in down at the corner, or maybe a golf course planned for the far side of your property line. It's the nature of hamlets, towns, and cities: they grow and grow.

One thing that may come out from a town or city right away is dirty air. Are you dreaming of breathing clean, fresh air under vast, clear blue skies? Maybe you will, and maybe you won't. Where do you think all the city's polluted fumes go? They go where the wind or the slightest breeze carries them, and they may very well end up where you live.

Finally, if you wish to send or receive any mail, instead of your mail being delivered to your door, it may be deposited in a mailbox on a post down at the corner or on the main road blocks away. Uninsured packages languish on the ground beside your box unless you have an unusually cooperative postal worker who takes the time to deliver packages to your door.

At the age of ten, little Danny quickly solved the daily newspaper problem with his bike by taking over the delivery of the paper from another boy who lived down on Foothill Road. His goal was not only to get a better bicycle, but also a BB gun. I soon added to my list of chores helping him fold papers whenever time ran short. Dad and I worried because many of the papers had to be delivered along Foothill Road with its busy traffic.

Of course, some city dwellers dream of country living so they can raise most of their produce and avoid foods grown countless miles away with harmful chemicals, pesticides, fertilizers, and preservatives. Other farmers have the compassion and good sense to raise animals without using growth hormones or antibiotics and to avoid causing animals to suffer in pens that are too small for them to take even a few steps, and that prevent them from ever even getting outside, feeling the sun, or even walking on actual soil or grass.

Not many who raise or grow their own food have time to sit around and just watch the grass grow. To raise farm animals and their feed takes enough fertile land, sufficient water, and more hard work than most people can possibly imagine. Nevertheless, it has always been worth it to some crazy souls, such as Dan and me. When people asked why we wanted to live out in the country, I always replied, "Because, in spite of all the negatives, it's wonderful! It's a different world!" Most farmers and ranchers seemed to agree and tried to hang on to their land as long as possible. It's things like working for yourself, being home with the family, dressing and living informally, raising crops and animals for home use, and being surrounded by the weather and land. It's eating food you've grown that's fresh, flavorful, and free of additives. And Hallelujah, it's not being crammed up against others on a narrow lot or in an apartment house and hearing the noise of neighbors and the city twenty-four hours a day.

Still another nice element, and one that I hadn't realized I missed, were country people—they're usually friendly, and it's nice to be near to, and occasionally join forces with those who share your interests. I found that those who live rurally and drive mostly pickups on lightly used roads tend to wave and smile to all who pass. I've heard such friendliness is repeated in most small towns and in the countryside across America—it's a nice custom and a habit of great significance: a reaching out to others and making them feel better, even if it's by a slight nod of the head or a hand barely raised from the steering wheel. Everyone needs to foster interconnectedness with others. So, if you move to the country, forget some of the harsh realities and wave to your rural neighbors in the bucolic countryside.

Nowadays, most people want to be friendly, but increasingly they seem afraid to wave or speak to strangers, especially in cities. Yet a curious thing is also happening—people with common interests often greet each other and wave. Recreational vehicle owners chat in campgrounds and often wave to one another on the roads. People who walk a dog or two find that other dog walkers are usually friendly and will sometimes chat for ages, especially if their dogs are of the same breed as yours. Runners, bicyclists, cat or horse owners, gardeners, and fishermen—all people with an activity in common are often happy and willing to greet one another and strike up a conversation. I always felt I could phone any farmer or rancher, even one I barely knew, to ask advice about some farm animal or crop, and they would always try to help. When I think of these acts of kindness, there still seems hope for civilization.

I also felt that besides being helpful and friendly, country people tend to be sincere and real, as opposed to pseudo or fake. And often, against terrible odds, they try to be self-reliant yet at the same time enjoy life's simple pleasures.

For me, one delightful (if small) benefit of country living was the chance to drive the kids to Halloween trick-or-treat in a town neighborhood where no one would recognize them in Mom's crudely made paper-sack masks and sheets. Halloween didn't usually come to the country unless it was a planned party, because of the long distances between the dark farms and ranches, usually with a number of roaring, protective dogs daring costumed kids to open their car doors. In fact, Halloween in the country put Dan and me out of work—out of his Halloween work, that is. When we had lived in town, he or I had to either escort the kids to dozens of front doors nearby, or stay home to hand out the week's grocery money in the form of concentrated sugar treats.

On O'Connor Farm, I soon had lawns on my mind. Fortunately there were no near neighbors for any lawn competitions over the degree of greenness or the number of weeds. Dan, therefore, remained puzzled over the size of the lawns I always promoted: "Why do you need a golf course-sized lawn around the house when you'll be the one to water and mow it?"

I never had a very good answer. "Maybe it's to partly make up for the tiny living space. A lawn can be like an extra living or romping room—kids can play croquet, badminton, or toss a ball on it; and there's less mud tracked into the house. But this time, you don't need to worry—there's not enough water for a big lawn."

Dan also continued to worry about my rural life. "You're really stuck out here day after day. Are you OK? Maybe you could hire a bookkeeper-housekeeper-cook and get out and teach. Are you happy? I'm still going off in a suit and tie every morning, and I often chat with grown-ups, or at least with college-age kids, while you stay here in ditch-digging clothes and those awful sneakers, and only talk to yourself, or the kids, or the dog."

It was true; our division of labor put us in two different worlds. But I always replied, "Of course I'm happy, even if it's as you say. No need to keep up with the Joneses, and a new sun comes up each day, no matter where we live. I don't try for or expect perfection in anything, and I even enjoy the struggle. In fact, if I had wealth, I'd probably miss the need to overcome all the rocks on our trail. It just doesn't bother me that it's always dress-down day out here. I'm too swamped to dress up for this show, and good clothes wouldn't last a day. Also, there's no time to not feel OK. I even schedule my worrying for evenings while I'm ironing your shirts and waiting for you to come home. With no labor union protecting me, my bosses are this potpourri of kids, animals, and endless jobs crying to be done. As the only maid, cook, chauffeur, gardener, bookkeeper, mother, and part-time farmer, at least I'm starved more for time than for food this go-around. It's fun and love under pressure to make things better."

I took over a small area near the back door for the vegetable garden, which had to be planted before I put in the lawn. Nothing had been planted on this land for years, so I decided to buy the seed and plants and try skipping fertilizer for a year. Later, I would be able to use cow and horse manure.

This planting would be a fall garden of beets, carrots, chard, onions, peas, and radishes. Corn, tomatoes, and all the other produce might be planted in the spring. Harvesting still seemed like giving birth—forever amazing to find brightly colored vegetables appearing on the plants. Again, my "vertical-integration production" would go from earth, to kitchen, to dinner table.

While the overlapping seasons of a mild climate had made continuous gardening possible, I decided that here one big spring planting and another smaller one early in the fall would be hard enough. With three children, another on the way, and all the needed house and farm tasks, Dan was right—I was understaffed.

Fortunately, no one saw me doing these first projects—I was visibly pregnant, awkward, and dressed in faded, out-of-style maternity clothes, now being worn during a fourth pregnancy.

I found immediate joy in the fragrance of the Los Osos Valley's rich, dark soil as I turned into a machine, a robot, and shoveled and shoveled. Even with a dull shovel blade, the more I turned the soil over, the higher my spirits lifted. Once more I got strength and vitality from knocking myself out. Happiness was in trying, just trying, and not in getting perfection. Bursting with success, I showed my first day's garden work to Dan and asked, "If only everyone could feel the joy of being connected to the earth by feeling the seasons come and go by with sun, rain, and growing plants, they'd be happier and more satisfied, don't you think?"

"Maybe," he responded, "but it's a good thing the seller's kids didn't think so, or we wouldn't be here."

With the garden planted, I switched and wished for rain instead of fog. From my childhood days in a village not too far away, I remembered that some years we received no autumn rains, and my world could remain brown and golden until Christmastime or later. Other years, we received the special blessing of early fall storms and the sight of the valley beginning to turn green. Then I had to pray that another rain would come before the short, tender, new grass and plants died. There wasn't the desert dryness of Arizona, but sufficient rain was never certain...yet somehow there was usually enough seed and moisture for the fields to come to life, no matter when the real winter began.

"Hello, hello. Anybody home?" People finally began to visit, and the roster of those who came was rather diverse. Alice and John, my first visitors from the college, drove up unannounced except for Treve's frantic barking. I hadn't forgotten the routine: I leapt to my feet, kicked various shoes and toys under the couch, gathered up the wash I was sorting on the dining room table, and carried it and the morning's scattered newspaper to the back room of the house, where I put everything on top of the washing machine and quickly closed the door. Unfortunately, I couldn't do the same with three kids, still in the front room with toys, juice glasses, and a half-finished puzzle.

Alice and John joined the bedlam and sat down on the sofa beside Doug.

"You're so beautifully tan," she complimented me. "But without a car, what do you do for fun and excitement way out here? I'd go completely bonkers without neighbors and transportation."

This was a common question. "Well, the tan, straggly hair, and the filthy tennis shoes come free with the work. With the excitement of three kids, plus one more arriving any time now, I don't require much transportation. Before the baby comes, I'm trying to finish the vegetable garden, plant a lawn, and help build a corral and shed for a horse and cow."

We all shared the plate of cookies she'd brought, plus my pitcher partially full of juice, but she and John didn't stay long.

I'd had no quick and witty reply to these friends' questions about boredom, at least not at the moment they asked. Yet nothing I said would have sounded rational.

Later, I got to talking it over with Dan. "Things here are not what they seem to others. Even if some of the work is simple and routine, I have the medicine for that—there's no time to mope; there are dreams to reach if we have a bit of luck, and there are sudden surprises and obstacles—like the overflowing sewer and lack of water—to spice things up. Alice was also wrong about no car. I get the car by being a taxi driver when needed—taking you to work and picking you up in the late afternoon in order to take kids here and there. Anyway, with our past experiences, this place may again be just a stopover. Taking chances and moving on seems to be our style."

Besides the water witcher, the septic tank specialist, and the mailman who never came farther than the mailbox unless there was a package, our visitors were either friends from the rental neighborhood where we had lived, the wives of the college staff, or old acquaintances who came from out of town.

If three's company and four's a crowd, then what are six in such in a tiny house? Baby Jeff arrived on Valentine's Day, and the interior of the house quickly broke out with about triple the chaos. Although I felt I was managing remarkably well, I soon realized that others might wonder. All those who came calling to bring a baby gift and to see the new infant seemed surprised, even amazed, by our tiny living room and two or four kids at home.

It didn't help my housekeeping work that new babies can be notorious insomniacs. Little Jeffrey Barnard got me up about six times a night. Trying to explain, I remarked to one caller, "As you can see, I'm light on domestic help right now." This comment resulted from our farm soon being considered "in quarantine" by those formerly friendly natives of the town or college.

"I'll be seeing you again real soon," one former neighbor suggested, as she hurriedly left to return to the comforts of town. I silently nodded and thought, "Sure, sure, when my last child leaves for college." This good lady had brought some home-sprouted petunias for me to plant, but even she had suddenly remembered an errand she needed to do in town. Other friends came calling, but they, too, stumbled out the front door as fast as they could without falling flat on their faces over blocks, toy trucks, books, laundry, the playpen, plus a bunch of live bodies with two or four feet—all in the two tiny front rooms.

Meanwhile, Treve was a great help and had found the rural areas out back lots of fun. He escorted Nancy and Danny on a number of exploratory trips when they got home after school. Treve also followed little Douglas around and chased tennis balls that only traveled a dozen feet or less.

Shortly after Jeffrey arrived, our dear friend Grace arrived from her home in Lake Tahoe to visit. So wonderfully and aptly named, she had always displayed both grace and tact, as well as love. Grace already knew enough not to stay overnight, especially when hearing of and now seeing our family of six.

As well-meaning as Grace was, she wasn't able to easily accept or see what I envisioned as she looked at our forlorn fields and the ugly, small, shoebox of a house without a single tree, flower, shrub, or even a roof above the small front porch. She saw the kids and me in grubby hand-me-down outfits, freshly laundered and ironed that morning, yet already mussed and spotted. And this visit was after I'd had two full days' warning she was coming and had hoed, washed, picked up, and vacuumed. I'd even gotten a coat of white paint on the house a few weeks before Jeffrey had arrived.

As Grace sipped a cup of coffee in our tiny dining room, she was perplexed and genuinely concerned by my rustic living, and hesitatingly suggested, "Judy, maybe you should reconsider and move back nearer to schools or the college at this stage of your life. I don't see how you're going to manage without a car and without more space in the house."

I could only repeat once again to her, "No, now that I'm back here in California, life takes place outdoors. How could you slave away in front of a desk with so many summer days passing by outside? I still have the pioneering genes, and I gave a great sigh of relief when we moved here. I see it as truly God's country—it's almost a spiritual feeling, and my little steps forward with hard work may lead to bigger things. It's funny—none of this ever seems dreary or dull to me, and I thrive in this stripped-down setting. It's merely that my work and dwelling are both in the same place. We'll get a second horseless carriage when we can. This scene summarizes as many of my dreams as is possible when starting over from scratch after getting our degrees.

"There's another thing out here...a feeling of peace and a connectedness with the land and the animals. I don't know how to say it. I feel fresh and inspired. I don't need many material things, and I instinctively seem to feel this is the way—a joy in action, even in shoveling or making dinner. Don't underrate the plodder—there'll be a turning point, and hopefully it won't take as long as it did on the two acres near Phoenix. Remember the time in Arizona when you came to dinner and I could do little more than boil potatoes, burn vegetables, and make tough fried chicken? I'm doing better now, both inside and outside the house. It wouldn't be good if everybody thought alike. However, I believe you do think a lot like me and can understand my love of the land. You grew up in the country, and I remember your telling me how you had a beloved pony. Nancy's heartfelt wish since she was a tiny girl was to own a horse; that wish has to be granted. Such deep desires should never die just because of the passing of time or for lack of trying. It will be here on this place, and soon, I trust, that she can finally have that horse."

With a puzzled frown, Grace still worried. Trying to be polite, yet probing a little deeper, she hesitated a bit and then again observed, "It still seems hard for you to be so isolated."

I nodded and explained, "Remember, I lived in town these last several years, and that was more than enough. But I, too, notice that this poor house seems out of place and a bit forlorn out here. With time, and if there's enough water, I'll anchor and soften its lines with trees and flowers. Just planting the clumps of bird-of-paradise flowers that Dan's father brought last week will make a difference.

"The place doesn't seem isolated to me; it's good living. However, Grace, you may be right—this farm may be another jumping-off place for one better. But, as I wrote you, I searched and searched for months to find this place. Small farms near the college are so few in number, it was almost impossible to find one for sale. Who knows, maybe someday we'll take off and live on a houseboat in a marina and feed gulls and pelicans, or we'll buy a log cabin in the high Sierras and keep a string of trail horses."

To Grace's husband, who had just arrived to pick her up, I laughed and tried to explain, "As you can see, old habits die hard—once again we're starting small, and are up to our ears in debt. We've got no worries about the stock market going up and down, but very soon I hope to have my own variety of 'stocks'—ones that baa or moo."

As the tiller of the land, I never needed time or money to bike, hike, jog, ski, lift weights, take karate lessons, or play tennis. My regimen was like holistic medicine—treating the whole body with countless activities and home-grown foods. My mind and body had constant workouts, with no time to be ill or to indulge in the midlife crisis that a few friends talked about. I'd take life as it came, but only after I gave it all I could.

Every day was Monday, and my "flexible" working hours were again roughly 5:30 AM to 10:30 PM. After I washed the supper dishes, there was little variation in my labor: I helped the older kids with their homework, read stories from the library to Doug, tackled the mountain of unfolded diapers, ironed Dan's shirts, and wiped up the floors in the kitchen and dining room. There was never time to complete all the chores. Meanwhile, the feeling of the blasted ticktock of time rushing by stayed with me as well as in the big alarm clock beside the bed.

The solitude imagined by Grace hardly existed. The TV we had bought before we'd left town sat unwatched in a corner of the living room. But the radio was a different matter. As soon as we finished breakfast, the clean-up act began, and I turned on the radio to listen to Guy Lombardo and his Royal Canadians, or to Merv Griffin playing the piano and singing songs like 'Ain't Misbehavin'.' Evenings I listened to the clear and wonderful voices of Fred Waring and his Pennsylvanians. With all that I had to do, I enjoyed the music, but there was surely no time for "misbehaving."

Everybody needs kind and helpful neighbors, and it's not good for people, or for the health of the country, for that matter, that fewer and fewer people recognize this. Most people take a variety of hard knocks over a lifetime: they sometimes need us, and we sometimes need them.

One whose help I definitely needed right then was Dorothy, who had lived one house away when we rented in town, and had helped me during the first week after Baby Doug and I came home from the hospital. Now, when Baby Jeffrey came into the world, she drove out each day to help me out again. Neighbors such as Dorothy cared, supported, and cooperated; they made kindness a lifelong habit, and everyone they touched was richer for it. In those days, people believed in their own "good-neighbor policy," and many children grew up with a sense of having an extended family composed of friends and neighbors.

But talk about togetherness! I blithely told everyone that Dan's and my riches were in the children, the animals, and the land. This was true, and a great blessing. Still, there was no getting away from these "riches," even for a day or two. In the early days on O'Connor Way, after Jeff was born, if I wanted to go anywhere by car, first I had to take Dad to the college to have the car and I got him about 5:00 PM. Since Nancy and Danny were in school part of the day, I took Doug and Jeff with me. Try to run errands or make a doctor visit with a tiny baby and a two year old! Doug and I quickly learned to just stay home on weekdays.

Moreover, after lunch each day, since I was the weary farm boss and mother, I always insisted that the baby and Douglas also needed sleep. The TV screen remained blank, and what might have been soap-opera time in other families was our naptime. On a few issues such as this one, I never was willing to budge.

In addition to the "Mom knows best" naps, I continued to take a hard line in pushing early toilet training for the two youngest kids, yet I did it with lots of laughing and handclapping over a child's successful minute or two on the potty. Often, the trainee grinned and clapped with me. However, before the toilet training for four kids, our dozens of cloth diapers went through thousands of washings. Now and then, I'd purchased a dozen more, especially if too many got used to clean the car, dry the windows, dust the furniture, or wipe up spills. It seemed as if there were a million mornings of our life when diapers hung on long clotheslines and waved and fluttered in the breeze. Modern moms can hardly visualize that, but then I can't believe that the whole modern world isn't now covered knee-deep in disposable diapers.

Naps renewed the kids' energy and mine, but even on Saturday nights, I never had any "umph" left for a "night on the town," and I had no clear idea of what those words even meant. Dress up? My dress clothes had slept in a closet or trunk so long they were permanently wrinkled and certainly out of style. Dine out? Dan and I simply ate whenever I fed the kids. And since we didn't have a babysitter, or even know the name of one, if we had gone out to dinner, we would have had to take four children along with us.

Instead, we delighted in our kids, their homework, piano practicing, games, hikes, and frequent weekends at the beach. There were also our domestic animals and an extremely large and varied bird population, including doves, quail, meadow larks, mocking birds, robins, and countless others to watch and occasionally feed. Without trees on our land we always wondered where these birds nested. However, we soon had oat, alfalfa, bales of hay, a lawn, and neighbors with livestock. There were also the nearby brush and trees up the mountains and around Bishop's Peak.

After our many years in Arizona, it was nice to have the more predictable rhythm and flow of the four seasons in this California Central-Coast valley: 1) a warm summer and a sunny fall, often with 2) an Indian Summer of cooling temperatures and an occasional light rain, then 3) winter rains that swept up the Los Osos Valley, and finally 4) a spring with cool weather and many mornings of soft fog that rolled down the valley from the coast and burned off by noon.

In come-as-you-are clothing, everyone rushed in when I shouted "Dinner's on; come this very minute!" With the neighbors we knew as friends not within easy hearing distance, I sometimes impulsively screamed and yelled at a kid or two 'til the cows came home. Of course, the rest of the family could also yell and shout as they pleased, and we became a boisterous gang.

And, glory be! Unlike our experiences in those harsh first years in Arizona, both the cooking and eating areas could now be cozy, warm rooms on cold days. And as my budget expanded, cooking and eating became fun again, with heaping plates and an abundance of second and third servings often on hand.

On most mornings, the tantalizing aroma of bad-for-you-but-savory foods like bacon or sausage and eggs filled the kitchen. At suppertime, there was often fried chicken, cooked to a hot, crispy brown, or roasts with gravy, plus potatoes and a variety of my garden vegetables. I grew lots of cucumbers and beets, and pickled what we couldn't immediately eat. Potatoes were cheap, and I cooked them a variety of ways, including sliced and deep-fried in bacon fat or lard. I still avoided cookbooks, and our meals were basic, plain, heavily larded, and sugary. I not only spooned out seconds and thirds, but finished off the evening meals with desserts. The kids stayed glued to their chairs, knowing that a sugary dessert was coming, often one of those pies I had finally mastered in Arizona. Even a bowl of jiggly red Jell-O was covered with whipped cream.

Unlike the hurried, desperate meals of earlier years, both breakfast and dinner were also a precious chance for a bit of congeniality, loud talk, and laughter. Now and then dad and I even finished a cup of coffee.

These days, many cooks try to ban all "homey" fragrances from the kitchen. There are exhaust fans and hoods above stoves, large sliding or swinging doors and windows bringing in fresh air, aerosol sprays, and outside grills for meats. Our house was often filled with wonderful homey aromas.

When living in town, the two older kids had attended a school where there was a teacher for each of the early grades, and both Nancy and Danny had a growing circle of friends. Now they attended a little two-room, two-teacher country school down at the corner of Los Osos Road and French Road (now named Madonna Road). One room held Grades 1, 2, and 3, and the other room held Grades 4, 5, and 6, with the youngest students always up front near the teacher. Having to make new friends was somewhat less difficult for Nancy than for Danny, because Nancy knew she would attend the junior high back in town in September, and also knew I was now starting to hunt for a horse. Her excitement was building, with the Mexican saddle, bridle, blanket, brush, and currycomb waiting in a heap in the corner of the dining room.

Faithful dog Treve was obviously born for this life. Full of heart and hope, he kept the belief that with the loving care of a kind family, life could be good. Yet he also found time to roam the fields and chase field mice, ground squirrels, gophers, and birds (although he never caught anything as far as we knew). Coming home tired and happy, he still considered it his duty to guard all of us from danger, and he carefully barked at the arrival of all cars. Then, as they left, Treve escorted them back down the lane, roaring and trying to bite the back tires to be certain they left the farm.

Nancy continued to sit on the front steps and talk to this great dog, probably telling him that Mom had better find a horse darn soon. The dog probably leaned closer to her and nodded in agreement. Once she came in to say, "Mom, Treve makes me feel good, really good, so I make him feel good too, and I give him hugs and kisses." She was onto something very valuable and true: both animals and humans need self-esteem through praise, attention, hugs, and maybe a cookie.

The less formal country school, with its smell of chalk dust, leftover lunch food, dirty shoes, flour paste, and crayons, had one big advantage for me: hand-me-down clothes seemed both acceptable and advisable. Few brand-new outfits had come our way. Family dressing reached a new low, with "casual clothes" for the two youngest being clothes that we had received as hand-me-downs from family friends in Arizona. Little Doug, arriving nine years after Danny, now wore Danny's toddler outfits, and new Baby Jeff was starting out with the smallest and oldest hand-me-downs—tiny shirts, stained bibs, and nighties that rotated in and out of the cedar chest as each of the children grew to fit them and then outgrew them.

I fared no better—after I packed away my maternity outfits, my clothing reverted to my rather aged high school and college attire. For me, I had enough ancient outfits to span all changes in style forever. Some of my pants were skin-tight, and others big and baggy, while hemlines ranged from far too short to far too long. My dad once repeated an old saying that went something like this—"Use it up, wear it out, make it do, or do without." It was the only thing to do, and we all accepted this philosophy, except Dan, who, as our breadwinning Dr. Dan, required good clothes to make a favorable impression on his colleagues and students.

The cedar chest Dan had given me when we became engaged hadn't held dresses, fancy new tablecloths, towels, doilies, and such—in Arizona it had held all the woolen items that we wouldn't wear and didn't want devoured by the voracious desert moths. For most of the years, the chest began a second life of holding the rotating outfits worn by the kids. If "outfit" means matching and coordinated clothing, that's the wrong word. Nothing matched. Just last year, I finally gave the last hand-me-downs to our youngest grandchild, and convinced Nancy to give the cedar chest a new home in her home. The five trunks were actually put in the three bedrooms in the house with spreads covering them.

Chapter 33

Shandy Who Walked Alone

The fields appeared to grow nothing but sage, countless weeds, and lots of wild oats; but it was increasingly evident that field mice found both fine food and shelter on the land and in the small new barn, and as time went on, I realized that we had acquired a regular army of the critters. To my to-do list, I added "get a cat."

Out at the animal shelter, as always, there was a large, confusing selection of felines; it took willpower not to adopt dozens of these frightened, desperate cats. My specifications should have been for a good-sized, short-haired, alert and friendly cat—an ordinary, no-nonsense kitty who would catch the mice and rats and still be able to put up with a dog, children of various ages, and soon a horse.

Still, one large orange cat held his head high, and out of a round face his intent, yellowish eyes quietly looked me over with a thoughtful stare. I had the impression he was doing a better job of sizing me up than I was of figuring out what he was like. He looked strong and healthy, with a thick, glossy coat of reasonably short hair. His mouth seemed pursed, as though he were thinking, "This whole affair of cages and buildings is a madhouse and has frightening odors. I'm just going to sit here and have no part of it." Finally, he was the one that Doug and I chose. Jeff was still too small to be part of the decision. The information on the card hooked to the cat's pen stated he was two years old, neutered, and went by the name of Shandy.

I asked to have him taken out of his cage and put on the table in the office where we could meet without all the other feline voices complaining and begging as the cats stretched their paws through the wire or padded around in their cages. Shandy seemed fairly friendly and unafraid, and he politely let me pet him. Doug thought he was "really neat" and decided that orange fur was ever so funny—Shandy came home with us.

As I'd done with Sage, I kept Shandy in the house for the first week to be sure he wouldn't try to return to his former home, wherever that might be. The puss prowled the house to study every aspect of it—floors, furniture, windows, and closets—as though he were buying the place and I was just the salesperson. He then scrutinized each of us with his round yellow eyes. He observed and sniffed the cat box on the back porch and had no trouble accepting a slice of fried chicken from our dinner that first evening.

Doug had a fast course from Nancy and Danny on petting the cat and playing with him, but not lifting him. The very first night, Shandy caught a mouse on the laundry room's back porch and left it by the door to the hall for us to find.

Everyone had to watch the doors constantly to make sure the cat didn't break out to freedom too soon. Shandy couldn't understand why he had to be housebound, and he often sat or stretched out beside the front or back door. When the kids were home, I kept him in our bedroom with the door shut until the continuous opening and closing of outside doors ended for the night.

This cat was the strong, silent type. He seldom spoke during the first days when he was confined to the house. When he did speak, he used a rather deep and to-the-point brusque voice. This turned out to be his regular voice, although I almost never heard it after he was allowed to be outside. Since much of my inside work was in the kitchen and laundry area, he followed me around some, but mostly he preferred solitude, and as soon as he was fed, he padded off to an empty bed to sleep, or sat in a splash of sunshine on a windowsill.

Shandy had actually given me clues to his personality before I brought him home. The other cats at the shelter had noisily begged for release from their jail cells, while Shandy had held back, quietly sitting in the center of his cage. Not a demonstrative fellow, he still appeared a self-reliant sort, even when things were totally out of his control.

I didn't know whether Treve had been raised with a cat, but he was excited about the newcomer. He seemed more intent on having a pal to play with and to chase, rather than to harm. Shandy squashed the play idea right away. When Treve started to come close, the cat snarled and quickly swaggered right up to Treve and boxed the dog's face on both cheeks. Unable to even say hello, Treve retreated, and that was that. No friendship, but a sort of truce to leave each other alone.

While Shandy might prove to be tough and rowdy in an outside situation, any inside playing was not for him—a string pulled along the floor or a small ball rolled slowly under his nose seemed to bore him, and he would close his eyes or look away. Had he been on his own? Had he lost his mother too early to be taught games of chase, bat-the-string, and hide-and-seek? I soon found out that his mom had at least given him good lessons on how to hunt.

Independent Shandy stayed on our farm when turned loose, and he aggressively and relentlessly began to spend most of his time stalking game. With his orange coat, he melted from sight into the front and back fields of wild oats and dry weeds. Only by a few waving stems of oats would I know where he prowled, ambushing field mice, gophers, and birds. Shandy seldom came to see me when I was working in the yard or hanging out the wash. Occasionally he remained near, but it was usually to watch a crack between bales of hay for the appearance of a careless rodent. Most cats are natural hunters, and they usually consider it their job, but Shandy carried this pursuit to an extreme.

For me, every day during that time was frantic. With not even a car on most days, new Baby Jeff and two-year-old Doug, and eight acres of property to develop into a farm, I had my hands full. Shandy fended for himself and never sought any attention or affection, running off whenever one of the children tried to pick him up. With their school, sports, and other activities, the older children were almost as busy as I was, so there was a lot of food for Shandy both morning and night, but little hugging and petting. It didn't help our friendship that I'd kept him a prisoner in the house for the first two weeks. Moreover, he harbored lots of fleas, and I had to repeatedly dust him with flea powder during that two-week period. I put a folded blanket in a corner of our bedroom for him to sleep on, but, like Sage, he never used it, and at night he either disappeared outside our room or slept on some unsuitable surface such as the dining room table, the kitchen counter, or my basket of clean wash. Shandy did manage to work up a smidgen of curiosity, however, about what I cooked in the kitchen.

The cat truly loved to be out at night, and I suspect that as soon as he was released he traveled far and wide on his special hunting trails. On the steps in the morning, there was often a house gift of the prey he'd captured. Sometimes, he didn't bother to come home for breakfast, but remained far off, perhaps feeling free as the Los Osos wind that blew through the tall grass where he prowled. Once in a while he came home with his fur full of the fragrance of sage, and I'd know he had traveled way back to the chaparral on Bishop's Peak mountain.

Shandy would always be happiest as a free spirit and a hunter. If this cat had a philosophy to live by, it was probably to be self-confident and never become dependent upon anyone. Maybe he had just never had a home with take-care-of-cat people.

One night, Shandy slept in the backseat of the car, and the next morning he made a surprise trip to the college. Not being the vocal, complaining type, he didn't bother to get up or let out his deep meow until Dan pulled into the parking lot. Since the day was hot and sunny, Dan couldn't leave Shandy in the car all day, so Shandy had to be rushed home and a class met without their teacher and soon left.

Even when this cat wanted to eat, his meows never came out loud, but rather like a hoarse whisper. Sometimes his mouth moved, but I would hear nothing.

Shandy "owned" the yard and continued to boss around confused Treve. This cat was definitely "top dog." Treve tried a number of times to make friends with this strange creature, but finally he gave up after numerous times of meeting up with Shandy's aloof, superior stare, low growls, hisses, and puffed-up fur.

In contrast to Shandy, Sage had been an easygoing, affectionate cat, but, even so, I saw some of the same behavior in both of them. Both craved independence, and both always had time for a nap in some out-of-the-way spot while still leaving plenty of time for their hunting and other exploring pursuits.

Chapter 34

Blondie and Others

The time had come. The years of hearing "You're too young," or "There's no place to ride," or, "We can't afford a horse yet" were over. Our young girl knew all about deferred satisfaction, but she had kept her passion and dream. A horse still tugged at her heart, and she still insisted, "I only want a horse." It had better be soon—gotta find the horse before Nancy starts wanting lipstick and thinking more about boys than about horses.

The horse would have about six to eight barbed wire-fenced acres on the backside of the property, and mom and dad would put in a separate gate to the pasture. An additional two acres were adjacent to the road on the other side of the house. Collections of horse stuff were everywhere in Nancy's room and in the dining room. They filled boxes in her closet: small horses made of clay, cloth, metal, plastic, porcelain, or wood; books of horse stories; horse-head bookends; horse pictures on all the walls; and her bedspread and curtains patterned with running horses. She and I scanned the classified ads for a horse for sale as soon as Danny brought us our paper each day.

Weeks passed and there were no interesting prospects. I stayed away from any livestock auctions: I knew we were too green to get a good, sound horse that way. Buying from a private party seemed best. Finally, we saw an ad for an older palomino mare in the north county. After Dan got off work, we all drove up to see the horse. We could certainly tell she was old. Her hip bones were showing, her back was somewhat swayed, and her teeth were long; but she was rather pretty, and she was certainly patient and careful with her inexperienced rider when the owner let Nancy ride her around the corral after giving her just a few suggestions about stopping, starting, and turning a horse.

The owner, a leathery-faced and wire-thin old man named Jack, explained his reasons for selling: "I bought the mare at an auction, but I know she's gentle and sound because I've had her for some time. She was to be a gift for my granddaughter, but my daughter and her family had to move to the Central Valley."

There were a couple of younger looking horses in the corral, and three or four in an adjoining field. Jack's old cowboy boots; his ancient, stained, western hat; and his faded jeans made him appear knowledgeable about horses. He assured us we could bring the mare back if she didn't work out. The rather low price seemed quite reasonable, and he could deliver her the next day. Nancy finally had her horse!

We named the horse Blondie. Nancy began getting up at daybreak to rush out and brush, currycomb, and feed her before going to school. The mare would nicker a greeting to Nancy as soon as she ran out the door. The buttery-colored mare had a long, shaggy winter coat, which began to shed as soon as Nancy began combing her. Horsehair soon floated around and covered most of the backyard, and the mare eventually sported a new and glossy coat. However, now her bony frame and deep swayback from advanced age were more obvious. She often slept while standing, with one back leg slightly bent, or occasionally a front leg resting, and stayed near the area where we fed and watered her.

Still, the golden horse was Nancy's dream come true. She quickly learned to ride, with me leading the horse around the yard and field, showing her how to rein a horse, hold the reins while mounting and dismounting, and a few other basic things. Most of the Christmas and birthday horse equipment Nancy had received over the years was put into use, and before long I let her and the mare wander around the back field alone. Usually Treve ran ahead of them, hoping to surprise a bird or a rodent in the grass and brush.

Breakfasts did wonders for Blondie. Her morning feedings literally made her "feel her oats" and seem more youthful. If Treve or one of us went out to her as she finished munching the last of the hay and grain, she snorted, tossed her head high, and trotted a little ways. Treve would bark and chase her to make it a game, but she would turn the tables and trot toward him with a lowered head. The dog would then decide he had to run for survival and that looking for ground squirrels or chasing tennis balls was safer than trying to play with a horse.

This should have been a time for continuing great celebration and fireworks. Nancy finally had her horse and was clearly on cloud nine. Yet this was not the end of the tale. The mare was an underachiever and only liked to walk, not run, in the field. Within a month or two, I became sure that she was also lame. If her front foot or leg hurt her, no wonder she was no ball of fire.

I talked to the seller, and he claimed that, with such a light, young girl riding her for short outings, he had thought the mare would "get over her limp." I'd been warned about "horse traders" and began to wonder if we had been taken in by one. It also occurred to me that we should have had a vet check her out, even if this would have meant additional money, time, and delay.

With endlessly long workdays, neither Dan nor I had time to make good decisions; I let Nancy try riding the horse a while longer. Some days the horse seemed better. The rest of the time, Blondie would only walk, and Nancy didn't have the training to make the horse trot, gallop, turn, or stop. Most of the time the old mare and the blissful young girl simply explored the pasture, and all went well, except for Nancy's dropping the reins a few times when Blondie got her head down to feed on the weedy grasses. For Nancy, riding bareback seemed more fun and less work than riding mounted on a saddle. I was only needed to help put on the bridle, since it took a tall person to put it over Blondie's ears.

Sometimes Nancy took out a book, and somehow mounted the mare bareback and then stretched out, tummy down, along the horse's back, with elbows out on each side. Then she would prop the book on Blondie's mane and read as the horse ate her hay.

However, gradually the mare's lameness increased, and the mare began to stumble and limp even while walking. At the same time, Nancy's skill at riding improved, and she found that a friend living down on Foothill Road owned a horse and that she and this friend could ride together. Before letting Nancy try to go on these longer rides, I decided Blondie would have to be checked out by a veterinarian. The diagnosis was that the mare had a diseased bone in her left foreleg, and the vet's final verdict was, "It won't get better over time, only worse. This horse should never have been sold to you and might eventually fall on the pavement out front."

Patient and gentle Blondie had had a long life. Maybe she had been a rental horse at a stable, with too many years of hard usage and a lot of wear and tear on her joints, bones, and ligaments. When we gave up on the lame mare, Nancy felt that Dan and I were betraying both her and the horse. Nancy had taken on almost all the chores of feeding, watering, and brushing the mare, or at least the lower parts of the mare, which were the only parts she could reach; she had completely given the horse all her pent-up love. Thus it was terrible for her to hear the vet say that the mare would not recover.

Jack, the former owner, agreed to take the mare back, but provided some solace by saying he had another mare that was younger, much smaller, and a very pretty bay. He would make it an even trade, and he could bring Little Foot down to us when he picked up Blondie. As he was willing to take the mare back, I decided he wasn't an entirely unscrupulous trader.

Again, we drove up over the Cuesta Grade to look at a horse. This one was supposed to have come from a neighboring ranch when that ranch was sold. Again, since this was an even trade, we had little choice. Again, I skipped having the horse looked at by a vet, and I didn't even get on her for a test ride.

Little Foot was a lovely gray colored small horse and seemed calm. She had a small, chiseled, and intelligent-looking head, and large, very observant brown eyes. Her ears alternated between being in an alert position and then being laid back against her head. I wondered why, but we'd said we'd try her.

"Dan, I don't understand why it's an even trade for a younger and apparently better horse. Maybe she came from an auction, not from a neighbor. But it's suspicious that once again there are no previous owners for us to call."

The very next day, my suspicions were justified. Little Foot wasn't just cranky or moody—she was a determined kicker and sometimes a biter, and she struck out at Nancy or me every chance she got. Often the mare didn't even bother to put her ears back and get in a good kicking position. She practiced her jerky, fast kicks, which could go straight back or somewhat sideways, even when no one was near and sometimes while she was just eating her hay.

Little Foot's front end was as dangerous as her back, because she had some long sharp teeth which she used for biting. When Nancy's friend Karen rode up on her horse, Little Foot tried to kick the other horse and then bit a chunk out of its rump. It was a challenge to get her bridled and saddled without her trying to wheel around and lash out with her hind legs. She seemed to be high-strung, moody, and perhaps fearful.

Someone suggested that Little Foot's kicking might be due to poorly fitting shoes. I had her reshod, and I warned the blacksmith about her biting and kicking, but he soon forgot both my warning and that young Nancy was present. At one point he suddenly straightened up, stepped back from the horse, and exclaimed, "Shit! This little sonofabitch just bit me—look at my shirt—it's shot! She's not safe on either end! Where'd ya get her?"

Little Foot was also barn-sour, which made for irreconcilable differences: the mare would stubbornly try to wheel around and head for home and dinner whenever Nancy tried to ride her down O'Connor Way to Karen's house. Nancy needed to win those arguments, but she didn't have the riding skills to make it easy. At least the mare didn't buck.

The thought that Little Foot might hurt little Douglas as he wandered around the field scared the bejeebers out of me. I became convinced that before long, Nancy, Danny, Doug, Dan or I would be terribly hurt. This little mare also had to go back to the seller.

Nancy protested, "What if we just pet her more and give her lots of sugar cubes and apples? Maybe she doesn't know we're friends."

"Hon, that's the right idea, but changing her attitude will take more than feeding her treats for a few months. She'll never be fun to ride, because she might still be looking for the chance to hurt one of us or one of the animals. Her ears aren't happy, forward-pointing ones; they're almost always laid back on her head. She's probably learned to kick and bite because someone abused her, and now she's kicking out of fear. I think I've read that fear can turn to hate. I don't know how to rehabilitate or train horses, and I don't have the hours it would take to work with her. She may have been fearful and a kicker for a long time. Goodness knows what she may have been through. Little Foot may never become a truly trusting, peaceful, and reliable mare for you to care for and ride. You'll surely grow up to want animals, so may I explain something right now, something that this mare's first owner, or owners, probably didn't know enough about? Horses and all critters need proper shelter from cold and heat and rain, and they need their stalls or barns kept clean. They also need plenty of good exercise each day; they need clean and proper food and fresh water; they need times to play; they need lots of love and companionship—they don't like being alone. That's a lot of needs. Moreover, no horse ever deserves to have cruel humans beat, whip, or kick it, or to be subjected to ropes and spurs. Someone ruined this mare by destroying her trust in the human race. There should be a movement on a grand scale, maybe worldwide, for the basic rights of all living creatures—a campaign for laws against cruelty, and demands that animals live free of fear."

Before Little Foot left us, she made our decision easier by leaving her teeth and hoof marks on Julie, the new nanny goat we had recently brought home, and one morning she just missed kicking Treve's head when he got too close to her.

There would be no truce as long as she was with us, but it was heartbreaking for Nancy to give back another horse. I tried to comfort her by saying, "Nancy, when one door closes, another door opens, so try to be patient. Fairy tales do come true—just you wait and see."

At that time, Dan had been told about a horse trainer in another part of the county who might take Little Foot in trade for another horse. Thus it came to pass that Big Red came to us.

For some reason, Nancy loved Big Red at first sight. I don't know why. Maybe her reaction came from her earlier disappointments and her desperation to get a horse she could keep. Maybe it was just the need she'd long bottled up inside—the need to care for, ride, and love a horse.

The owner rode Red around his large corral to show the horse's leg action, easy reining, and other training. Big Red's name described him. He was reddish brown, huge, and seemed full of tremendous power and energy. Then we were told he was blind in one eye. The owner insisted the horse could see just fine with one eye and that it wouldn't matter, saying, "Red is one smart horse and not easily frightened."

I certainly had no knowledge about one-eyed horses, but decided we had better wait for another horse, even if Little Foot could be given in trade. At that point Nancy cried and cried for weeks, especially at bedtime. "I love him. Please let me have him. Please, please let's take him!" I couldn't get her to stop crying, although she almost never cried. Finally, Dan and I decided to try Red for a week.

Big Red seemed an even bigger horse on our little farm, and Nancy needed help to mount him. She'd need the saddle at first, and maybe always, in order to get on such a tall, heavy horse. I watched her ride out around the field at a walk that first evening, and the horse seemed steady, but oh so big. Why did she love this monster? I kept wondering. Maybe one's spirit feels stronger and one's more in command of life on a horse than on the ground, the bigger the animal the better. My first horse had been almost as large, and I'd loved him dearly when I was about her age, but I had always believed it was because of his fine training at Thatcher School, where all the students had well trained horses. That horse had a love of life, a happy disposition, and constant companionable feelings for me.

The next evening after supper, Dan went down the lane to the front of the property to mend the fence and fill some potholes that the gophers had created in the lane. Nancy was anxious to ride, so I bridled and saddled Red. Horses often fill their stomachs with air while the cinch on the saddle is being tightened, so I tried to make sure the cinch was truly tight. Then I started to boost Nancy up. She put one foot in the stirrup and pulled herself up to stand with her weight on that stirrup. Then she started to swing her other leg over Red's back. She had one hand on the horn holding the reins, and the other hand on the back of the saddle. At that moment, Red bolted—a full-out run down the lane with the reins flying loose around his neck. Nancy was clinging to the saddle horn, both legs on Big Red's left side, with just her left foot in the stirrup. She was wearing tennis shoes.

I screamed and screamed for Dan to help. Fortunately, he heard me and immediately stepped into the middle of the lane, spread his arms wide, and waved them back and forth, up and down, and yelling, "Whoa, whoa! Whoa, boy!" Dan stayed right in the path of the racing horse as it continued to run toward him and the paved O'Connor Road just beyond.

I'll never know why, but Big Red suddenly stopped in front of Dan. Nancy still had both hands gripping the saddle and saddle horn, and her whole body was still on the left side of Red, with her one foot in the stirrup.

I was weak and shaky as the three of them came back to the house. This was one of the worst waking nightmares of my whole life, and it still comes back to haunt me from time to time. With all of Nancy's weight on the left stirrup, if the cinch on the saddle had loosened a little and the saddle had then slipped under Red's midsection, Nancy might have fallen off under those thundering hooves. Or her foot, in only a tennis shoe, could have slipped through the extralarge stirrup. Then, if she had lost her grip on the saddle horn or had tried to jump off, or if the saddle had slipped around, her foot would have been caught in the stirrup and her body would have been dragged and kicked repeatedly under the horse until it stopped.

This huge, half-ton horse could also have been frightened enough to run much farther on the slippery asphalt of O'Connor Way if Nancy's dad had not happened to be down at the end of the lane.

We could only whip ourselves, saying over and over, "Dumb, dumb, dumb!" Red left the next day. It was much later that I learned about the characteristic behavior of horses—they are extremely sensitive and easily stirred to action, and they instinctively run from danger if they have the opportunity, rather than staying and fighting with teeth and hooves.

Horses' eyes are also somewhat to the sides of their heads; so they see two separate pictures, and their vision isn't great unless both eyes can focus directly on an object. Certainly, one-eyed Big Red would feel more stress and would tend to run if he imagined he heard danger on his blind side.

This one-eyed horse realized he was in new and completely strange surroundings. He also had a new rider, a stranger, on his back. Perhaps Nancy didn't swing her right leg over the horse fast enough. We had no real knowledge of his past behavior and his sensitivities.

"Jeez, Dan, how could it have gone from my endless, irrational worries, such as making the children wear sweaters in July or having them take rain slickers if there's a foggy drizzle, to this?" I had been constantly full of admonitions, "Don't fall in the creek," and "Dry your hair before you go out." Now, with these choices of horses, I'd made three horrible mistakes.

Even more than Blondie and Little Foot, the huge red horse had completely captured Nancy's heart. Not fully understanding the peril involved in riding this gigantic, one-eyed guy, she blamed me for not still keeping Big Red. Her face again became a storm cloud at dinnertime, and she shed a flood of tears at bedtime.

Dan also tried to talk to her. "Nancy, Mom and I both agree Red is a very dangerous horse for you. I'll talk about these horse fiascos in my classes. Since the students are mostly aggies, many of them must have horses back home, and one of them may know of some safe, good horse."

"I want Big Red back!" she sobbed and shouted with shrill desperation.

"Why do you want that dangerous monster who could hurt you?"

"Just because."

"Why because?"

"I just do. He wouldn't hurt me."

Buying a horse is a risky job. In spite of their size and strength, horses can have ever so many things wrong with them. Careless or ignorant breeding has created animals with nasty temperaments and weak body parts—bad legs, feet, lungs, or hearts. And the big hazards in getting a good horse involve more than the breeding: they also involve the way the horse has been treated and trained. Some horses have been underfed, left in small, dirty stalls and not given enough exercise, and some have been cruelly and poorly trained. Other horses have been ridden too hard or too long by inexperienced riders—countless abuses can occur.

Horses that aren't sound in body and mind, or that are abused, may become fearful or lame; they may be biters, kickers, or buckers, or they may be hard-mouthed, barn-sour, or runaways. Horses have good memories, and with harsh or ignorant care, they may develop a contempt or dislike for all humans. Where, oh where, I wondered, would we be able to find the horse to fulfill Nancy's lifelong dream?

Chapter 35

Fame of Julie Goes Worldwide

Meanwhile, as we began our search for Nancy's horse, other animals had arrived. As soon as we bought the O'Connor Way Farm, Dan's mom made the decision that we should take one of her family's milk goats that had been bred not long before. Momma had allergic reactions to cows' milk, and her family, after years of driving great distances to buy goat milk for her, decided to buy her a goat. Their Ojai home was near town, but that didn't seem to prevent their owning livestock, just as I had kept my great horse in that same town for many years when I was young.

The children's grandma spoke almost poetically about the beauty of goats and the fun of owning them. She believed that eating the right foods and drinking goat milk would cure almost anything.

Grandma always gave away everything other family members and I gave her for her birthday and for Christmas, as well as much of what she owned. Now she wanted to give us goats. Once we had outfoxed her, though. We drove down and arrived at her house at dawn one Saturday morning, bringing cans of paint, brushes, and spackle, and food, cold drinks, and sleeping bags, and we painted the entire inside of her house before we left on Sunday evening.

On both days of that weekend, it was well over a hundred degrees in the shade, and we were quite a sight—the boys and Dan took off all their clothes except for their shorts, and I wore just a shirt and shorts. We worked barefoot, and, working as fast as we could, we spilled paint all over the tarps and ourselves. On the second day, after we finished painting, we washed the windows and the stove, and cleaned and waxed the floors. The work done that weekend was one gift that Grandma could never give away.

Julie, the goat that Grandma wanted to give us, was an offspring of the nanny goat Dan's folks kept to milk, and I had a suspicion that Dan's mom had kept Julie just in order to give her to us. Julie was a white Saanen goat, a breed known for giving lots of milk. We liked cow milk better, but we seldom won any verbal skirmish with Momma.

While Dan continued to say no, I soon took Momma's side. "Dan, remember Mrs. Lincoln, the wealthy lady you wrote an article about for the Arizona Republic? She felt goat milk was such wonderful milk, and even with all her wealth, she took the trouble of owning those Toggenburg goats that she kept in that beautiful barn? Remember how you fooled the staff at the high school, by getting some of the milk from her goats served to the teachers by the cafeteria staff? You even wrote that the milk can taste almost the same as cows' milk if the animals are fed and cared for properly. People throughout the world drink more goat milk than any other kind—at least that's what you wrote in your article about them."

Dan took an awful lot of convincing and reminded me, "Look, I've already gotten to know a dairy farmer who told me he would sell us one of his Jersey cows. With a family of six, we'll need lots of milk, you know."

Momma repeatedly told Dan that Julie would give three quarts of milk each day for almost a year—well, for ten months of each year, anyway. As Momma petted Julie, she reminded Dan, "You've been telling me how broke you are, and how you barely managed to buy the farm. She won't eat nearly as much hay as a cow. Not only that, we'll take her back someday, if you wish." As if on cue, Julie poked her head over the fence and looked at Dan as everyone laughed.

I quickly added, "Look, she's a gift, she's free, and, in addition to the milk, in a few months she'll give us one or two kids. I've read that goats have great personalities and are both fun and intelligent. I'd love to know a goat during my lifetime. This friendly sweetie can surely become part of the family."

Julie was intrigued with so many of us trying to pet her, probably hoping that at least someone had something edible somewhere in a hand or a pocket. As we continued to stroke Julie, the "in favor of goat milk" opinions became the rest of us, against Dan's lone hesitation. The next weekend, we went back to Ojai for Julie, who rode home in a rented trailer pulled behind our car. She wore her new halter, carefully tied with a new rope, and she stood on a thick matting of hay spread on the floor of the trailer. Still, her terrified "baa-baa-baa" cries followed us all the way home.

Although we still had the extrafine recently baled oat and alfalfa hay that we had bought for a horse, Momma made us take a bale of "Julie's alfalfa" plus a small bag of grain, and a salt-lick, so that Julie could have "her own salt" inside the corral. We all set out to make her feel at home, and most days, the children fed her bits of celery, carrots, apple slices, or even pieces of bread. Julie would stay either in the new shed or in the sturdy corral we had built, and any horse we got could live out in the field, at least until the winter rains arrived.

When a new horse arrived a few days later, the goat, who was friendly by nature, became completely astonished at the sight of this huge animal. For a while, we heard not one more "baa." After several days, Julie seemed to realize that the horse couldn't reach her in the corral or the shed, but she did a lot of looking at the mare, and seemed to reserve judgment.

In the days that followed, I learned that Julie was quite affectionate and liked company and being talked to. Goats, like dogs and cats, are especially expressive, and this delightful animal liked to talk, especially when I walked out to visit her. All animals that make sounds seem able to communicate, to express things like "yes," "no," "watch out," "get away," or "please." In addition to audible language, they talk with their eyes, ears, tails, posture, and actions. I swore that Julie often fluttered her eyelashes when she was in an interrogatory mode, such as when our dog Treve tried to meet her and she seemed to be asking, "Just what sort of animal is that one beside you?" There had been no other resident animals in her former life.

Sometimes I led Julie around on my now green lawn, or I tied her with a long chain to one of the redwood fence posts that we'd set out around the yard—these were posts that waited the entire time we lived on O'Connor Way for the horizontal boards that were to be added to make it a real fence. On the patio, I used to sit and try to both read the paper and hold Julie's long chain so that she could browse around the yard. One morning, she suddenly came up to me, brought her face up close to mine, blew a kiss in my ear, and nuzzled my face. Lovely!

Even when I held her by the chain, Julie loved to scamper up on the new stack of baled alfalfa or on a separate stack of oat hay, where she probably felt she was Queen of the Mountain. Although she was pregnant, Mrs. Goat usually hammed it up and acted like a rambunctious or moody teenager. Her feed box had to be nailed to the side of the shed, and her watering bucket wired to the fence; otherwise, she would have destroyed them. Lacking other toys, she had begun to use the bucket and the box as play equipment in the corral.

Like our rabbits, Mrs. Goat also chewed on wood, mainly on the wood of the shed and the corral. She was also a master at opening the gate to escape from the corral, and she got into the yard a number of times. Mrs. Goat always enjoyed tasting and testing new things, such as clothes and sheets hanging on the clothesline. With all my other jobs and family I seldom witnessed her buffoonery; if I wasn't around to catch her, she pulled the wash off the clothesline and ran around with it in her mouth, or she pushed her way under the sheets and other items to scratch the itch on her back, or maybe just for the fun of it. On the porch she sometimes found shoes and socks (or even a sweater) to carry around and chew to smithereens. Nothing could be left outside after Julie arrived. Julie also liked to nip and nibble on clothes while we were wearing them. For her, life was to be enjoyed, and she made the most of it. I thought her philosophy sound, but expensive for my budget in terms of replacing destroyed shoes, sheets, and my vegetable garden.

At first, Treve had no use for the goat, but gradually she won him over. Both Treve and Julie loved life and fun, but they never did figure out quite how to get their games going right. They tried. Julie chased Treve around the yard and butted him with her head a few times, but when Treve tried to chase her, she jumped up on the haystack and looked down as though to say, "Come on. Playing tag all over the stack of hay is even more fun."

I bought a metal garbage can to hold Julie's grain, and wired and staked it securely, for I knew she could make herself seriously ill if she ever got out and ate all the grain in one grand banquet. She often jumped onto the top of the can to view her domain. Being that high put her eye-to-eye with me as I held her leash, and we would gaze into each other's eyes, each of us probably wondering what the other was thinking, and each of us wishing we could talk to the other. Ever so quickly, Julie became family to me, not just a source of milk.

Dan made a crude milking and feeding station for Julie designated the "milking stool" with a wooden box from the dump. Soon after, Dan came in one morning to report, "Well, my carefree time is more scarce than ever—this morning there are three goats out there." Fortunately, Mrs. Goat had managed the births without assistance, since neither Dan nor I had any knowledge or experience as a midwife to a goat. But mom and the two babies were fine—Julie had instinctively cleaned them up and was ready for food and water when we all rushed out to congratulate her and see her kids. In an agitated state, she fretted about so much company and positioned herself between her babies and us that first morning.

My little oasis of new green lawn on two sides of the house quickly became a goat entertainment center. It seemed just a matter of days before the baby goats began to weasel under the bottom board of the corral and act like playful, high-spirited children—jumping, running, bumping their hard heads against each other, and leaping over boxes and the milking stand.

Julie had given birth to one son and one daughter, and Nancy promptly named them Jack and Jill. These pixies were as pretty as could be, with snow-white coats, sturdy little bodies, legs as agile as ballet dancers, and elflike faces with bright, inquisitive eyes. The goats obviously relished company, needed and cared for each other, and took joy in their play together. I suddenly realized that their mom had been lonely. Like horses, sheep, and dogs, goats are herd animals, and they savor companionship. When deprived of the company of their own species, they may become buddies with other animals. At my friend's ranch years ago, a monkey had actually hung out with a horse. Here our dog Treve tried hard to play with the goats and the cat, but met the greatest success by just staying around the children and me most of the time.

I complained, "These goat kids are acting like about a dozen of the human kind. They and their mom continue to outwit all our efforts to make the gate and corral goat-proof, and they're now chewing up the cross-boards. While Momma Goat studies and figures out the multiple gate latches, her kids crawl or wiggle out under the corral fence." The first time the youngsters escaped, Momma Goat became so frantic to be out with them that she broke two hooks on the gate in order to join them in the fun. Dan finally decided to nail hog wire around the entire inside of the wooden corral.

Julie's dietary needs and her curiosity changed little as time passed. The stomachs of goats have four chambers, like those of cows, but goats are able to eat more weeds and plants and nonfood items than cows could tolerate—I found the horse's new halter and rope chewed almost beyond use, as Julie, with her milk bag swinging, was running around the yard carrying the halter in her mouth.

Jack and Jill were such pretty animals, and it seemed as though they and their mother all loved compliments and laughter. Maybe it was my imagination, but I began to wonder if my laughter didn't signal them permission to do more damage and to perform daring exploits willy-nilly. I tried to laugh lots.

Before the woven hog wire could be bought and nailed up on the corral fence, the stunt actors danced and bounced from the baled hay to the wood pile to the lawn. One day I looked out a window and caught sight of the young kids on our car roof, with Momma Goat on the hood. The youngsters had jumped from the hood to the roof. They were sitting and soaking up the view and the warm sunshine on their improvised decks. Only the thick mud on their hooves saved the car from bad scratches.

The second car that the goats jumped onto was not ours, but one of an acquaintance who had come on business. This woman drove a glistening black car, and she herself was a model of high fashion from head to toe. As she came to the front door, even before gazing at my cast of characters and the whole homestead stage set, I think her lips were already curling, the way the goats' lips did when they were annoyed or unhappy.

The front room was now always a minefield of baby clutter, preschool kids' clutter, school kids' clutter, and grown-ups' clutter. Even without the children themselves in the room, it was a mob scene of family belongings, and, as usual, I was a reactor rather than an actor in this crisis. As our friend found a spot on the sofa where she could sit down, I rushed to scoop up an armload of toys, newspapers, and drinking glasses nearby. I was like a stagehand still getting props in place as the curtain goes up.

When this woman left the house just a short time later, she and I saw an astonishing sight. Momma Goat was on the hood, and the two babies were on the roof of her shiny black car. As I yelled and ran toward the car, the goats jumped off. The woman and I inspected the car and discovered long muddy scratches on the hood and roof. I also noticed that the nose of this enraged female was turned up and that her upper lip was forming a distinct curl. Dan and I paid to have the fender, hood, and top of her car repainted. She never came to the house again.

I hadn't given much thought recently to what this person would see in our small living room, but even when I thought about it, I knew that a social, conventional way of living would have to wait a long time. There was no alternative: that room was the only room in which to stuff a sofa, three chairs, the large upright piano, the floor-model TV, and two bookcases. This was the way it was, and so be it—a daily soap opera of undiscovered actors, who were without silk and chiffon clothes, divorces, glamorous sets, or the terrible problems of life that appeared on soap operas on the TV screen if I turned it on in the afternoon.

Actually, it could have been worse: the dog had been outside, Danny wasn't practicing his scales and finger exercises, and I hadn't begun to set up the playpen for Baby Jeff to roll around in. I managed to laugh about the visit that evening as I related the story to Dan while I got supper served.

"Well, we are what we are. I'm not her and she's not me. It would be better if I could lock a gate down at the road and avoid visitors like her for several years so I can struggle in privacy to beautify this place and add on a room or two."

On my farm stage set, the baby goats, Jack and Jill, and their mom, with lots of excess energy, continued to put on impromptu displays of gymnastics while dancing and playing follow-the-leader whenever they managed to escape the corral. Both baby goats, like their mom, began to chew up the wooden fencing, plus everything they could find in the yard or on the porches, and both Momma Goat and her kids spent hours pulling hay loose from the alfalfa bales.

Jack and Jill especially loved the two small porches and the front and back steps of the house, and they invented stunt games there—running up the steps to the porch, jumping off on the sides, and then running up the steps again. They performed for each other, as well as for me. In fact, we were all avid fans, as long as the destruction was limited, and they seemed to know we were laughing at their slapstick skits.

Once they found the front door ajar, and I suddenly had the goat kids storming through the living room where Doug and Danny were sitting on the rug. The human kids screamed, and the goat kids turned and went flying back out by the same door.

Procrastination of even a day or two doesn't work well on a farm; our delay in installing the hog wire meant a series of costly performances involving irrepressible fun and "baaaing." Goat youngsters and mom grazed on my several new trees and shrubs, and ran repeatedly through the bed of my newly prepared vegetable garden. I tried to monitor them from the window over the kitchen sink, but their current prank was usually in progress before I could scream, "Julie, Jack, and Jill, stop it!" This time Julie was carrying one of Doug's new white shoes in her mouth, and the kids were trying to grab it from her. Only extra servings of alfalfa got them back into the corral, but Doug's left shoe was never the same.

With Julie giving more milk than we could drink, we brought home two baby Hereford calves to drink the extra, and feeding the calves became another of my several-times-a-day jobs. Dan milked Julie before he left each morning, and again at night, but I fed the calves after he escaped to the college each morning.

It was fun to teach those reddish-colored baby calves to drink out of a pail, but, as I'd discovered in Arizona, this chore usually meant a change of clothes. I remembered the process—after putting a rope on the calf, I would hold his body tightly between my knees, pick up the pail of warm milk in one hand, and with the other hand push the calf's head down into the milk. As his mouth sank deeper into the milk, I put my hand farther down into the milk and quickly pointed one finger up toward the calf's mouth. He pranced and nudged the pail around, splashing me all over, maybe smelling the milk and getting some of the milk in his mouth. He desperately wanted breakfast. When he eventually started to suck on my finger, I lowered it still deeper into the milk, and soon he was drinking instead of just sucking on my finger. A baby calf is often as much fun as a baby goat. My zoo had expanded to include baby calves, baby goats, Julie the momma goat, Treve the dog, and Shandy the independent cat outside, plus six of us inside the little house.

Yet, in spite of the "funny farm" chaos provided by this large clan, Dan sometimes invited guests home who were visiting the college. On one occasion, Dan invited a Mr. Francis to dinner. This man was an official, from either the Agency for International Development, called AID, or from the USDA office in Washington—I can't remember which. While I cooked dinner and gave the children an early supper in the kitchen, Mr. Francis, still in a dark suit, white shirt, and navy blue tie, followed Dan out to watch him feed and milk Julie. That evening Dan also did my feeding chores and poured part of the goat milk into another pail to take to the Hereford calves—nothing very unusual.

Maybe Mr. Francis was looking for material for an article, or maybe his visit to Cal Poly's campus hadn't been particularly instructive, for our guest suddenly became enthusiastic and excited at the idea of how we were benefiting from our goats. At dinner, since it was Mr. Francis's birthday, we drank a toast to him with goat milk. That toast was very appropriate, as he then lost no time in telling us how our "farming operation" could be copied in many other parts of the world, especially in countries like Israel and Jordan. We tried not to laugh as he talked about our "great farming operation."

In those days, when meat was considered so necessary for good health, Mr. Francis and others like him spent a lot of time thinking of ways to increase the supply of meat in developing countries. In many of those places, people owned and farmed small plots of land like ours. On those plots, Mr. Francis decided at dinner, people should have goats, not only for milk, cheese, and meat, but to help raise beef calves. No matter how long the calves were kept, they would put on far more weight than goat kids. Voilà! There would be less poverty and better health worldwide. Mr. Francis said he would write up our methods and get the word out.

Actually, goats had originated some ten million years ago in the part of the world he was talking about, so maybe those lands would once again host goats, and calves as well. Even so, I felt, as I knew Dan did, that this idea of giving goats' milk to beef calves seemed a bit simplified. Where would those countries get all the calves, for instance? But we kept from laughing, and I even explained that goat and calf fertilizer would be like gold and help make small vegetable or grain plots grow like crazy. Goats can readily adapt to many types of food. Some goats, I'd read, even pull small farm carts and furnish hair for clothes—all sorts of possibilities.

The official publication eventually came out for distribution, and we received a copy along with a glowing letter of appreciation from Mr. Francis. During the next year, several teams and single men from abroad came to see our part-time farm. Israel and neighboring countries apparently had land and weather similar to California's Central Coast, and maybe even weeds and brush similar to those growing on our "back forty."

One summer Dan even took one group from Yugoslavia that was visiting Cal Poly around the state in a bus for ten days, visiting farms, ranches, and other agricultural businesses. The members of that group all had dinner at our house the last evening. With such limited seating, some of the guests ate outside, balancing their plates on top of the red-wood fence posts and watching the goats while eating. They had heard about the goats. We laughed about our internationally famous Julie for many years.

Like cows, goats have to be bred each year if they are to give milk. Eventually it was time to find a suitor for Julie. I phoned feed stores and asked around, since there were no goat ads in the telephone book. This didn't seem to be a county of goat fanciers. I was considering placing an ad for matrimonial assistance for Julie, when I finally located a small farmer in the north county who had goats. "Yes, you can bring your nanny and take her home the same day; there should be no problem," he told me. We had just acquired a horse trailer, and I volunteered to drive it over the Cuesta Grade, with Julie in the trailer and Doug and Jeff with me in the car.

True to form, I could have been better informed before driving up there with one goat and two little boys. As it turned out, the goat farm was small and squalid, the buck was brown and smelly with filth, and his long curling hooves hadn't been trimmed in ages. It seemed a miracle he could even walk. His appearance scarcely marked him as a bearer of good ancestral genes for beauty, brains, brawn, or sweetness. Still, maybe he had good qualities that weren't visible—it wasn't his fault that he lived there, and he probably looked much better in earlier years.

I unloaded Julie, whispering to her that she'd get a good antiseptic bath once we returned home, and I led her into the corral, as directed by the elderly goat owner, who seemed to live alone in a small house nearby. I hoped Julie's terrifying ride in the trailer and this strange, unromantic setting wouldn't make her too reluctant.

"Behave, Julie, think about having some cute children in about five months," I mumbled to her, as I pulled her farther into the corral, where the buck's odor was almost overwhelming.

Lo and behold, in about an hour's time the old buck managed to become Julie's husband of the day. The farmer helped me load Julie back into the trailer and tie her properly, and we started for home.

Within a hundred feet or so of the fifteen hundred-foot high Cuesta Summit, the car suddenly quit. No warning—the motor just stopped. I let the car glide to the side of the road and began to try to flag down cars. For a while, no one stopped to help, and no policeman drove by. The day was windy and chilly, and little Jeff began to cry for food and milk. I finally flagged down three different drivers and gave each of them the Auto Club's towing phone number to call. About an hour later, a tow truck finally arrived. I asked the driver if one, two, or three people had reported me. He said just one. Even back in "the good old days," not everyone was a good Samaritan. The driver of the tow truck took all of us home and then towed the car to a repair shop.

As promised, Julie got a good soapy bath on the lawn the next day. Mostly, animals like to be clean, just as humans do; though many, like cats, like to wash themselves. Certainly, Julie had never had a bath before, and she was one impatient, grouchy nanny before I was through with the pail of soap and water, a bar of Fels Naptha for extra measure, and a cold-water rinse from the hose.

It had been a wretched two days, but in due time, Julie had two snow-white and beautiful kids. I don't know if it was partly the bad trip over the mountain or what, but when Dan suggested we get rid of the goats and buy a cow, I very quickly said, "Why not? One neighbor buying milk, plus an additional calf or two, will more than pay for the larger feed bill."

I phoned Dan's mom and told her we were going to get a cow. The timing was just right. We had a relative, married only a few years, who said he would love to take all five of our goats if we could deliver them. So Julie and her kids went to a new and good home, one with a little girl to give them treats.

Saying goodbye to friendly, intelligent, and bright-eyed Julie and her smart-aleck kids was ever so hard, but so was milking her twice a day for much less milk than a cow gives. Having to breed a goat and then needing to get rid of her offspring were also increasing problems, since we loved the kids too much to have them butchered. In contrast, there were plenty of bulls around to service a cow, and if ever that failed, artificial insemination service was available.

The following week we all piled into the car to go pick out the new Jersey cow milk maker, while Dan repeated his tired joke, "Kids, I guess you know that the white goats gave us white milk, and now we'll get a brown cow to give us chocolate milk." We laughed, and we were reminded that happiness isn't just "a warm puppy," as Charles Schulz would have you believe, but all close relationships—including a partner, kids, and many kinds of animals.

Chapter 36

A Very Special Jersey

Dan had a friend by the last name of Righetti who owned a very fine dairy farm south of town and up toward the hills. The day we went to purchase a cow from him, a number of beautiful Jersey cows were grazing in a green field near his farmyard where we parked. It was midafternoon, and lengthening shadows warned that the cows would soon be streaming in on a well-worn trail to the barn in order to be milked.

Mr. Righetti met us with a welcoming smile as he walked quickly over from the house to meet the six of us at the fence. "I have to give some thought about which cow I can spare, which one will make this nice young family of yours with lots of kids a good family cow." It had to be his decision; we all remained quiet, but each of us probably tried hard to spot the best one as he was considering which cow he would choose.

Maude, our huge Holstein cow in Arizona, had become a nice cow for us, but she gave so much milk it was hard to get rid of it all, even when two neighbors each bought a gallon or two each week and I fed all I could to our calves. Jerseys are a much smaller breed and give less milk. They are colored a bit like deer, and have wonderful, big, liquid-brown eyes. The cow Mr. Righetti chose for us was beautiful, and we immediately named her April for the month of her birth. I fell in love with her right then and there.

Once back at O'Connor Way, it was easier to unload April from the truck than it had been to put her into it back at the dairy. Now, she actually seemed quite tame and was willing to be led into the corral, where she would meet the horse for the first time. I wanted their first encounter to take place where we could monitor their reactions before I let them live together in the back field.

The arrival of this lovely, small Jersey cow was an exciting event in our normally low-key, informal, and casual drama. However, even with a smaller cow, within days, not our cup, but our whole kitchen, was running over with milk. The neighbor's children came to collect gallon jars of it for their large family down the road, our two new calves slurped it out of a pail, and the six of us drank it morning, noon, and night.

Treve was discovering that his family grew and diminished in mysterious ways. He had never met a cow before, and several of our horses hadn't stayed with us for very long. April sometimes followed Treve when he headed toward the back of the field hoping to flush out a bird or a rabbit to chase. The dog usually came home and stayed beside April while Dan milked her.

In addition to companionship, critters need space, lots of it, just like people do, to be healthy and happy. The needs of these sensitive animals got me thinking, as I talked to Dan while we watched April's reaction to her new home. "Maybe it's what I got from those political science classes I took, but I'm sure all animals, as well as humans, need the same rights 'to life, liberty and the pursuit of happiness.' They yearn for liberty, for freedom to roam, discover, and form groups. It's amazing that the dog and the cow seemed to become friends. I'm sure all critters strive to be happy, to have fun, and, from tiny fish to huge elephants, try to enjoy life.

"But it's harder and harder for them as so many of their habitats are increasingly threatened. Not all dairies have those nice big fields April enjoyed back at Mr. Righetti's dairy, and I suspect more and more horses are being kept in corrals instead of being able to run free in fields or being exercised every day. None of us can individually save the planet and all the animals and plants on it—yet each human being can do a lot, even on a small scale, by treating every animal, both wild and tame, with compassion and caring.

"What squares you and I are! Thank heavens there are still lots of us around, especially in the field of agriculture. The president and other politicians trying to win elections should make up a slogan, 'Make this a country of squares again,' with values of hard work, honesty, and caring for everyone and all living things. I think it's likely that your nice dairyman friend has sold us one of his best cows."

"That's probably true," Dan replied, "but right now I've got to get April milked, and I need a square meal before I go teach."

I sensed that Dan felt much better about milking a cow again, even though all of us missed those bright and happy-go-lucky goats. April had freshened recently, so once again, I'd be buying young calves and teaching them to drink out of a bucket, and filling one-gallon mayonnaise jars with milk for us and the large family nearby. Maybe it was a feeling of passage, of relief, that inspired Dan to take the goat-milking station and break it up into firewood that evening.

As April settled into her routine of feeding, grazing, and being milked, Treve could see that she didn't want to run or play the way the goat or horse had. Still, the dog was forever kind, and seemed determined to make friends with her. Treve demonstrated so many fine traits, ones that I hoped our four kids would take to heart as the years passed. These traits could all come under the heading of "kindness," a word that usually encompasses other concepts such as loyalty, compassion, sensitivity, love, concern, giving, trust, understanding, and praise.

Chapter 37

My Blue One

After the Christmas holidays, Dan jokingly, and at the same time worriedly, mentioned to his students our dismal luck in getting a good horse. He told them the story about one-eyed Big Red, who could have killed Nancy, explaining that "my wife and I bought the wrong horse three times in a row."

Surely it was wonderful fate that had placed in one of Dan's classes a student who was already a superb horseman—a top trainer not only of horses, but also of their riders. Eventually, he owned his own large training facilities and a stable of riding and racing horses. Monty would also become world-famous for his gentle, successful methods of training horses, and he would write a number of best-selling books. Even while attending college, he had taken on the development of a small riding facility nearby.

After class, Monty came up and told Dan that he knew some people who had two gray horses for showing and wanted to sell one. "She's not the sorrel color your daughter wants, but a fine horse is what's important—color doesn't make the horse. The gray mare they're replacing is a great little horse, but not quality enough to win in big shows. These people will only sell their mare to a very good home." He promised to talk to them.

Later, Monty reported that his friends would sell us the mare, whose name was Blue One. Monty agreed to help Nancy learn to ride properly, and was willing to advise us about our tack. As soon as he looked at Nancy's saddle and bridle, he was obviously shocked, and I watched him search for words to tell us. He decided to be frank, saying, "You couldn't have bought anything much worse." Our bargain saddle from Mexico was too long and too wide in the seat, and the cinches and stirrups were wrong. The bridle and bit were as bad as the saddle. Nothing was right. Not only would we be paying more than we had planned to spend for the mare, but all the tack had to be replaced.

Saddles are often made for different uses, such as roping, barrel racing, or pleasure riding. The saddle we got for Nancy would be made for pleasure riding. It would be safe and comfortable and fit Nancy's tall and slender shape. Saddles also need to fit the horse, and Monty spoke of Blue's "center of balance."

Monty sent off an order for us to the Garcia Saddlery Store in Salinas for a new saddle, saddle blanket, bridle, and bit—equipment good enough that Nancy could use it even in shows, if she ever decided to do that. The saddle had a nice padded seat and was decorated with touches of silver. The new saddle blanket fit properly between the horse and the saddle. Even I could tell that the new bit and bridle were totally different and much better than what we had bought. In fact, all the new gear looked elegant, comfortable, and right for both horse and rider.

With all this activity, we decided to buy a used horse trailer, and Monty kept us from making mistakes on that purchase. It would be a single-horse trailer, well-made and sturdy, with wheels far apart, and balanced properly to make for a level ride. There needed to be a manger in front for hay or grain, and it would be nice if there were compartments for Blue's saddle and other tack, and for storing a bit of hay. The tailgate had to be fairly low when put down, so it would be easy for a horse to walk up the ramp into the trailer, as well as to back out and down. And the gate needed a strong metal latch. Other features of a good trailer I've forgotten, but Monty gave his OK to the used one I finally located. The new horse would now have wheels.

Towing our new trailer behind the station wagon and feeling very tense, we drove down to Santa Maria to buy the horse. We hadn't even seen this mare yet, other than in a snapshot that Monty had brought to school. Still, with three bad mistakes haunting us, it was hard to get our excitement and expectations up. "Honey, let's stay cautious, just in case."

As the stable door was opened, Blue and another gray mare came spilling out, both horses trying to get out the door at the same time as we walked up to the corral. A sudden shiver raced up and down my spine: both horses were beautiful and happy and had been properly chosen and trained by Monty—it looked as if our history of horse-buying boo-boos was definitely over!

At first glance, the mares looked like twins. There was an intense moment of waiting, during which I tried to figure out which mare was ours. Both horses were medium-sized dark grays, with alert, nicely chiseled heads, big dark eyes, and ears that pricked forward with curiosity and friendship. Their legs seemed straight, their backs were level, and they looked strong. These were contented and joyful horses, and they both trotted up to the fence, probably looking for an apple or a carrot. Nancy seemed mesmerized and said nothing, but she pulled two carrots out of her pants pocket.

"The one on your left is Blue One," Monty observed, as he carried the new halter and rope we'd brought through the gate of the corral. The mare was barely five years old, not seven or more, as Monty had much earlier suggested would be a good age for a horse who would be ridden by someone of Nancy's age, but Monty assured us the mare was a whole list of good things, saying, "Unlike some horses at five, this one's gentle, trustworthy, reins beautifully, and is very obedient. She has a steady personality and is a 'thinking horse.' See her wide forehead and wide-spaced bright eyes?"

Blue, whose breeding was half Morgan and half quarter horse, had been gently and carefully trained and was a sensitive, intelligent mare. Unlike Little Foot, she obviously felt all was right with the world. Both the horses remained near us against the fence. At that time, fortunately, it was becoming more common to "train" horses than to "break" them with brute strength, a whip, and ropes. This mare was talking with her body—with gestures of her ears, tail, and head—and again I felt a great wave of relief. In addition to the mare's obvious qualities, there were the honest and nice family selling her and Monty's advising us.

It was an emotional time for Nancy and me, as well as for the owners. Even though Blue wasn't top-star quality for shows at such places as the San Francisco Cow Palace shows, they had loved her and would miss her.

The young mare had been well-schooled in loading. I'd brought a coffee-can of grain, and Nancy shook the oats into the manger. Blue willingly walked right up the tailgate and into the trailer, as she had been taught to do. Then, with Blue whinnying her excitement, we drove away with our precious cargo.

Blue whinnied and whinnied all the way home, with the melodious sound drifting clearly into the car. Was it her delight at the thought of going somewhere, or was it an anxious goodbye to the other gray horse who wasn't coming with her? As it turned out, in all the years we owned her, this easygoing and happy mare would continue to whinny while being trailered. We were getting the news straight from the horse's mouth—I thought Blue liked to go places, especially to horse shows (unlike many horses, she always walked quickly into the trailer and never needed any prodding).

Glory be! That afternoon, every one of us suddenly knew that Nancy finally had her dream horse. We could sense that this mare would become part of the family, and Dan and I also knew there just might be another horse before too long...I had realized my dreams! Years later, one of our Arizona friends remembered that I had once confided to her that I had a lifelong wish for four kids, a station wagon, a collie dog, and a farm or a ranch with a horse or two.

Actually, I was already making new plans, since it had become clear to me that loneliness can be devastating—that animals, like humans, need companionship. Our sheep had needed other sheep, our goat had needed other goats, the chickens had banded together, and humans need other humans. Blue would miss the other gray mare and would need a friend. But in the meantime, the soft clop-clop of Blue's hooves on our lane would be a happy sound, and each time Nancy and Blue went out together, they'd have each other.

I turned around to wink at Nancy and whispered, "Ooh la la, she's awesome! At last everything is coming up roses!"

Nancy sat unusually quiet in the backseat, as though she were still barely breathing from all the suspense and final success, and she moved over beside the door, away from Danny and Doug, while Jeff sat in the front seat with Mom and Dad. She was certainly full of this special moment, yet was visibly relaxed and had a wide grin glued to her face. This lovely, dark blue-gray mare, with her refined head and alert eyes and ears, would become Nancy's "Blue One" in more than name. Even the sky blue day appeared brighter to me as I contemplated our good fortune.

Danny, meanwhile, was handling his new paper route and scout activities. I finally relented with the warning, "Just remember—you're the paperboy! Your mom's too old to be folding papers." That sounded good, but I was soon folding papers on the days the deliveries had to be done in a hurry so the whole family could go to the beach and to other activities on time.

Danny's next request was even more frightening and frustrating. He wanted a gun—a BB gun. Both Dan and I hated guns, but Danny countered that with "Mom, I won't shoot anything that's alive. I'll just practice with tin cans out in the field, way back in the field. All my friends have guns." I was sure that not all families gave their little boys real guns, but most of the boys who went to the rural school down on Los Osos Road probably had them. Danny begged and begged.

So there was a BB gun under the Christmas tree that year. Our hope and plan was that this might be a passing phase.

"You must go out to the back of the field. Don't shoot anywhere near the house. Your sister and your little brothers all need their two eyes—a BB gun could blind them. Let me see you cover your eyes with both hands for a full minute so you can feel how that would be."

Fortunately, Doug and Jeff were still small, and their "wants" were red wagons, a big set of building blocks, and a kitten. Physically, they looked as if they led the most dangerous life of all our children—they always seemed to have skinned knees, skinned elbows, and cuts on their fingers and toes, making it look as if they'd walked into a field of land mines, especially after I coated all their "owies" with Mercurochrome. The land mines were usually our red-rock lane, our barbed wire fences, the climbable oak trees up on Bishop's Peak, and the baled haystacks in the small barn.

When Doug started collecting bugs, as Nancy and Danny once had, my worries about that were small compared to those I'd had over the activities of the older two kids. I did take note, however, when Doug held up one of his many jars and asked, "Shall I take the lid off?" or "Boy, is this a big spider!" or "Look at this guy's stinger!" or just, "I've got to show you this, but be careful!" Still, these challenges were nothing compared to those presented by the older kids.

Would the saying that "The outside of a horse is good for the inside of a man" apply to a young girl? I was very sure Blue would be good for the inside of Nancy. Nevertheless, I had a daughter riding bareback, at a lope or a gallop, on top of a thousand pounds of horsepower pounding alongside a paved street on four iron-shod hooves. And Danny was riding his bicycle on a paper route that took him beside fast-moving traffic on Foothill Boulevard and O'Connor Way.

I'd devoted my entire life to keeping these kids safe and in one piece. Now, they could kill themselves. Oh, my! Not until they learned to drive a car and Doug started experimenting with a big chemistry set in the laundry room did it get any worse.

In the twenties, when I was very young, my dad had taken me up for a plane ride with a barnstorming pilot while Mom stood and agonized beside the landing strip. I can still see her there, withstanding a brisk wind, shading her eyes with one hand to look up, and holding down her billowing, long brown coat with her other hand, and I remember that I felt sorry for her and her fear for my safety. Maybe that marked me for life, keeping me from ever enjoying living dangerously. Many years later, two of our sons, one grandson, and one daughter-in-law learned to pilot small planes. All three sons ski off steep snow-covered mountains, now with grandchildren leading the pack or following close behind. Worse, worser, and worsest! Those aren't laugh lines around my mouth—they're whimper lines!

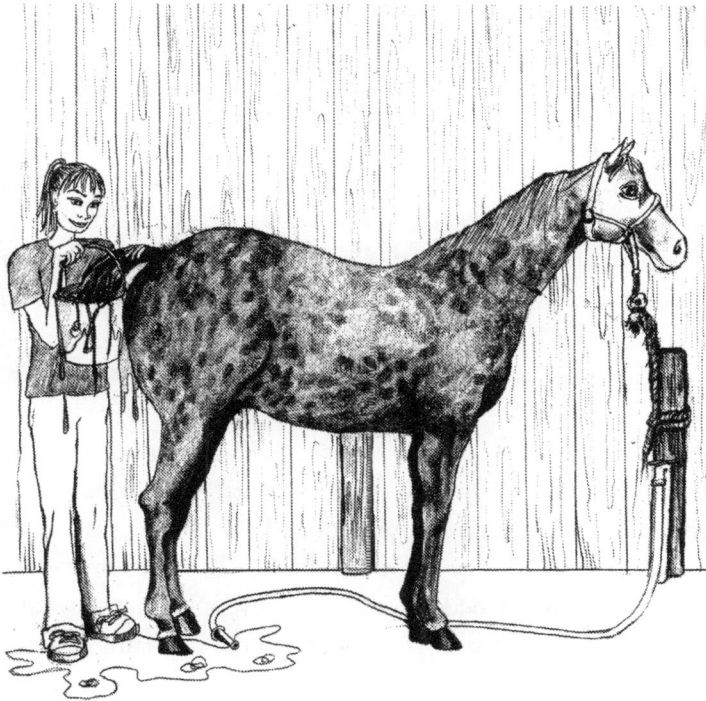

Chapter 38

Life with Blue—Who Needs Schooling?

Countless things changed, and we had much to do in connection with Blue entering our lives. Nancy, of course, was in heaven, but unexpected bills kept coming in. While the purchase price of the horse was far more than I'd planned, it was only the down payment. Just as when you buy a car, you must also pay for insurance, gasoline, oil, new parts, and other repairs, buying a horse requires paying the bills for hay and oats, shelter, a watering trough, gates, and fencing, among other things. Blue had to receive new shoes periodically, and there were occasional vet bills. The new custom-made equipment of a saddle, a blanket, and reins had arrived from the saddler in Salinas. There were ropes, a pail, a brush, and a currycomb to buy, and time had to be found to exercise the horse daily and to train both horse and rider.

Now that we had the horse trailer, Blue and Nancy could go out to Monty's training stable south of town and take lessons. The mare had obviously received a lot of schooling, but Nancy had not. Even as a five-year-old, Blue had already shown her stability, her desire to please, and her easy gaits, with a soft, springy trot and a slow easy lope, but she needed refresher lessons, especially in working with Nancy.

While watching a lesson, little Doug remarked, "I already know how to ride. You kick 'em to make 'em go and pull back to make 'em stop. Then you steer 'em like this with the reins." He showed me a plausible imitation of reining a plow horse, and then asked, "Why does Nancy have to go to school?"

"Nancy has to learn to ride the correct way. Just like riding your first bicycle doesn't teach you to drive a real car, Nancy has to learn the safe and correct way to ride a real horse. Even horses can forget some of their training, so Monty can teach Nancy how to remind the horse what they both have learned. Actually, honey, only part of what you say about riding is correct. Pulling back hard on the reins might make Blue's mouth hurt, because that bit in her mouth is made of metal."

The next week the two younger boys and I went to watch Nancy's first lesson with Monty. While I'd had a horse growing up, I would learn by listening, not riding. Monty asked Nancy to back the mare out of the trailer, and he showed her how to make a slipknot and tie the horse to a hitching post. He showed her exactly where to set the blanket and saddle and how to firmly cinch up the saddle. Nancy and I had practiced a little of this, but Monty had more needed instructions and authority, and the weight of his words was far more than a mere mom's. He showed Nancy a better way to put the bridle over Blue's head, and although many horses are touchy about this kind of attention, Blue stayed calm. I think the mare liked being near the other horses at the stable, and she may even have enjoyed the training.

Monty's first statements said so much: "Like best friends, both you and Blue will develop a partnership, and it will get so you know what to do with just a few small clues. You'll trust each other. However, as Blue's rider, you'll always have to remain firm and yet kind. To be firm, you need to be both confident and patient, but never try to use force.

That means you need to learn how to ensure proper horse behavior and to understand what that is."

Somewhere, maybe as a child, I had learned how to mount correctly, and I had taught Nancy to do that as best I could. Monty showed all that to Nancy again, and then how to dismount as well. He explained it step by step: "Nancy, turn and face the rear of the horse. Stand close to Blue. Now put your left hand over the reins and hold on to them while grabbing the saddle horn. Using your right hand, turn the stirrup around so it faces you and…"

From that point on, Nancy began schooling that was new to her. Once in a while, Monty got on Blue and made sure that the horse was reacting quickly and in the right manner. The boys and I sat on the bleachers and watched. I remembered a lot of what was in the lessons, since Monty repeated instructions so many times, but they were far more complicated and detailed than Doug had expected: "Don't slide your foot in as far as it will go. Keep the ball of your foot on the stirrup, so if you stand up in the stirrups, you'll be on the balls of your feet. Now, point your toes straight ahead toward the horse's head. Keep your heels down slightly lower than the rest of your foot. Keep a little weight on your feet, but sit down squarely in the saddle. Your knees should be bent about as much as they are now. Animals are a lot like people: they'll do a lot for you if you ask politely."

Nancy learned to barely move the reins against Blue's neck when she needed to turn her, and to press one leg against her side to signal her. She barely pulled the reins to stop or back up, and gave lots of softly spoken praise when the horse understood and obeyed. She learned to keep her body centered, tall, and balanced while Blue loped her figure eights.

Monty continued, "It's good to talk to Blue. Horses have good hearing, and she'll hear a very soft command. If you decide to enter her in shows, you'll want her to obey your instructions immediately and smoothly. So you can quietly say 'walk,' 'trot,' 'lope,' 'whoa,' and 'back' each time, if you wish."

After a number of lessons, I decided Nancy was learning so much, and Blue seemed so happy while being trained, that it might be fun for them to enter some of the small, county shows that Monty had mentioned. Nancy too had begun to wonder how well the two of them would do in a show.

First, Nancy would have to get some proper riding clothes. Monty turned us over to his wife, Pat, and beautiful riding attire began arriving in the mail from the Salinas store. There were a stylish, pearl-gray, western hat; a long-sleeved, blue-gray shirt with pearl buttons; a pair of light gray leather chaps; and soft, two-tone gray boots with decorative stitching. None of this came cheap.

With the prospect of showing her horse, lessons took on more fun and meaning for our tall and slender twelve-year-old. Monty stepped up the schooling on Blue's weaker points, along with giving more directions to Nancy: "You've got to work on Blue's leads—she's never changed them quickly or easily. Being on the right lead helps a horse with her weight and balance as she turns. The judges will want Blue to change leads correctly as she lopes a figure eight. When you ride Blue around the barnyard area by your house, get your mom to tell you whether Blue is changing properly. Soon you'll be able to feel when she switches."

This last suggestion turned out rather badly when Nancy put it into practice. One evening, Nancy rode Blue at a faster lope than usual in the parking area, heading toward a different section of the fence. As Nancy turned Blue, the horse slipped, lost her footing in a small pile of gravel, and fell down on her side. I happened to see the accident. Blue got to her feet and stood perfectly still right beside Nancy, who stayed on the ground briefly, holding her leg. She had been thrown free from Blue's body and a moment later was able to pull herself up to a standing position by grasping a stirrup. Then, gathering the reins in her hands, they walked over to the house as she shouted, "Mom! Mom!" Although Nancy still carries a small scar from that incident, she was not badly hurt, and Blue suffered not so much as a scratch.

Chapter 39

A Trail to the Irish Hills

We had owned and lived on O'Connor Farm for about three years when out friend Grace phoned to ask us to help her and her husband find a ranch to buy in the area of San Luis Obispo. After recently buying two ranches in the north county, they were now interested in one closer to San Luis, and they thought Dan and I and the kids might live on it and manage it. And so we began a long search, which finally led us to a wonderful property only a few miles from our eight-acre farm. This property was about seven hundred and sixty acres and had been used in the last few years as a turkey farm, but we would be able to find a cattleman to lease most of the land for a grazing range.

I assured Grace and her husband that the ranch would be an excellent investment, with the town eventually growing out in that direction. We went to inspect the property by driving up Prefumo Canyon Road and turning into a rutted dirt lane to the right that led to the ranch house, sheds, and barns, which were scattered around on the level top of the hill except for one very old barn down the hill on the west side.

All was serene and beautiful as we looked at the ranch. Down the valley, to the south, only a couple of ranch houses were visible, along with the little two-room schoolhouse at the far side of the corner beyond Laguna Lake, which we could see from the ranch house. Most of the ranch hills were gentle and rolling, with fields of golden oats and wild grasses bordering Los Osos Road, which extended west to Baywood Park and beyond that to Morro Bay. Behind these lower hills were the steeper mountains known as the Irish Hills, covered in oak and chaparral. Moisture-laden air from the ocean kept these hills green longer than the rest of the area.

Raising turkeys had been a hard undertaking on this land, and the owners were just not going to try any longer. That winter, our friends purchased the turkey ranch, and our family began to get ready to move. At first, we sold our back five acres, with an easement that would share the lane to our front acreage and our house. That let us keep a place for our animals as we moved, and it kept our access to our house, which we would live in until we could move in early spring. After we left, we planned to keep the house as a rental.

O'Connor Farm had never been fine-tuned or even changed very much in the three years we'd lived there. Except for a new well, a new septic system, and a fresh coat of white paint, the house was still the same, though my lawn and vegetable plots were green. As in Arizona, there were few souvenirs as reminders of this farm; I'd been too busy to even take snapshots.

Still, countless memories were made on that land, and it became a stepping stone to more exciting years to come. Our goals and dreams to this point hadn't been reached by racing down wide ribbons of freeway with our eyes glued to the road. We had followed a long, slow, steep trail of byroads and detours, with some primitive stopover homes for a number of years along the way.

The new address would not involve a change of schools for the children. From our new location, the Laguna School with its first-through-sixth-grade classes in two rooms would be only a few blocks away, and the junior and senior high schools in town would be several minutes closer.

Sometimes, moving is the only way to survive from mounds of trash when a "save everything" mom runs the household. I had always intended to save five trunks of books, but for the rest of the mess, there was no excuse. There were no antiques or treasures such as cut glass, valuable paintings, old clocks, or even a cowbell. My collections were of broken equipment—toasters, irons, an electric blanket, two pots with broken handles, and a noncleaning vacuum cleaner—as well as the new ones. Besides the books in the original five trunks, we had enough additional books to fill the space on every wall in the new home all the way to the ceilings! I had saved every piece of clothing, furniture, and ranch equipment we'd ever owned, and every old letter and magazine since the day we were married. Every closet, every cupboard, every cranny, was filled with the stuff we had accumulated over the years.

Fortunately, we never had put anything other than Christmas tree ornaments in the attics of the houses we had lived in. These attics had always seemed filled with enough electric wires to light up a theater. And the wires were invariably old, stiff, and scary-looking, going in every which way across and between the rafters. Whenever we moved to a new house, I brought a stepladder to consider the amount of the new attic space. Usually I was already holding a full box in my arms, but I would quickly back down the ladder after seeing the attic, saying, "Nope, there's already enough of a clutter of wires up there to start a five-alarm fire."

And, as usual, I excused my huge collection of worthless items by saying, "Oh, you know, it's a common malady in all Depression-era kids." Even with the prosperity that had followed the war years, I always felt hard times might come again. I might have just been born this way and the collecting was related to my nesting instincts or to the gene for survival.

One friend, who always had a ready laugh when observing my previous farm, and who tried to be both comforting and polite, suggested,

"I think that imaginative, highly intelligent humans have this saving disease, because they've read of or can imagine such things as forty-day floods, loss of jobs, no money, or new careers where they might need a front-facing back hoe, or a Palm Beach suit from the Roaring Twenties." She knew Dan still had his white Palm Beach suit from his high school days as a dance-band leader.

The what-cha-ma-call-its were becoming an awesome mountain of lifelong dimensions, yet I could always imagine a thousand happenings that would call for something from my collections. To the maxim "Waste not, want not," I had added another: "Throw away not, want not." Still, if the things in the boxes had been stored for decades without being used or missed, why keep the stuff?

This hoarding was even more deplorable because, with no attic or garage, we had stored much of the stuff outside on pallets and boards. The "too good to throw away" mountains of stuff had been covered with sheets of plastic, tarps, or sheets of tin roofing. Bicycles, wagons, scooters, shovels, and a wheelbarrow had lounged around on the lawn or dirt through rainy winters and foggy summers until they were more rust than metal. No thrift store would let any of it through the door. Luckily, Dan almost always pretended to be unfazed by his pack rat spouse.

Before moving, I tested of my genes by telling the two older kids, "I'm putting this box right here in the hallway between your doors, and I want it full of stuff you're throwing away. There are more boxes when this one's full." It could have been worse: the box got one sock, some candy wrappers, some gift-wrapping paper that looked like some I'd used back in Arizona, and half a dozen lunch sacks that I didn't dare investigate further. I could see the kids would be savers, as I was, and perhaps for the same reasons—the kids, especially the older two, had experienced poverty for years.

We had no choice of moving days, because we'd rented the O'Connor Way house and the front three acres to people moving in on a Monday in March. There was only a fine mist falling as we got up before dawn on the preceding Saturday morning to get ready to move, but soon a last, fickle-minded, hard storm moved in and made for a cold, wet, and miserable weekend for this stage of our life to end and a new stage of life to begin on a different ranch. The Los Osos Valley gets about twenty inches of rain each year, but the storm that weekend would make for a far higher total. All day, rain pounded down and a cold wind numbed us as we made the many moving trips using just the station wagon and the horse trailer.

To anyone who'd listen, I said—not once but several times—"Well, I surely did save everything for a rainy day." No one bothered to laugh—we were all too cold, shivery, and soaking wet as we sloshed back and forth in more and more mud and rain, and I speculated that at this point, the family members must surely resent my mountains of flotsam and jetsam.

The first day, we moved in all the remaining bales of hay, the piano, the deep-freeze, the trunks, and the sofa, along with Nancy's mare, Blue, and April the cow. I'd stupidly vacuumed and mopped the house at the new ranch several days earlier, not foreseeing the downpour and the muddy feet bringing in mountains of wet boxes and furniture. The weather was everywhere and got into everything.

Nancy turned Blue loose in the south end of the long shed, one that opened to the lower field adjacent to the lane leading to the house. The horse whinnied a welcome to us with every load we brought both days, clearly enjoying the green field and happy to see her family arrive. She seemed afraid of going back into the shed, but I enticed her with a big flake of oat hay that evening. If she had bloated up on too much green grass, it would have spoiled her fun, and ours, too.

Some years in this central part of the state, Californians spend a lot of time praying for rain, but this was one of those rarer years when the storms had been heavy, and people wished the rain would go away. Everything became wet as we carried it from house to car or horse trailer. Cardboard boxes were soggy and falling apart by the time they were carried inside the new house. It didn't help that at the top of the trailer, on three sides, there was an open area of about fifteen inches.

A student from the college helped us both days. I had to wonder what he thought of Dr. Dan, usually in a full suit and tie at school, out mucking in the mud, rain, and wind that blew up the valley all weekend. I also wondered if this lad had ever been so wet or worked so hard.

Hunched over, heads down, and thoroughly soaked, we all continued to pack the trailer and car and then unload our belongings at the new house. Feeling guilty about the working conditions, I raced back into the kitchen at the old house, rinsed out a pot and cups from the still-dirty sink of breakfast dishes, and made hot coffee and cocoa for the crew before the stove was unplugged and moved. With plastic cups full, we sat on the bare floor of the living room and enjoyed an interval of rest.

Blue had been easy to move, but the piano, the deep-freeze, and the cow were unruly monsters who didn't want to be loaded. Claustrophobia can affect animals as well as people, and they don't like to be cornered with no way to escape. To April, the trailer was a closed box on wheels, a box that made her unsteady on her feet. And she definitely preferred solid, flat ground to the slippery incline of the muddy tailgate.

The neighbor who had been buying some of April's milk came to lend us a hand loading her, but even with four of us pulling and pushing, April danced a muddy waltz. The neighbor suggested "twisting her tail," but when he tried that, April kicked his shins and swung her tail across his neck. That ramp was the scariest thing she'd seen since she'd been delivered to us in a cattle truck. Her second method of protesting was to plant her feet as if they were in cement, while she shook her head back and forth and up and down so that we could hardly hang on to her halter and ropes. The cow's third strategy was to turn and stand sideways to the ramp. Oats and hay were not a good bribe that day. It didn't help that Dan and I had a lot more backbone than muscle, and that our children took after their parents in lack of brawn.

It was just as hard to push our piano up the trailer's ramp. The full-sized piano rocked and swayed, and there was just no room inside the single-horse trailer for a person to stand alongside the piano and pull—if one of the men went in first to lift and pull, then there was no way for him to get back out once the piano was in there. There were a lot of shouts of "One, two, three, PUSH!" before the freezer, cow, and piano were all transferred to their new location.

In this manner, we moved down the Valley a few miles to the Oak Hills Ranch. Oak Hills was happiness to me: each time we arrived pulling a trailer load of stuff, Oak Hills made me feel wonderful. Sustaining me and entertaining my imagination all through that rainy and windy storm were visions of sunny days on a real ranch with its barns to contain all our stuff, and a ranch house with four bedrooms and plenty of closets and nooks and crannies. We would have the freedom of seven hundred and sixty acres to explore and be a home to us and all our family of critters. There would be birds to hear and watch, deer coming down from the mountains to feed at dusk, and someday, perhaps, more horses, calves, dogs, and cats. It might as well have been spring.

Chapter 40

After the Storm

It was late afternoon by the time we took the last load down the valley to the new ranch. By then, the endless trips in the rain with car and trailer had made the muddy lane up to the new house so slippery and rutted that it was almost impossible to drive. Treve and Shandy came with this last load, and both jumped back and forth from front seat to backseat, greatly relieved that we weren't leaving them in the O'Connor Way house any longer.

Now that we had finished moving, the storm had pretty much blown away. At the back of the barnyard, the leaves of the olive green eucalyptus trees were shining with a coat of raindrops as the late afternoon sun filtered through their branches. The cleanly washed fields and buildings also sparkled and felt fresh and new.

Down the hill from the house, across the Los Osos Valley Road, Laguna Lake brimmed full from the rain and soon began to reflect the vibrant colors of the setting sun, while San Luis Mountain, just beyond the lake, turned rose and purple in the canyons. Far off, the higher Santa Lucia Mountains were becoming dark silhouettes.

I've never forgotten those early scenes after we locked the house on O'Connor Way, put the key under the mat for the renters, and drove home to Oak Hills. Even if beauty and happiness exist mainly in one's head, I couldn't help but feel this ranch life would be a great, if challenging, time. Already the new place had become an affair of my heart, and I was certain it would give back all I would be able to put into it. This land did not need taming, just lots of nurturing and protecting.

Nancy asked if she could take a quick ride bareback out over the trail to the west behind the eucalyptus trees, and the boys immediately wanted to explore with her. It was such a special time for them, I couldn't not let them go, but I got a bit of help from them beforehand by saying, "Sure, go ahead, but first, you have to bring some of the dry wood from the shed and stack it on the back porch. Be sure to look for spiders on each log. I'll need your help soon or you won't have beds tonight." Several of the beds still had to be re-assembled, and they all still needed to be made up.

There was no Bu-Gas in the outside tank, so we couldn't light the one wall heater to warm the house. It was cold, and the many loads of boxes and furniture were wet and already smelled musty. Dan built as large a fire as he dared in the one fireplace, and I turned the electric oven on and left the door open for warmth.

Through the window above the kitchen sink, I watched the children file out between the rows of dark eucalyptus trees in the early twilight. Blue and Nancy were in the lead, while Danny and the younger boys chased behind her, encouraged by a gleeful and excited Treve. I belted out an enthusiastic, "Ride 'em, cowgirl!"

It suddenly occurred to me that it wouldn't be many years before all of them would be off on trails of their own, toward new goals and in the pursuit of happiness—life is a continual closing of old chapters and opening of new ones.

I was still just as hooked on country living as I had ever been, and I prayed I had enough "get-up-and-go" for whatever lay ahead. As Dan headed out to milk April, I remarked to him, "Hard work's going to be fun in this beautiful setting!" He smiled, and I began rifling through the wet boxes, looking for dry bedding and for clean school clothes to lay out for the next day. For all of us life should be a great adventure, with lots of happiness. To accomplish that, live fully, work hard, and be a winner—remember, there is always tomorrow.

If you enjoyed this book, please consider browsing our current selection of classic and contemporary works! Available for purchase online, from your local bookstore, or directly from the publisher at www.bramblewoodpress.com

www.ingramcontent.com/pod-product-compliance
Lightning Source LLC
Chambersburg PA
CBHW031236090426
42742CB00007B/225